Multiracial Identity and Racial
Politics in the United States

Multiracial Identity and Racial Politics in the United States

NATALIE MASUOKA

OXFORD
UNIVERSITY PRESS

OXFORD
UNIVERSITY PRESS

Oxford University Press is a department of the University of Oxford. It furthers
the University's objective of excellence in research, scholarship, and education
by publishing worldwide. Oxford is a registered trade mark of Oxford University
Press in the UK and certain other countries.

Published in the United States of America by Oxford University Press
198 Madison Avenue, New York, NY 10016, United States of America.

CIP data is on file at the Library of Congress

ISBN 978–0–19–065746–8 (hbk.); 978–0–19–065747–5 (pbk.)

9 8 7 6 5 4 3 2 1
Paperback printed by Webcom, Inc., Canada
Hardback printed by Bridgeport National Bindery, Inc., United States of America

CONTENTS

TABLES AND FIGURES

Tables

Figures

ACKNOWLEDGEMENTS

This book is the product of many conversations, arguments, events and experiences I encountered since first enrolling as a graduate student. The general topic of multiracial identity started first as a course paper on comparing political attitudes across racial groups that later turned into a dissertation focusing on the opinions of multiracial Americans. But as I began publicly presenting this research, I received such a wide variation of questions and challenges that it was clear there was something more complex about multiracial identification that couldn't be limited to a focus of the unique attitudes a specific group. Slowly, I began to use multiracial identity more as a case to understand racial formation more broadly and so this book, in many, ways reflects this journey.

But beyond the intellectual, this book holds just as much, if not more, personal satisfaction because it is the product of the long process I went through learning how to write a book. More importantly, I look at this book and see how many very special friendships that I have developed because there have been so many generous and thoughtful people who each helped me wade through what oftentimes was a frustrating writing process.

I was able to initially start research on multiracial individuals because Janelle Wong generously took the time to talk to a random graduate student about available data sources and Katherine Tate saw the scholarly potential of multiracial politics. My dissertation committee, Bernie Grofman, Louis DeSipio and Russ Dalton helped steer the initial project, some of which can still be seen in the pages of this final manuscript.

Behind every scholar, there is a special mentor who helped to nurture intellectual talent. I was able to write the book I wanted to write because Jane Junn has been a wonderful friend, mentor and role model. Jane's encouragement helped me survive graduate school and the tenure process. I also took the much needed detour to write *The Politics of Belonging* with her which firmly imprinted the scholarly style that is reflected in this book.

I also thank the many people who have offered insights along the way: Marisa Abrajano, Matt Barreto, Jeff Berry, Niambi Carter, Dennis Chong, Jamie Druckman, Dorothy Fujita-Rony, Lisa Garcia Bedolla, Christian Greer, Kerry Haynie, Rodney Hero, Vince Hutchings, Alisa Kessel, Jennifer Lee, Taeku Lee, Pei-te Lien, Paula McClain, David Meyer, Charlie Morgan, Carrie Nordlund, Stephen Nuno, Saba Ozyurt, Nimah Mazaheri, Catherine Paden, Chris Parker, Efren Perez, Mark Petracca, Karthick Ramakrishnan, Ricardo Ramirez, Kathy Rim, Reuel Rogers, Gabe Sanchez, Debbie Schildkraut, Ron Schmidt, Willie Schonfeld, Becki Scola, Gary Segura, Christ Stout, Dara Strolovitch, Linda Tickle-Degnen, Carole Uhlaner, Alix Van Sickle, Candis Watts-Smith and Kim Williams. Thank you as well to the many departments who invited me to present sections of this book: MIT, University of Michigan, University of Nebraska-Lincoln, University of North Carolina-Chapel Hill, Northeastern University, Northwestern University, University of Washington-Seattle and Tisch College at Tufts.

Thank you to all of the multiracial activists who took out time to tell me about their political efforts and personal stories and who made Chapter 3 of the book possible. Although you remain anonymous in the text, I hope you find that the presentation of your interviews offers readers new insights into the multiracial activism. Thanks to Hester Cheng for her help transcribing all of these interviews.

At the Oxford University Press, I thank my editor, Dave McBride, for seeing very early on that there was potential in this project. When this book was ready for publication, he offered a supportive environment as I finalized the text of the manuscript. Additional thanks to Katie Weaver and the rest of the Oxford University Press team for their help throughout the publication process. I was lucky to receive feedback from three generous reviewers who offered a thorough read of the manuscript and offered a number of useful suggestions for improvement. The book is a better product thanks to their feedback.

Of course, my final thanks goes to my family. My parents, the Tygh family and the extended LA-based Masuoka family have long been the cheerleaders of my life who have offered support and words of encouragement (and many times a bed to sleep on). This book is dedicated to Gordon, who has been the perfect partner and is the one who is always there to push me to stay positive through life's many challenges.

1 | Identity Choice

CHANGING PRACTICES OF RACE AND
MULTIRACIAL IDENTIFICATION

IN 2000, THE US CENSUS Bureau made a small change to the wording of its racial identification question. Question number 6 on the census form asked: "What is this person's race? Mark one or more races to indicate what this person considers himself/herself to be." The directions *mark one or more* replaced the words "fill ONE circle for the race" that had been used in the prior census.[1] When census data were released, officials found that more than 6.8 million Americans, or 2.4% of the population, opted to check multiple races. This mark-one-or-more option on the racial identification question was again employed in the 2010 census. Reports show that, over this decade, the number of Americans who checked multiple races grew by over 30%: to slightly over 9 million, or 2.9% of the population. These statistics suggest that the population who identifies with two or more racial categories, or what will be referred to in this book as *multiracial*, is growing faster than those who identify as either (only) white or (only) black.

Reports such as these offer a sense that the multiracial population is a *new* demographic subpopulation in the United States. Today, the federal government distinguishes those who checked multiple races as a separate racial group and labels them the "two or more races population." Statistical tables distributed by the Census Bureau that present data on the racial diversity of the country include the two-or-more-races population as a unique group alongside the categories of "white," "black," and "Asian." Rising rates of interracial marriage combined with documented populations of individuals who report to be multiple races lead many to equate multiracial individuals with other new populations such as immigrants. In the mainstream media, multiracial Americans are framed as having their own lifestyles, challenges, and characteristics. For example, starting in February 2011, the *New York Times* began running a regular series called "Race Remixed" that primarily highlighted the unique challenges of young adults who identify as multiracial. *USA Today*'s website also features a section on race and the Census that includes stories such as "Multiracial No Longer Boxed in by the Census"[2] and "Attitudes toward Multiracial Americans Evolving."[3]

Yet, while some herald the rise of multiracial identity as a new advance in society, the fact is that racial mixing is an enduring feature in the United States. Marriage between partners of two different racial groups has indeed been outlawed for most of American history, but intimate interracial relationships have existed since the first settlers arrived to the Americas in the sixteenth century.[4] The notion that different racial, ethnic, or other ancestral peoples did not reproduce across group lines does not square with demographic evidence: demographic simulations estimate that all human beings alive today likely share a common ancestor (Rhode et al. 2004). Moreover, Anthony Perez and Charles Hirschman (2009) report that most native-born Americans have ancestors from different parts of the world. F. James Davis (1991) estimates that at least 70% of African Americans are of mixed racial background. Moreover, colonization and other migration patterns lead to the interracial mixture of immigrants even before they arrive to the United States. Take, for example, today's Latino immigrant population. Latinos represent descendants of those Europeans, Asians, and Africans who intermingled with the indigenous peoples in the Americas (Menchaca 2001; Rodriguez 2000). Thus, the contention that multiracial Americans today represent a *new* demographic development often fails to acknowledge the complex history of interracial interactions that have occurred inside and outside the United States.

It is indeed true that interracial marriage rates in the United States are rising and that the children of these marriages is a growing population in the country. (Wang 2012). However, the typical emphasis on the novelty of interracial mixing in this country does not fully capture the true significance of what today's multiracial population reflects about race relations in twenty-first-century America. These views take an ahistorical approach to understanding race relations because they focus only on the current circumstances rather than considering how past practices and long-standing institutions influence those relationships documented in today's society. These typical approaches thus deflect our attention from the more important lessons and insights that we can and should draw from the documentation of a multiracial population in today's society. Multiracial individuals show us that our norms surrounding race and racial classification are indeed changing, but that the implications are more complex and nuanced than what is commonly discussed.

This book advocates for a new conceptual approach for understanding the significance of today's multiracial population. I argue that we can document a sizable multiracial population today for two reasons: there exist institutional opportunities to assert a multiracial identity, and there are some Americans who choose to take advantage of this opportunity. Those who self-identify as multiracial are not the only Americans who are of mixed racial heritage; rather, they represent individuals who choose to designate themselves as such. In contrast, there are many Americans who are clearly aware of the fact that they have ancestors of different racial backgrounds but who choose not to self-identify as multiracial. These individuals follow the more long-standing American norm of racial classification by identifying with (only) one of the established racial categories, such as "white," "black," or "Asian." Therefore, what an officially extant multiracial population really demonstrates is a growing flexibility in how Americans understand and choose to describe their race. Just as importantly, Americans are growing more tolerant and accepting of this identity flexibility. Although the majority of Americans identify with only one established racial category, we have seen no major public rejection of those individuals who choose to claim a multiracial identity.

When viewing the multiracial population through this lens, what becomes clear is that there is a growing tension between the perceived roles of *assigned classification* and *identification* in how Americans understand the application of race. Since the advances of the civil rights movement of the 1950s and 1960s, a subtle but important shift has developed, from viewing race as a characteristic that is primarily the product of social assignment (classification) to one that reflects a person's sense of self (identification). As a result, race is increasingly seen as a marker of personal identity, which has cultivated the belief that individual agency and choice should determine how one is to be racially identified. In this context, we find more individuals asserting their own racial identity or preferred identity label, resulting in increased public visibility of multiracial identities. Yet conceptualizing race as identity is a distinct contrast to the norm of the early twentieth century, when individuals were assigned a racial category based on existing social rules. In particular, the socially established rule of hypodescent, also commonly referred to as the "one-drop rule," dictated that a person with a nonwhite ancestor would be assigned to the relevant nonwhite category and never as white (Davis

1991). In many ways, those Americans who use one established racial identity to describe themselves rely on historic racial norms to define their relevant assignment into a racial group and embrace an identity that matches that racial classification.

Because it is argued that those who self-identify as multiracial do not follow historic social norms and instead assert their preferred multiracial identity, these individuals most clearly demonstrate what will be called in this book *identity choice*, or the expression of race as a reflection of personal identity. But self-identified multiracial individuals are not the only individuals today who practice identity choice. Americans who identify with only one established racial category have also, in many ways, made a choice to express a particular racial identity. However, for multiracial individuals, their decision to express race as a hybrid is in distinct contrast to historic practices and represents a new and modern form of racial identity. Moreover, identifying as multiracial is a behavior that social scientists are increasingly able to document and systematically analyze because of the way we collect data on race today. For this reason, multiracial identities will be the key case used to understand the formation and implications of identity choice.

This book proposes and develops a distinctive approach to understanding and interpreting the empirical findings presented in the forthcoming chapters. Readers should understand "multiracial" as a form of self-identification that individuals assert when there exist opportunities to do so. Therefore, rather than accept an individual's race as a given fact, this approach to the term encourages readers to instead question why some choose to identify as multiracial while others adopt an identity attached to (only) one established racial category, in particular white, black, Asian American, or Latino.[5] This approach emphasizes the importance of explaining multiracial identification as in contrast with attachments to established racial categories.

It should also be noted that this book makes a specific empirical choice to focus primarily on the ways in which Americans report their race on official forms such as the census and in private data collection efforts such as public opinion surveys. This is one of many arenas where individuals can promote and represent their racial identities, but this particular context is consequential because these types of data collection efforts are well publicized and are often framed as important "facts" about the population that in turn can influence how Americans understand the social features of their nation (see also Prewitt 2013; Yanow 2002). This book thus offers a unique perspective on how to interpret the empirical patterns that are often reported about multiracial individuals and those who identify with one established racial category.

The lessons provided by this book address how we can understand, more broadly, the new directions in racial formation in the twenty-first century. Our ability today to document the existence and growth of a self-identified multiracial population alongside the persistence of populations who identify with established racial categories serves as a unique empirical opportunity to understand a process of racial formation. We live in a time in which racial categories are being contested. This book thus employs a multimethod design in order to uncover the many complex forces that explain this racial formation process. First, I employ historical analysis and qualitative interviews to unveil exactly how contemporary racial norms have shifted from those in the past and how norms become integrated into governing institutions. After establishing this context, I examine survey and census data to understand how changing racial norms are revealed through individual behavior. This book will demonstrate that by contrasting historical approaches to race with those practiced today, we can see that what are often framed as "new" developments in American race relations are not exactly novel but are, in reality, direct responses to social norms about race from the previous era.

Tracing Racial Norms: From Assigned Classification to Personal Identification

This book will begin by employing historical analysis to explain why the rise of identity choice appears at the end of the twentieth century. Today, it may be common to find expressions of multiracial identities in many different areas of public life such as popular culture, the arts, and even political campaigns. But multiracial identities are increasingly visible because Americans are living in a political and cultural environment that allows for the expression of these identities. Central to this argument is the historical claim that Americans have witnessed a cultural shift from viewing race as a process primarily of *assigned classification* to believing that race can be primarily a product of *identification*. This cultural embrace of race as identification is, in many ways, consequential to how we understand the implications of all racial categories, but has provided a unique opening for the expression of multiracial identification.

If we first begin by reviewing the origins and political purpose of race in the United States, we recognize that, historically, race has been practiced as a process of classification: a racial category is assigned to individuals.

Most importantly, racial classification served a particular purpose: it was the primary feature used to defend the social order that upheld one group, whites, as superior and all other groups as inferior. Because race is central to understanding group relationships, reliance on racial categorization became institutionalized and deeply embedded in social practices (Haney Lopez 2006; Marx 1998; Sidanius and Pratto 1999; Smith 1999). Both institutions and individuals sought to preserve and defend the boundaries that defined each racial category. Individual interactions that policed who could be "white" enforced the racial categorization system in everyday interactions, while laws such as those promoting "separate but equal" facilities sanctioned local practices that physically separated racial groups. Racial categories represent powerful social tools used to serve the political objective of maintaining an explicit social hierarchy of racial groups.

To buttress this social hierarchy, race has been understood to be represented by a small set of discrete categories. Categories such as "white," "black," and "Asian" have been used to designate a range of rights and liberties such as who is a full citizen, what rights can be exercised, or where someone can own a home. To uphold these associations, racial categories have been assumed to be mutually exclusive, so that a person cannot be a member of more than one racial category. To maintain durability of these categories, people were sorted into discrete racial groups based on socially defined rules prevalent at a given time. For example, the rule of hypodescent was asserted to create an inclusive category of "black" (Davis 1991; Hollinger 2003). Historic mixed-race populations such as "mulatto" and "octoroon" were rooted in these assumptions of hypodescent. Alternatively, whiteness was defined by phenotype and what was labeled "common knowledge" understandings, which effectively equated whiteness with certain European heritages and were used to maintain both the perception of exclusivity and the privileges associated with the white racial category, such as citizenship (Gross 2008; Haney-Lopez 1996). By comparing the methods that determine who is classified as white or as black, we can see that racial categories were first defined by different social rules. Then individuals were sorted into those categories based on those rules. In turn, one's racial classification was attached to a particular social status, and rights were bestowed based on that status.

Although race has historically been assigned to individuals, this is not to say that race has never been conceived as an identity. Because race represents a salient social marker, individuals recognize that their assigned classification is an important characteristic in describing who they are and their place in society. Individuals largely accept their racial classification and adopt that racial status as a feature of their individual identity. Historians have reviewed early slave narratives and document the powerful influence of race in determining how people understood their sense of self (Berlin 2000; Blassingame 1979; White 1999). Furthermore, group identities have developed among individuals who recognize their shared racial status. One would be hard pressed to contradict the assertion that members of the Ku Klux Klan strongly embraced a white racial identity (Blee 2002). Groups have also emphasized and expressly highlighted their racial status so that they could be differentiated from others. For example, when waves of new immigrants from Eastern and Southern Europe arrived to the United States in the late nineteenth century, they were assumed to be inferior to native-born Americans, whose ancestors were largely from Northern and Western Europe. To distance themselves from low-status blacks and other minorities, these immigrants downplayed national origin by expressly highlighting their designated white racial status (Jacobson 1998; Ignatiev 2009 Roediger 1991). In all of these cases, however, racial and ethnic identities were not necessarily direct products of personal preferences or choices but rather were developed as a response to an imposed classification.

The shift from conceiving race primarily as a process of assigned classification to one that can be asserted through personal identification did not happen abruptly, but was slowly cultivated as the result of multiple political, cultural, and demographic shifts that happened over the second half of the twentieth century. While chapter 2 will cover these in greater detail, one example is the advances attributed to the civil rights movement that have weakened the government's and individuals' ability to explicitly discriminate on the basis of race. Although studies confirm that racial tensions and discrimination still exist today (Massey 2007; Oliver and Shapiro 2006), there have been important and notable gains in racial equality since passage of civil rights legislation in the 1960s. These advances have, in many ways, challenged the pessimistic outlook on race relations in our contemporary era and have thus encouraged the outlook that one's race is less likely to be a structural barrier than it has been in the past (for example, see Thernstrom and Thernstrom 1997).[6] Alongside an emphasis in federal policy on racial equality, there have been cultural developments, such as the growing discussions on "multiculturalism" and "diversity" (Glaser 1998; Kymlicka 1996). These new values reframe racial difference in a positive, rather than in a pejorative, light. Inclusive practices in which Americans are not simply asked to accept but also to encourage and celebrate racial and cultural differences are often found in pop culture and the mainstream media.

Collectively, these social, political, and cultural changes are highlighted because they cultivated the public perception that, contrary to previous eras, individual agency can challenge and possibly overcome the constraints of race. Alongside these changes is an increased emphasis on personal self-expression that is reflected in practices of racial identification. In-depth interviews with multiracial activists presented later in this book will reveal an embrace of individual agency that is bound up in one's preference to self-identify as multiracial. By asserting a multiracial identity, activists advocate the view that personal preferences in racial identification should and can play a role in how people are racially classified by others. This agency-oriented perspective is a distinct contrast to the historical logic applied to racial categorization, in which identity was rooted in the experience of assigned racial categorization. While these activists hold a distinct multiracial group consciousness and so represent a unique class of political activists, their ideological perspectives and personal experiences offer qualitative insight into the narratives that uphold the practice of multiracial identity choice.

By tracing the historical development of race, we can see a subtle but important shift from perceiving race primarily as assigned classification to perceiving it as a characteristic influenced by personal preferences and identity. What becomes apparent is that today's rise of a self-identified multiracial population is largely a response to the assumptions cultivated in the early twentieth century, in which racial categories were strictly assigned and immutable. The belief that race can be claimed by the individual and primarily reflects one's personal identity develops as a belief that historic practices should no longer apply. Yet, at the same time, the belief that race is a practice of assigned classification has not disappeared and, many might argue, is in no way a waning practice. Thus, the findings in this book show that, while identifying as multiracial is an increasingly visible practice, the established racial categories, particularly the distinction between "white" and "black," continue to influence the meaning of multiracial identities. So while some argue that the rise of multiracial individuals is fundamentally changing how Americans understand race (see, for example, Hochschild, Weaver, and Burch 2012; Lee and Bean 2010), this book demonstrates that multiracial identification must instead be seen as a product of historical processes in American race relations.

Institutional Opportunities: The Option to Mark One or Many Races

In addition to being reflected in changing cultural norms, the transition from conceiving race as assigned classification to an indicator of personal identity can also be documented in how the federal government has shifted its collection of racial statistics over time. When officials first began collecting racial data, the race of the respondent was determined by the enumerator (Anderson 1988; Snipp 2003). The federal government outlined its definition of each racial category and directed enumerators to classify Americans based on this template. But starting in 1960, the census began using a mail-in form in which each American was instructed to self-report her own characteristics to the federal government. Race was then characterized as a report of how a person understood her own race rather than a government-defined characteristic. The opportunity to express one's own conceptualization of race was then expanded in 2000 when the Census Bureau changed the instructions by offering the opportunity to "Mark One or More" races on the racial identification question.[7]

One of the unanticipated implications of these institutional changes in the census is that it has created an environment where race is conceptualized as a form of personal identification (see also Nobles 2000; Prewitt 2012; Williams 2006). In addition to declaring your own race, the ability to designate multiple racial categories offers many different options: Americans can declare the race that others think they are, they can follow historical precedent and self-identify with one established racial category, or they can mark multiple race boxes (see also Bailey 2008; Roth 2012; Saperstein and Penner 2012). However, while many options are offered, we cannot assume that all individuals use the same logic or have the same motives when they declare their race. An example that reflects the competing logics to the race question is the contrast between the multiracial identities expressed by the activists who sought to change the racial identification question on the 2000 census and the racial identity of President Barack Obama.

Contrasting Two Cases of Racial Identification

The 2000 census change was the product of lobbying efforts by organizations that represented interracial couples and their families (Williams 2006). These activists framed race as an expression of one's heritage and background (see, for example, Root 1992). They promoted "accuracy" in racial reporting, and so their lobbying strategies targeted data collection by the Census Bureau (Williams 2006). Carlos Fernandez, then president of the multiracial advocacy group Association of MultiEthnic Americans (AMEA), testified in favor for a change on the racial identification question by stating:

> We believe that every person, especially every child, who is multiethnic/ interracial has the same right as any other person to assert an identity that embraces the fullness and integrity of their actual ancestry. . . . Each and every time we confront one of these [government] forms, we are faced yet again with the awkward, irrational, and for many of us, the offensive task of selecting a "race" or "ethnicity" which does not truthfully identify us and has the further result of failing to count our community.[8]

Multiracial advocates argued that the existing method used to collect racial identification, which required that respondents select one racial category, not only discriminated against those with multiple racial backgrounds but was also outmoded. Advocates argued that government collection procedures should keep pace with the growing racial complexity of American society. Advocates believed that offering the option to claim multiracial identity would help raise public awareness and encourage people to express their own perceptions of racial identity on official forms. They also emphasized the role of family ancestry: those who have two white parents would classify themselves as white, while those who have parents of two different races would be able to declare those two races. In this way, activists conceived racial categorization as an indicator of both identity and family ancestry. Once given the option, activists proposed, Americans would take the opportunity to report the nuances of their race.

Yet once the new question wording was implemented in 2000, it became clear that how a person identifies herself is not dictated by parental ancestry alone. Contrary to expectations, it became apparent that many Americans with parents of two different races did *not* select multiple racial categories on the census. To the disappointment of many multiracial activists, the most prominent child of interracial parents in the United States, President Barack Obama, selected only "black" as his racial identification on his 2010 census form. Obama's family background was well publicized when he ran for president in 2008. Americans are well aware of the president as the child of a white mother from Kansas and a Kenyan immigrant father (Obama 2004 . Although Obama often described his mixed racial background in campaign speeches, he explicitly self-identifies as African American.

Obama's reasons for identifying as black are given in his 2004 autobiography. But he offered another revealing reflection during a Democratic presidential debate in 2007.[9] When queried about his black racial identity, Obama stated, "You know, when I'm catching a cab in Manhattan—in the past, I think I've given my credentials." With this statement, Obama communicated the persistent constraints imposed by race. For him, race is not a choice but rather a feature imposed on him by society and one that has clear implications for how he is treated as an individual. The example of hailing a taxi speaks not only to the basic, everyday implications of assigned racial classification but also to race's impact on how individuals experience the world. By identifying as black, Obama asserts his recognition that classification as black distinctively characterizes his life experiences.

This contrast between Obama and advocates of a multiracial option in the census demonstrates how different personal understandings of race correspond with decisions about racial identification (see also Campbell, Bratter, and Roth 2016). Some children of interracial parentage define their race as primarily an indicator of family ancestry and choose to self-identify as multiracial. In contrast, some individuals follow existing rules of racial classification, such as hypodescent, and identify with an established racial category. Thus, different definitions of race encourage distinct forms of racial identities. Some multiracial activists argue that their race should reflect family ancestry, but this is their personal approach to race, not a universal definition of how race operates. In contrast, Obama's racial identity demonstrates considerations beyond family background. Obama's position reflects how social processes that have defined race create meaning for each racial category. Cab drivers perceive Obama as black because they rely on characteristics such as skin color, phenotype, common knowledge, and other social cues to racially classify individuals (Cornell and Harmann 2007; Hattam 2007; Omi and Winant 1994). This example perfectly illustrates the racial environment in which Americans operate today and the complexity that characterizes processes of racial identification that can be largely attributed to the new opportunities to assert multiracial identity choice.

Race as a Reflection of Personal Identification

Building from this contrast, this book adopts a more nuanced approach to understanding what it means when a person reports her race as one established category and how that differs from the decision to assert one's race as multiracial. In the United States, individuals commonly declare their race and interact in an environment where racial identity choices are institutionally sanctioned. In this environment, race is not simply a marker of one's demography but more appropriately a feature asserted by an individual. I contend that today's multiracial population exercises the identity choice to be multiracial. At the same time, like President Obama, those who self-identify with only one established racial category are also making assertions about how they want to be racially classified by others. Both multiracial activists and President Obama are given different options through which to express their race, but they chose different racial identities that were guided by different ways of conceptualizing race.

Because we typically collect racial data using a measure of self-report and giving the option to check multiple races, how a person declares her race is a useful empirical measure for understanding how that individual chooses to racially identify and how she understands her place in the racial order. This book thus adds to the literature by asserting that racial identities are important reflections of how a person approaches race.[10] Because race represents a socially and politically consequential feature in the United States, Americans do not take their racial identification lightly and are well aware that their racial identification is an important social marker.[11] Racial identification has not been typically described as a representation of a person's approach to race because it was assumed that an individual identifies with the racial category to which she was assigned. As a result, most research focuses on how race encourages attachment to particular *group* identities (for example, Conover 1984; Dawson 1994) because it was not certain that an individual would develop identity attachment to an assigned category. However, because the census now presents individuals with different racial identity options, such as the opportunity to self-identify as multiracial, scholars now must explain *why* a person makes her identity choices.

Given this argument, I adopt a methodological strategy and analytical framework that highlights racial *self-identification*. Therefore, only those who so self-identify will be considered multiracial in this book. Those who self-identify with one of the established racial categories of "white," "black," "Asian," or "Latino"[12] will be labeled by that term or as "monoracial." Self-identified multiracial individuals choose monikers such as "mixed," "multiracial," or "biracial," or, like the golfer Tiger Woods, they create their own term ("Cablinasian").[13] This book does not focus on a particular term, but rather their embracing of an identity that reflects a hybrid of two or more established racial categories. There are other ways of identifying a multiracial person, such as relying on genetic background, distinguishing those with an ambiguous racial phenotype, or selecting individuals who have interracial parents.[14] However, these definitions emphasize the role of imposed social norms and are not analyzed in this book.

Highlighting race as self-identification, the empirical analyses herein are oriented around understanding the processes that lead individuals to declare a racial identity and around revealing the possible political conse quences of their identity choice. I argue that individuals *decide* to identify as multiracial; they are not automatically adopting a social identity. The contrast between President Obama and multiracial activists illuminates how individuals can arrive at distinct conclusions about their racial identity. For many Americans, racial identity is not straightforward, but rather a complicated choice amid conflicting ideological and normative consid- erations and social contexts. Although this book highlights multiracial identification, because self-identifying as monoracial can also be under- stood as an identity choice, I highlight the contrast between multiracial and monoracial identities. I will examine the evidence to understand how particular logics, social contexts, and personal resources are correlated with the decision to identify as multiracial, and contrast these patterns with those that are correlated with the decision to identify as monoracial. The evidence will show that, even though multiracial identification is a rel- atively new option for Americans, distinctive patterns differentiate attach- ments to a multiracial identity from attachments to a monoracial identity.

It should also be recognized that within the multiracial population there is significant racial diversity. Multiracial individuals can declare them- selves to be white, black, and Native American, or white and Asian, or Asian and Latino. Importantly, census data show that the majority of self- identified multiracial individuals denote two races, with one of the races being "white." These patterns inspire many hypotheses: there may be more opportunities to declare certain types of multiracial identity today, or, alternatively, certain types of multiracial identity may be more desirable than others. The evidence in this book will show that there are distinctive demographic and attitudinal differences based in the racial combinations reported by multiracial individuals. So while I assert that the multiracial population shares a common decision to self-identify as racially hybrid, the historically established racial hierarchy is still important for under- standing the social and political implications of multiracial identities.

An important lesson gleaned from the evidence is that, while choice exists, not all racial identities are fluid. I do not find evidence that iden- tification as "white" is understood as a flexible option. Moreover, racial choice is not an option for all Americans. It may be made available by institutions such as the census, but only certain individuals can actually practice multiracial identities. In other words, a person might think of herself as multiracial while her interactions with others lead her to identify as a monoracial. Like the processes that have created the established monoracial categories, multiracial identity is also structured by social and political circumstances. In this way, multiracial identities share an important similarity with established monoracial identities, since structural and cultural barriers continue to dictate racial categories. Thus, multiracial identification is not simply an indicator of a person's attitudes toward race but also reflects the surrounding context and the resources available to that person.

Implications of Identity Choice

Having made the connection between race and self-identification, we can take different paths to evaluate the social and political consequences of identity choice. This book offers three ways of thinking about these consequences: the role of multiracial identification in development of political attitudes, citizens' reactions to and evaluations of racial identity assertions, and the lessons gleaned about racial formation in the twenty-first century.

Racial Identity and Political Attitudes

Long-standing research comparing the political attitudes and behaviors of blacks and whites—and more recently that of Asian Americans and Latinos—shows that racial classification and identification matter for politics (Bowler and Segura 2012; Fraga et al. 2011; Masuoka and Junn 2013; Tate 1994; Wong et al. 2011). The pivotal study by Michael Dawson (1994) demonstrated that because blacks share the historical experiences of discrimination and status as a marginalized group, they are more likely to take racial considerations into account when forming their individual political opinions. Dawson's study shows the impact of being classified as a racialized, nonwhite subject on a person's political attitudes. If multiracial individuals do, in fact, conceive of race differently than other Americans, we cannot overlook their growing presence and so should include them in an analysis of political behavior and attitudes.

Studies have shown a distinct difference between the political attitudes of whites and the political attitudes of racial minorities (Bowler and Segura 2012; Fraga et al. 2011; Masuoka and Junn 2013; Tate 1994; Wong et al. 2011). Scholars explain these persistent findings by pointing to the structural and institutionalized nature of race as it is practiced in the United

States. Whites enjoy a privileged status largely bestowed by their racial classification. In contrast, racial minorities respond to the political system based on the social and political constraints to which they are subjected. Race is a persistent consideration for racial minorities because it acts as a constant force in their daily activities, whereas for whites, race is rarely at the forefront because it does not often present personal obstacles. Making this comparison between whites and racial minorities, we can see that our theories explaining the connection between race and political attitudes assume that individuals' attitudes reflect their assigned position in society.

Self-identified multiracial individuals thus pose a challenge to existing assumptions. They have chosen their racial identities and, as I claim, multiracial identification reflects an embrace of agency in racial classification. If we adopt an identity choice approach, then we should expect that multiracial individuals may not entirely view race as a constraining feature. Accordingly, it is an important question whether the logics commonly used to explain the connection between racial minorities and political attitudes also apply to multiracial individuals. This book uses a comparative approach to examine if multiracial attitudes align more closely with whites or with racial minorities (specifically blacks and Latinos) on issues related to racial redistribution. I argue that if multiracial attitudes align with those of whites, this supports the argument that multiracial individuals view their race as personal identity rather than a structural feature that constrains individual life chances.

Racial Identities as a Political Cue to Voters

By highlighting the tension between racial classification and identification, we become more aware that a person's racial identity may not match the racial classification that others impose on her. Multiracial identities represent an obvious case, especially given the fact that, until recently, it was not common to assert a multiracial identity. Given the lack of precedent, may individuals want to self-identify as multiracial even though other Americans would classify them as white or a monoracial minority. But self-identification as monoracial is also subject to this same tension. As in the example of President Obama, many Americans who are seen as of mixed race because they have interracial parentage self-identify with only one established racial category. While identification as monoracial could signal acquiescence to historic racial norms, in a growing culture of self-identification, we can also recognize monoracial identification as an identity choice.

However, the possible mismatch between how one chooses to identify and how others perceive one's race raises questions about the influence of racial identification on interpersonal interactions. To what extent do we pay attention to the racial identity a person asserts, and to what extent do our own perceptions of race inform how we interact with that person? Does one process override the other? Those who embrace identity choice may believe that a person's asserted identity should guide how others perceive her race. However, social science research shows that individual quickly assign others to racial groups (Allport 1954; Brewer 1988; Macrae and Bodenhausen 2000).

In the context of politics, racial and ethnic groups are linked with particular political stereotypes that others use to make decisions about their own interests. For example, blacks are overwhelmingly Democratic and tend to support governmental intervention (Tate 1994, 2010), and studies show that white voters use these assumptions to determine their vote for or against black candidates (Lerman and Sadin 2016). Moreover, studies show that race is used as a political tool by elites to mobilize or demobilize voters (Barreto 2010; Mendelberg 2001). Identities, in particular, serve as mobilization tools. For example, when a candidate emphasizes her ethnic background, she seeks to engage voters with a similar background who assume that she will demonstrate loyalty to coethnic constituents (Dahl 1961; Parenti 1967).

Therefore, it is questionable whether assertions of racial identity guide interpersonal interactions and decision-making. By examining to what extent a person's racial identity preferences align with how others perceive that person's race, I can determine how assertions of racial identity can override processes of racial assignment. This book will consider how voters racially classify political leaders and to what extent these perceptions guide their evaluation of leaders. By noting the tension between assigned classification and self-identification, we become aware that race may not be a shortcut for individuals to rely on when making political decisions, as has been typically assumed in the scholarship. Messages about identity may conflict with other definitions of race, forcing voters to process multiple pieces of information when they evaluate their political leaders.

New Questions for Racial Formation

Finally, in addition to the implications of identity choice for individual political attitudes, identity choice pushes us to think more conceptually about the meaning of racial categories and future developments in American race relations that may result from more dominant claims of identity choice. By developing the identity choice framework, I raise awareness about the growing emphasis on personal preference that many Americans are beginning to adopt in their approach to race. The narratives generated by multiracial activists that emphasize agency and self-expression promote the view that race is becoming a more flexible practice. Yet each of us experiences the tension between assignment and identification differently, so individual responses to this tension will be central to how we understand the role of race. The evidence in this book pushes readers to think about how individuals navigate the gap between norms that characterize race as assigned classification and those that characterize race a product of personal identification.

An even larger question is whether the rise of identity choice changes the meanings attached to established racial categories. The evidence presented in this book indicates that the rise of multiracial identification do not change, or even problematize, the existing racial order. Framing race as identity offers Americans the ability to assert hybrid racial identities, but these identities only make sense when contrasted against established monoracial categories. This book discusses the implications of identity choice and identifies systematic patterns but also presents findings that inspire new questions. The empirical patterns reflect what can be known at this stage of racial formation and offer future scholars the opportunity to develop new evidence and hypotheses about the trajectory of race in the United States.

Overview of the Book

In the pages that will follow, I further develop the identity choice approach and employ multiple methodological strategies in order to reveal the process of racial formation occurring today. The analyses presented in chapters 2 and 3 develop the claim that Americans increasingly perceive race as a product of personal identification. Chapter 2 lays the foundation by outlining the events that explain the rise of identity choice at the turn of the twenty-first century. This chapter traces the curious evolution of racial classification practices in the United States by charting historical events and cases that established the American racial classification system. I then trace how different events during the modern civil rights movement created a norm that framed race as a product of personal identification.

Although the shift from assigned classification to identification influences all Americans, chapter 3 analyzes narratives that defend the assertion of multiracial identities. Past studies have shown that public visibility of multiracial identities can be attributed to a small number of activists who sought to mobilize multiracial identification (DaCosta 2007; Williams 2006). These activists propose that racial identity should be a product of individual choice. This chapter presents data from 27 in-depth interviews with multiracial activists representing some 20 nonprofit advocacy organizations or activities that I conducted in 2006. My objective is to outline how narratives posed by activists argue that individuals should self-identify as multiracial. The interviews show that activists not only assert a multiracial identity but reflect a group consciousness in which their identity is connected with a distinct set of ideological beliefs. The interviews reveal how this group responds to historic practices of race and has developed a narrative of identity choice that justifies the decision to self-identify as multiracial.

To substantiate the claim that multiracial identities exist because there are social and political opportunities to assert them, chapter 4 presents evidence demonstrating that multiraciality is a form of identity rather than an objective demographic trend. Using data from the *Washington Post / Kaiser Family Foundation / Harvard University* survey *Race and Ethnicity in 2001: Attitudes, Perceptions, and Experiences* (WKH 2001) and the 2009 survey *Racial Attitudes in America II* collected by the Pew Research Center for the People and the Press (Pew Research Center 2009), I demonstrate that multiracial identification is a complex identity, not simply an essentialist reporting of one's family background or heritage. I also argue that multiracial identification is most likely to be asserted when there are opportunities to do so.

Chapters 5 and 6 offer two different ways to understand the possible individual-level implications of identity choice. Chapter 5 focuses on the influence of racial identification on individual political attitudes. Using two datasets that include sizable samples of whites, blacks, Latinos, and self-identified multiracial individuals—the American National Election Study 2008 Time Series Study and the 2009 Pew—I compare the responses across monoracial and multiracial groups on partisanship, public policy preferences, and racial attitudes. I consider to what extent racial background influences political attitude formation among multiracial individuals by evaluating the extent to which the racial combination reported by a multiracial respondent explains the variation in political attitudes found within the multiracial population. This chapter also considers evidence on speculation that multiracial individuals perceive a shared racialized experience.

Chapter 6 assesses how individuals react to assertions of identity choice by examining how voters understand Barack Obama's race. President Obama represents one case of identity choice: he publicly identifies as African American yet consistently highlights his interracial familybackground. The first half of the chapter compares how whites, blacks, and Latinos racially classify Obama. Because a sizable number of respondents identify Obama as of mixed race rather than black, the second half of the chapter examines whether those who classify Obama as of mixed race evaluate him more favorably than those who classify him as black. In particular, I test the *deracialization* hypothesis: the expectation that minority political leaders who de-emphasize their loyalties to coethnics will generate greater political support among the white electorate. This chapter explores whether perceptions of Obama as a mixed-race person had the effect of deracializing the president among white voters.

The concluding chapter takes stock of the politics surrounding identity choice and multiracial identification. In this final chapter, I review and assess how today's multiracial population offers an ideal case study of racial formation. I also discuss societal implications of the rise of identity choice, as well as new questions that are stimulated by the ideas and evidence in this book. The conclusion emphasizes the importance of evaluating the implications of multiracial identification in contrast to monoracial identities. Rather than seeing multiracial individuals as a harbinger of dramatic change in the practice of race in the United States, I argue that multiracial identification and identity choice are ideas in direct dialogue with long-standing established racial categories.

2 | Exclusive Categories
HISTORICAL FORMATION OF RACIAL CLASSIFICATION
IN THE UNITED STATES

TODAY, AMERICANS OF MIXED-RACE BACKGROUND are commonly pointed to as evidence that race relations are fundamentally changing. This idea draws from many different sources: some of the original writings on assimilation theory pointed to interracial marriage as one of the final steps in the assimilation of ethnic immigrants into mainstream America (Alba and Nee 2005; Gordon 1964). Other scholarly theories, such as those that seek to explain group conflict, hypothesize that intimate, personalized contact between racial groups reduces prejudice and intolerance (Allport 1954; Pettigrew 1998). One can also draw conclusion about changing demography from social practices such as the tracking of the two-or-more-races population by the US census. Some pundits and scholars argue that multiracial Americans are evidence of a weakening reliance on race. For example, historian David Hollinger (2005) contends those who reject multiracial identities are using outdated attitudes that encourage balkanization. By contrast, others speculate on an entirely new racial order to come (Gans 1999; Hochschild, Weaver, and Burch 2012; Lee and Bean 2010). In either case, there is an implied claim of transformation.

Yet these proclamations of fundamental change rely on an ahistorical lens on American race relations. While scholars generally accept that race is a social construct, the American racial system has experienced the dramatic overhauls that many have proposed. It is true that the assignment of individuals to racial categories has been modified over time, but these changes have not revolutionized the practice of race in the United States. Race continues to be used as a means to understand social status and hierarchy. As Sidanius and Pratto (1999) posit, hierarchy is a natural characteristic of human societies: some members are understood to represent the more privileged of groups, while those below vary in their desirability. While the most basic hierarchies relies on gender and age, advanced societies rely on arbitrary social markers such as class, race, ethnicity, or religion to order citizens in a social hierarchy. So rather than predicting transformation, we should think of race as a cyclical process of formation: the racial system of the current century is informed by historic processes of racial classification (Omi and Winant 1994). The modern racial system includes new adaptations informed by recent events, but race's historical role continues to inform the definitions of racial categories.

This chapter employs historical analysis to develop the argument that a multiracial identity, rather than being understood as a "new" racial group, is best understood as a form of identity expression that has emerged today because there are inviting opportunities to do so. I trace historic changes in political institutions and social norms to show how this environment came about. In particular, I argue that Americans have shifted from perceiving race as an assigned characteristic, to one that is increasingly understood as a reflection of personal identity. The objective of this chapter is to show how and why multiracial self-identification bloomed at the end of the twentieth century. Overall, this chapter offers the important lesson that multiracial self-identification is largely a *response* to existing practices of racial categorization that developed in the first half of the twentieth century. Self-identified multiracial individuals are therefore not overturning existing practices, but instead are in dialogue with existing racial norms.

This chapter begins by establishing that intimate interracial interaction is not a new practice in the United States, and thus that racially mixed people have always existed. It was the construction of discrete racial categories understood to represent distinctive groups that promoted the public perception that rigid boundaries divided the races and that minimal interracial mixing has occurred over time. By contrasting actual practices with the cultural narratives about race, we find that the rules that govern racial classification are the product of political motives rather than objective descriptions of demography or family ancestry. Building from this, the chapter then outlines how the opportunities to assert a multiracial identity developed in the second half of the twentieth century.

Interracial Interactions in the Early Colonial Period

In practice, intimate interracial interactions—those that create individuals of different racial or ethnic ancestries—have long characterized American race relations. Yet the overwhelming majority of Americans today believe themselves to be of only one race. How did it come to be the case that being of two or more races is declared by only a small segment of Americans today? Later sections of this chapter will outline why many Americans, particularly white Americans, have adopted the view that they are not of mixed-race descent. This beginning section will first establish that today's celebrations about a "new" multiracial population largely discount a long history of intimate interracial interactions in the United States.

Race relations during the early settlement era provide a useful contrast to the modern practices of interracial contact because an individual's social status was not yet directly linked with racial categories. Historians point out that during this period intimate interracial interactions were more prevalent, particularly among nonelite populations. Records documenting relationships between white settlers, black slaves, and Native American tribes show that racial mixing was a fact of life. Strategies for survival offer a partial explanation for these interracial relationships, but it is also true that the social hierarchy during the early settlement period was determined by class and servitude rather than race, and so less social stigma was attached to interracial mixing. It was not until race became more clearly linked with social status that interracial relationships became increasingly discouraged.

Colonial populations in the century leading up to the American Revolution were more racially diverse than many might think. These populations were quite diverse in terms of family and social status. In New England, colonialists from Europe arrived as families, while in Virginia most early European settlers were single men (Berlin 2000). In addition to those free white settlers, white indentured servants were also sent to the colonies to fulfill their required period of service. Blacks at that time also were diverse in terms of social status. African slaves were imported primarily from the West Indies to assist with labor, but exposure to black slaves was not consistent across the American colonies since black slaves lived in the southern colonies rather than in the North. There was also a small free black population, Atlantic Creoles, merchants and brokers who traveled the trade routes along the African and American Atlantic coasts. Finally, of course, there were the indigenous peoples of North America, who had significant contact with these new settlers and were recognized by the new European settlers as distinctive and autonomous peoples.

Life was challenging in the New World for European settlers. The long passage across the Atlantic kept the white colonial population relatively small. Disease was a real threat to sustaining a working white population.

In this context, racial segregation was not given the highest social priority. Rather the consequential social order was that between master and servant. The social divide between free and unfree, which characterized European societies, also became the most relevant for understanding the social order in the New World (Morgan 1975; Foner 1999). So even though African slaves and white indentured servants were understood to represent different races, they were perceived to be of the same social status (Berlin 2000).[1] These two groups filled the same labor roles and were subject to the rules of their master. As such, they shared goals of freedom from their master. The famous Bacon's Rebellion in 1676 mobilized both black slaves and white servants to rally together against labor injustices (Rice 2012).

Historical accounts suggest interracial mixing between whites and blacks was more common in the early settlement days than today (Berlin 2000; Moran 2003; Morgan 1999; Nagel 2003). Historians document high rates of interracial interaction and intimate relationships among those in the lower social classes. David Roediger (1991) argues that because historians often use records of the social elite and public legal records to document social norms, their accounts suggest a more stringent racial divide than that which held in everyday practice among the lower classes. Roediger (1991) argues that if one reviews court testimonies, partnerships in petty crimes, and practices during festivals, it is clear that relationships between nonelite whites and blacks were more prevalent than previously assumed. Joshua Rothman (2003) creatively documented divorce filings that revealed common claims that a white spouse was having an affair with an African American (see also Hodes 1997). These examples reveal that consensual white-black relationships were common. We must also recognize the other nonconsensual acts between men and women that were also common in the precolonial and antebellum period. It is now well substantiated that widespread rape occurred between white owners and black slaves up through the Civil War (Escott 1979; White 1999).

This is not to say that there did not exist social stigma against white-black racial mixing in the early settlement periods. In fact, laws barring interracial marriages had been enacted as early as 1661 in Maryland (Moran 2003; Nagel 2003; Roediger 1991). Interestingly, such antimiscegenation laws reveal that enough interracial mixing occurred that sanctions were deemed necessary (Rothman 2003). But, pragmatically, the challenges of living in the New World reduced emphasis on strict social mores because they were not essential to survival. Even traditional gender roles did not survive, since both men and women were forced to work together in order to survive (Berlin 2000). Small populations and gender imbalances made racial mixing more common. Thus interracial mixing was more common in the southern colonies because single men made up a larger share of the population than in the northern colonies, which had more families (Moran 2003). Indeed, evidence suggests that the social stigma that discouraged interracial relationships between whites and blacks was not yet in full force in the early colonial period because the correspondence between social status and race had not fully crystallized.

Whites and Native American peoples also intermixed in the early settlement period. European settlers perceived Native American peoples as a different and inferior race. Diaries kept by early European explorers of the fifteenth and sixteenth centuries reveal the tendency to compare Native American features and lifestyles to those of Europeans (Berkhofer 1979; Powell 2005; Smedley and Smedley 2012). Native Americans were described with distinctive phenotypic characteristics such as hair type and skin color and were characterized as savage and lecherous (Berkhofer 1979; Powell 2005; Smedley and Smedley 2012; Smits 1987).[2] On the other hand, tribes' status as autonomous nations meant that Native Americans were a free and independent people who competed with whites for territory (Deloria and Wilkins 2000). Intermarriage between whites and Native Americans was thus often encouraged because such relationships would help solidify alliances (Moran 2003).[3] This perception became more predominant as tribes were increasingly viewed as military threats against the newly formed United States (Deloria and Wilkins 2000).[4]

There was also significant interracial mixing between blacks and Native Americans. Native Americans were also enslaved, and thus contact between blacks and Native Americans was frequent. Runaway slaves formed maroon communities and often created alliances with Native American tribes against white settlers (Aptheker 1939; Berlin 2000). Nonslave Native Americans were legally free peoples, and so many blacks attempted to assert their freedom by claiming Native American heritage. Because heritage is difficult to disprove, if black slaves could convince a jury that they had Native American maternal ancestry, they could be emancipated (Gross 2008).

Later, when Native American peoples were awarded the right to private land titles during the allotment era, proving Native American ancestry became more politically consequential.[5] Upholding Native American racial segregation became increasingly important to control the distribution of resources, such as land and slave status. During the antebellum period, whites began to emphasize a distinctive Native American racial identity and officially sanctioned Native American and black intermarriages

(Gross 2008; Woods 2003). To protect resources and ensure their own status as free people, Native American tribes themselves discouraged members from marrying blacks and contested the history and existence of black ancestry among tribal members (Gross 2008; Woods 2003).[6]

While racial divisions between Europeans, Africans, and Native Americans did exist, race was not the most politically salient marker of social difference during this period. The precedent brought from Europe, which emphasized class status and in which one's level of freedom defined the system of social stratification, applied to life in the New World and thus governed social relationships. In this period, because race did not directly determine a person's status, interracial mixing was a more conventional practice. Comparing white-black, white–Native American. and black–Native American relations, we find that intimate relationships and marriage were more informed by the division between "free" and "unfree" and the distribution of resources than by race. More importantly, as the case of Native American and black contact particularly demonstrates, race was increasingly emphasized when there was a political imperative to ensure that social divisions were maintained. Life in the early colonial period thus undermines claims that mixed-race populations are modern developments in American life.

Construction of the American Racial Categorization System

Although interracial mixing is prevalent throughout US history, the American racial system is a categorical construct (see also Yanow 2002). Officially, individuals can be classified into the racial groups of white, black, Asian, and Native American / Pacific Islander [7] (i.e., the indigenous tribes or populations in North American and acquired American territories). Americans also see Latinos as a distinct grouping. However, Latinos have been awarded a different form of racial and ethnic classification by the federal government; its implications will be discussed later in the chapter (Dowling 2014; Miyawaki 2015; Prewitt 2013; Rodriguez 2000; Roth 2012; Schwede, Leslie, and Griffin 2002). But the most consequential feature is that the five groupings, white, black, Asian, Native American, Pacific Islander, and Latino, are understood as *discrete* categories. The American racial system gives a sense that there is no overlap or intermixing across groups, and so it can be assumed that membership in one category eliminates membership in other categories. In practice, the racial categories we use today seem almost intuitive, even though these racial divisions do not reflect an objective or natural social division. Rather, as this section will document, the social definitions applied to each racial category were created over the course of many political battles regarding citizenship and equality. How Americans developed this racial system is an important story that others have documented, but this discussion focuses on how and why Americans came to adopt a *categorical* racial system.

Scholars largely attribute the rise of the American racial system to elites' distinct political efforts to unify a diverse white population and thus develop a sense of group or national cohesion (see, for example, Key 1977; Marx 1998; Morgan1975; Smith 2003). Race and nationhood became firmly affixed as political elites used whiteness as the attribute qualifying one for full and equal citizenship. The social category "white" designated who was a citizen, while those classified as nonwhite were either noncitizens or partial citizens (Haney Lopez 2006). Yet interestingly, Americans did not create a dichotomous categorization system of citizen and noncitizen but rather more varied categories that at the same time aligned with distinctive forms of citizenship statuses. The historic racial diversity found in the United States created a context in which each racialized group was viewed as a distinctive population facing a unique set of circumstances. Blacks, Native Americans, and later Asian immigrants and Mexicans in the Southwest each challenged American notions of citizenship in their own ways. In turn, Americans came to conceive of each group as a separate racial category hierarchically ordered along a scale of citizenship status.

Early Foundations of the American Racial System: White, Black, and Native American

The distinction between "free" and "unfree," which characterized social relations in the early settlement period, slowly became aligned with the distinction between white and black as labor economics in the colonies began to change (Morgan 1975; Foner 1999). A significant difference between white indentured servitude and chattel slavery was that whites ultimately could earn their freedom, while blacks remained permanent property of slaveholders.[8] At the same time, crops such as cotton, tobacco, and indigo needed significant, cheap labor, particularly in the South.[9] This demand for labor fostered the African slave market in the United States (Foner 1983). In many areas in the South, black slaves began to outnumber white servants. Thus, as the black slave population grew, white Americans came to assume a near perfect linkage between slavery and blackness.

One of the major political divisions during the drafting of the Constitution was the role of slavery. The infamous three-fifths compromise has been understood as a political bargain necessary to ensure ratification of the Constitution (Foner 1999). In order to pacify those states with large slave populations (mainly in the South),[10] the Framers allowed slavery to continue in the country until 1808. This allowed the import of new slaves into the new nation for another 20 years. Furthermore, the Framers included a fugitive slave clause that required that slaves be returned to their masters even if that slave was found in a territory that had abolished slavery. The three-fifths compromise is often highlighted as a bargain struck between the North and the South, but it also be codified the idea that some members of the nation were not equal citizens. As a function of the common-law practice of birthright citizenship used in the colonies (Shuck and Smith 1985), blacks were assumed to be American. But with the three-fifths compromise, the Framers effectively defined blacks as only partial citizens. This decision set in motion a path to racial categories that were affiliated with particular levels of citizenship.[11] Those classified as white held full political citizenship, while those classified as slave (and later racially black) had only partial citizenship (Smith 1999).

The classification of blacks was not the only concern of the Framers. Native Americans were also defined in the Constitution as a distinctive racial category with a separate citizenship status (Deloria and Wilkins 2000). Although tribes were recognized as autonomous from one another, Native Americans were classified in the Constitution as one racial group, "Indians," all to be treated in a similar manner (Smith 1999). The Constitution recognizes Native Americans primarily as independent nations whose relations with the United States were to be governed by Congress (Wilkins and Lomawaima 2002). As with other foreign nations, Indian relationships were solidified through treaties. However, the Constitution points out that some Native Americans may not be considered sovereign. Article 1, section 2 states that "Indians not taxed" were not to be included in the population enumeration determining representation, which implied that some Native Americans (likely those who were enslaved or incorporated into white colonies) were considered American citizens. However, the Constitution did not specify the citizenship rights of these incorporated Native Americans (Smith 1999). Native Americans were thus recognized as a separate race and primarily characterized as members of separate nations who are not privileged with the same benefits and rights as white citizens.

After ratification of the Constitution, Congress quickly passed laws that enforced the connection between racial classification and citizenship. A racialized description of American citizenship was explicit in the Naturalization Act of 1790 (Haney Lopez 2006). The act limited naturalization to "free white persons." At the time, this naturalization law was considered generous since it provided relatively few requirements for white men to earn citizenship.[12] Yet the racial adjective used in this law excluded not only blacks and Native Americans but any person classified as non-white. By establishing the racial prerequisite to citizenship, Americans officially defined itself as a "white" nation or, more appropriately, a nation that limited full political inclusion to those classified as white (Gross 2008; Haney Lopez 2006). The attention to and preservation of the white category remained a critical area in legal jurisprudence, since defining whiteness was key to maintaining the perceived exclusivity of American citizenship.

The early institutional design that privileged the white racial category but designated separate nationhood for Native Americans and denied equal citizenship to blacks set in motion a path toward discrete categorization. What is so striking about the creation of racial categorization is that, in practice, Americans perceived ethnic variation beyond these three categories. Although blacks and Native Americans were often homogenized within their respective racial categories, white Americans assumed essential group differences and a hierarchy of European nationalities (Gerstle 2001; Jacobson 1998; Roediger 1991). Benjamin Franklin, for example, noted for his anti-German sentiment, strongly advocated ridding the country of this "swarthy" class of Europeans (Ketcham 2003). Individuals of "in-between" status (Higham 2002), that is, between white and black, such as the Irish and Southern and Eastern Europeans, strategically responded to structural rules by engaging in practices that would emphasize their whiteness (see also Roediger 2005). Oftentimes this meant that they shared social and economic circumstances with blacks, they engaged in racially discriminatory practices, such as forming racially exclusive labor unions (Roediger 1991; Ignatiev 2009). Europeans of in-between status also cultivated specific images of blackness through minstrel performances so as to disassociate their own group from blacks and encourage perceptual alignment with whites (Roediger 1991). So although those of various European backgrounds did not immediately identify with each other as one collective group, institutional rules ultimately created incentives to adopt a white racial identity.

Later institutional decisions not only upheld a system of discrete racial categories but also emphasized the link between race and citizenship. Legal rulings leading up to the Civil War further distinguished the citizenship awarded to blacks and that awarded to whites. Northern courts denied that citizenship implied equal rights, determining, rather, that it is characterized by multiple classes (Smith 1999). Lawyers in the 1834 case *Crandall v. State of Connecticut* established that citizenship afforded only the protection of law, not the assignment of rights. In this way, the court recognized the rule of birthright citizenship but denied that birthright would automatically entitle a person to all political privileges.[13] Moreover, federal policy toward Native Americans slowly stripped tribes of their land and, with that land, of their sovereign autonomy from the United States (Deloria and Wilkins 2000; Wilkins 2002).[14] The political significance of Native Americans declined, as they were no longer viewed as a barrier to white landownership. Over time, federal policy changed to view Native American tribes as wards of the state, rather than competing sovereign nations.

This contrast in treatment of blacks and Native American tribes in relation to whites demonstrates that early decisions to connect citizenship with racial classification were upheld not only by governing institutions but also through everyday activities of individual Americans. In practice, Americans did recognize diversity, such as the existence of separate sovereign tribes and differences among European-origin groups. However, because citizenship status and privileges of membership were connected firmly to the racial categories of white, black, and Native American, greater political and social emphasis was placed on discrete racial classification over time. This historical story also helps to explain how today we find that "white" and "black" mark the most and least privileged groups in the American racial hierarchy and that Native Americans are generally ignored in public deliberations about race.

Solidifying the Categorical System: Adding New Groups to the Racial System

The Constitution and early legal decisions established three racial categories, white, black, and Native American, but territorial expansion and new immigration forced Americans to adopt new rules to incorporate new groups. Two different trajectories explain the incorporation of Asian Americans and of Mexican Americans.

Asian Immigrants as Aliens Ineligible for Citizenship

The first major wave of Asian immigrants to the United States occurred when the Chinese migrated to California seeking new fortunes in the Gold Rush of the 1850s (Chan 1991; Takaki 1998). Other waves of Asian immigrants, including Filipino, (Asian) Indian, Japanese, and Korean, soon followed. In practice, whites perceived Asians as another inferior racial species who were used to fulfill a labor demand in the developing American West. However, because Asians were not a significant population in the United States before the mid-nineteenth century, there was no established rule determining their racial classification. Not until Asian immigrants began challenging naturalization and citizenship laws was there a need to create a distinctive classification for them. What resulted was an established practice in which Asians were recognized as a group distinct from whites, blacks, and indigenous Americans.

The naturalization rule in place since 1790 established that only "free white persons" could become citizens. Thus, in order to be a citizen, a person needed either to be born on American soil or to be racially white. In 1878, the California Circuit Court ruled in *In re: Ah Yup* that a Chinese immigrant could not naturalize because he did not meet the racial requirement (Hing 1994). However, the use of the term "white" left open the possibility that immigrants could petition to be classified as "white" since the category was never defined by law. Throughout the first half of the twentieth century, immigrants from various countries, most notably those from Asian countries, including Japan, Philippines, Korea, and India, petitioned for citizenship by challenging the definition of "white." Ian Haney Lopez (2006) documented a total of 52 legal cases that challenged the definition of white, with two involving Asian immigrants reaching the Supreme Court.[15] Using a variety of explanations that helped justify their decision, including the science of anthropology, eugenicist ideas about racial hierarchies, and common-sense understandings of race, the Court rejected the notion that Asians could be white.[16] These decisions firmly maintained strict boundaries that created a more exclusive white racial category and determined that those from Asian countries represented a separate group.

Asian immigrants' noncitizen status provided a legal justification for denying them equal rights. Since citizenship is equated with deservingness, noncitizenship status is a conceptual proxy justifying discrimination, since noncitizens are viewed as unworthy (Hing 2003, 1994). Asians' race, foreign status, and lack of citizenship were used interchangeably as justification in public policies that enforced their unequal status. Although white racial status was officially denied to Asians, there was also an understanding that Asians were different from blacks as well. Whites used Asian laborers to drive down wages for black laborers. Segregation in the West also supported the perception that Asian immigrants were distinct from blacks (Takaki 1998).

Asian immigrants themselves also asserted group identities separate from blacks. One revealing case of identity formation has been documented among a small Chinese immigrant population who had migrated to Mississippi after the Civil War (Cornell and Hartmann 2007; Loewen 1971). Chinese immigrants were recruited by white landowners in Mississippi to fill the labor shortages after black slaves were emancipated. The Chinese were at first considered to be of the same racial status as blacks. But, through their own chosen behaviors and community-imposed segregation from blacks, the Chinese of Mississippi sought to differentiate themselves from blacks. Ultimately, the Chinese established themselves as a middle group between whites and blacks. This case reveals that not only did the American public classify immigrants from Asia as a separate group, but in many cases these new immigrants wanted to be recognized as a distinctive group.

Mexicans of the Southwest: Incorporated Citizens

In contrast to Asian immigrants, Mexicans living in the southwestern territories gained through the Treaty of Guadalupe Hidalgo were not assigned to a new racial category. Their initial assignment to the white racial category was a product of treaty negotiations, but this racial assignment did not consistently apply to Mexican immigrants entering the Southwest after the Mexican-American War. Thus, the racial classification of Mexicans shows how it can change over time.

To end the Mexican-American War, the United States and Mexico signed the Treaty of Guadalupe Hidalgo, which stipulated the terms of land transfer from Mexico to the United States (Gomez 2008). In this treaty, the Mexican government outlined protections for Mexican citizens living in the southwestern territories at the time of the transfer. Mexican nationals residing in the Southwest would have the option of remaining in their homes and would be eligible for American citizenship. But the classification of Mexicans as citizens disrupted the carefully constructed white racial prerequisite to citizenship established in the law. As newly incorporated citizens, Mexicans could thus be considered racially "white." In the 1897 case *In re Rodriguez*, the state of Texas attempted to deny Ricardo Rodriguez, a Mexican citizen, the right to naturalization on the basis that Rodriguez was not white. Using a twist of logic, lawyers for Rodriguez claimed that because the United States had awarded Mexicans citizenship through the Treaty of Guadalupe Hidalgo, Mexicans were classified as white by virtue of their citizenship status (Gross 2008; Haney-Lopez 2006). Although the judge ultimately upheld Rodriguez's right to naturalization as promised by the treaty, he was also quick to note that in everyday practice, Rodriguez would normally not be classified as white. Rather than challenging the whiteness prerequisite to citizenship, the courts allowed Rodriguez to keep his citizenship status.

Whereas Asian immigrants were quickly seen as a distinct racial group, the classification of Mexicans as a separate racial group was thus complicated by the fact that they were originally incorporated into the United States as citizens. Since race was used to justify unequal citizenship status, there was no imperative to racially classify Mexicans as a distinct group. This historical perspective explains why the racial classification of Mexicans has been inconsistent over time. The federal government only once considered Mexicans a separate racial group, when the U.S. Census in 1930 listed "Mexican" as a racial category. Mexicans have also been classified in cultural terms, such as "Spanish speaking," and today are officially subsumed under the "Hispanic/Latino" ethnic category. Yet historians have shown that even though Mexicans were not officially classified as a distinctive nonwhite racial group, in practice they have been treated as if they were non-white (Bender 2005; Menchaca 2002; Rodriguez 2008). In western states like California, racial segregation rules applied to Mexicans just as they applied to blacks and Asian Americans (Camarillo 1984). Thus, official classification and social practice do not always align. However, the official designation of Mexicans and other Latinos as a distinctive racial group continues to be deliberated today, demonstrating that new groups are not always classified in new and distinctive categories.

Social categories based on race ultimately came to correspond with the different levels of citizenship awarded to each group. At the founding, the categories of white, black, and Native American each designated a specific citizenship status. Later, we see this unique American practice at work when we review the incorporation of new groups, such as Asian immigrants and Mexicans, into the polity. These cases of incorporation show how both citizenship status and race have been deployed to assign status to new groups. But what is most striking about the American racial system is that it is characterized by a small set of categories. The United States has witnessed a dynamic history characterized by extensive diversity, but the general culture has sorted individuals into a handful of racial groupings. This a direct contrast to cultures such as those in Latin America, where there are a larger number of racial categories (Nobles 2000). The correspondence between race and citizenship explains why there are so few racial categories in the United States: since the American objective was to award full citizenship only to a select group of people, there was no political imperative to construct a complicated web of citizenship statuses, only a need for a small number of racial categories to designate specific levels of membership.

Biology, Blood, and Segregation: Imposed Racial Classification

Alongside the national conceptualization of race as a set of discrete categories, Americans developed a logic that guided social norms for how individuals were to be sorted into categories. Early writings in anthropology reflect societal or cultural beliefs that there exist inherent and biological differences between civilizations (Powell 2005). The cultural norms thus established upheld the belief that intrinsic traits direct assignment of a person into a particular racial category. Individuals did not choose their racial classification; rather a person could be *assigned* a race since racial categories reflected fundamental traits. Over time, two general logics have been employed to govern racial classification: one relies on a logic of ancestry or descent and the other relies on a logic of visible phenotype or physical biology. The norms governing racial classification through the first half of the twentieth century reflect a strange amalgamation of these two logics.

In the early founding period, race was often assigned on the basis of visual appearance and phenotype. It was also assumed that race could be legally determined through "common knowledge" (Gross 2008; Haney Lopez 2006). An individual's race was considered visibly obvious when his or her physical features conformed with existing stereotypes about what Asians, blacks, indigenous, Latinos, and whites looked like. Early legal cases emphasized phenotypic traits. For example, in 1806 in *Hudgins v. Wright* the defendant's race was determined on the basis of particular phenotypic traits. The judge presiding offered a racial test: "Nature has stampt upon the African and his descendents two characteristic marks, besides the difference of complexion, which often remain visible long after the characteristic distinction of colour either disappears or becomes doubtful; a flat nose and woolly head of hair" (Haney-Lopez 1999, 2). The judge framed race as not only visibly apparent but also reflected in traits that did not disappear over generations.

However, given frequent racial group mixing, the visible difference between a white person and a black person was oftentimes difficult to decipher. In fact, in the antebellum era, many light-skinned slaves with European facial features attempted to escape slavery by claiming to be white (Gross 2008). Thus, there was a need for a stringent requirement beyond visual inspection to determine the difference between the races. Family ancestry offered a more direct indicator of racial descent (Davis 1991; Hickman 1996). It was intuitive to distinguish between whites, blacks, and indigenous tribes according to their family ancestry since bloodlines were used in Europe. Concepts such as "race," "nation," and "peoples" were once used interchangeably since they all denoted the idea of group difference (Gross 2008). Some European cultures believed that each nation descended from a common bloodline (Brubaker1992). Thus, early European ideas made strong associations between citizenship and parentage. Furthermore, the concept of "pedigree" could serve as a legitimate explanation for the assignment of social status (Berlin 2000; Foner 1999). American reliance on ancestry not only helped to clarify those cases in which phenotype was ambiguous but also was consistent with some early European traditions related to descent.

However, even a rule of descent could not reliably determine a person's racial classification. If a person had one parent who was acknowledged to be white and another parent who was acknowledged to be black, a simple rule of descent could mean that the person was white. For example, illegitimate children of white male slave owners could be considered racially white. In order to resolve this concern, the rule of "one drop," also called hypodescent, was implemented. The rule of hypodescent dictated that a person was given the status of "black" if that person had any ancestors who were African (Davis 1991; Hollinger 2003). This rule effectively created an inclusive definition of who was to be considered "black" and the perception of exclusivity of those to be considered "white." While this rule was most prominently applied to defining blackness, it was also applied to Native Americans,[17] Hawaiians, and Asians (Gross 2008, Spickard 1986, 1991). So in reality, hypodescent was primarily a rule to protect the exclusivity of whiteness but allowed for racial diversity within nonwhite groups: those classified as white showed no evidence of African, Asian, indigenous, or Latin Asian heritage, whereas those classified as nonwhite could have ancestors of different races. Racial mixing thus created nonwhite populations.

The rise of science led to further emphasis on the classification of living objects into typologies (Nobles 2000; Tichenor 2002; Yanow 2002). Because science was considered a rigorous and objective process, scientific theories helped to legitimate historically held ideas about white superiority and racial categorization. At the turn of the twentieth century, different scientific and academic disciplines began to take on the question of race and biology. Anthropology, especially ethnology, was committed to classifying cultures and races. The eugenics movement also gained prominence in this period. Eugencists sought to connect races with particular biological attributes, such as phenotype, hair type, and cranial size, and made inferences on the effects of these attributes on an individual's intelligence and personality (Hattam 2007; Nobles 2000). Even the idea that each racial group derived from a common ancestor corresponded with new ideas associated with evolution and Darwinism. These scientific theories not only helped to legitimize earlier reliance on phenotype and ancestry, but also made these logics appear to be scientifically rigorous and objective.

Cultural logics such as hypodescent, "common knowledge," and those offered by eugenic theories are not the only forces that upheld practices of imposed racial classification. When formal citizenship was awarded to blacks through passage of the Thirteenth, Fourteenth. and Fifteenth Amendments, the exclusive alignment between whiteness and citizenship appeared to be eroding. Because white southerners continued to believe that they were not only distinct from but superior to blacks, they enacted rules that maintained the racial hierarchy (Johnson, K. 2008; Marx 1998; Myrdal 1944). The practice of Jim Crow, a system of rules governing interactions between whites and blacks, maintained the idea that, even without slavery, whites were still superior to blacks. Under Jim Crow, both public spaces and social interactions were segregated. Although most historians highlight Jim Crow practices in the South, racial segregation was practiced in all regions in the first half of the twentieth century (Camarillo 1984; Hing 2003; Ngai 2006; Takaki 1998). If racial groups were separated, it was easier to differentiate whites from blacks and other nonwhites. When segregation was legally upheld as "separate but equal" in *Plessy v. Ferguson* in 1896, physical distance between the races was legitimized as an attribute of American life (Massey 2007; Smith 1999).

In addition to formal segregation, American society after the Civil War policed intimate interactions between the races. Intimate contact was dangerous because it blurred the line between white and nonwhite (Davis 1991; Moran 2003). Bans on interracial marriage had long been widespread, but under Jim Crow, intimate relationships were severely punished. The 1833 Civil Rights cases upheld the legality of racial discrimination when the justices ruled that the Constitution only protected federal or institutional discrimination, not personal discrimination (Smith 1999). Lynchings, workplace discrimination, and other social retributions maintained a strict distance between the races (Myrdal 1944). The severe social consequences levied against perceived integrationists made interracial interaction more rare. Collectively, Jim Crow and other forms of racial segregation outside the South created the national perception that the races did not interact. Thus, by the time a national movement began questioning the moral and legal implications of segregation in the 1940s, Americans had developed clearly segregated racial groups and the general assumption that racial groups did not intermingle in any intimate manner.

The practice of assigned classification also allowed for social recognition of historic mixed-race populations, in particular the "mulatto" population. Such categories were created by the white elite as a social buffer; they were socially ranked below whites but above blacks (Reuter 1918). Status distinctions within the black population helped control racial tensions, since competition could be redirected to occur between blacks and mixed-race groups rather than between whites and nonwhites. Mulattoes and other mixed-race black populations were also used as case studies to test eugenic theories about racial superiority. These theories had proposed that racial mixing created inferior species. To test their hypotheses, eugenicists convinced state officials to collect data on mixed-race blacks, resulting in the inclusion of racial categories such as "mulatto" and "octoroon" in post–Civil War censuses (Nobles 2000). Thus, while Americans have in the past acknowledged racially mixed populations, the recognition of mixed-race blacks was a product, not of personal choice made by black Americans, but of categories deployed by whites to warn against interracial mixing (see also Spencer 2010).

The American assumption that individuals can be assigned to racial categories is upheld by the belief that there exist fundamental and intrinsic differences across groups of people. Even historic mixed-race groups like mulattoes were tools to uphold ideas of racial difference. The collection of beliefs ranging from ancestry, phenotype, and biology used to define racial categories demonstrate the efforts expended to maintain a social hierarchy. The rise of racial segregation shows that even when the relationship between race and citizenship has been challenged, such as through legal efforts to formally include blacks in the citizenry, social practices simply reform to accommodate new rules. As a result, the belief that race reflects inherent differences became so ingrained that assignment of individuals to racial categories has been a standard practice in American life. Finally, the cultural narratives of hypodescent and the practice of racial segregation that upheld the racial hierarchy after the Civil War have helped create the modern perception that intimate interracial interactions and mixed-race heritage are uncommon features of American society.

The Civil Rights Movement: Shifting Ideas about Race

Given the dominant practice of defining race as a small set of discrete categories and the assignment of an individual to only one group, it is striking that we today see a growing number of Americans who assert racial hybridity. How did we reach a cultural period when individuals perceive, and take advantage of, opportunities to assert a multiracial identity? I argue that this shift is an unanticipated consequence of the modern civil rights movement. While this movement led to institutional changes that combated racial inequalities, these changes also encouraged Americans to embrace different social values: rejection of racism, "diversity" as a positive social feature, and recognition of the critical role of racial identity in the formation of self-esteem. These beliefs foster open and inviting environments in which individuals can embrace nonwhite racial identities, in particular, multiracial identities.

Changing White Racial Attitudes

The civil rights movement led to institutional changes that sought to improve the life chances and citizenship status of nonwhite Americans. These changes included the 1964 Civil Rights Act, which ensured equal protection of the laws for all racial groups, the 1965 Voting Rights Act, which both protected and increased voting for racial minorities, and the 1965 Immigration and Nationality Act, which eliminated racial quotas that sought to exclude non–Western European immigrants from entering the country.[18] One of the most important outcomes from these laws has been the shift in white racial attitudes. For example, a 1942 survey conducted by the National Opinion Research Council (NORC) found that less than half (47%) of whites believed that blacks were the intellectual equals of whites (Kinder and Sanders 1996). This survey also found that 68% of white Americans believed that white and black children should go to separate schools (Schuman et al. 1997). Today, a relatively small number of whites support the idea that blacks are intellectually inferior to whites. NORC found that as early as 1956, 80% of white Americans believed that whites and blacks were intellectual equals (Kinder and Sanders 1996). Americans today also strongly reject practices of racial segregation. Data show that in 1995, only 4% of white Americans supported segregating whites from blacks (Schuman et al. 1997). White racial attitudes have become more liberal among all age cohorts since the civil rights movement.

Changes in public attitudes reflect new values and norms practiced by white Americans. Prior to the civil rights movement, racist viewpoints and discriminatory treatment were rarely disavowed since the white public generally accepted that racial minorities were inferior to whites. But as the public began to reject racism, discriminatory attitudes and activities no longer were acceptable, institutionally sanctioned practices. It is socially undesirable to express openly racist views today. Tali Mendelberg (2001) argues that white Americans increasingly support the "norm of equality": the belief that all Americans should be treated equally. Americans are thus expected to value racial equality and want to be perceived as practicing this vision.

Americans have also grown more supportive of interracial relationships, including marriage. When racial segregation was the social norm, intimate interracial relationships were not only culturally unacceptable, but illegal. Interracial couples in the past were disowned from their families, subject to discriminatory treatment, and often segregated from others (Moran 2003). However, in 1967, the Supreme Court ruled that state anti-miscegenation laws were unconstitutional. Moreover, given the growing public belief that whites and blacks are equal, racial intermarriage has become a widely accepted practice. In 1958, 4% of respondents approved of white-black intermarriage, while in 2013, the approval rate was 87% (Newport 2013). In turn, there has been a dramatic growth in the number of interracial marriages. In 1970, there were an estimated 300,000 interracial marriages, whereas in 2010 that number was approximately 5.4 million (Lee and Edmonston 2005; Lofquist et al. 2012). Although interracial marriages are still exceptions to the norm,[19] their growth is nonetheless an important feature in American life.

The liberalization of white racial attitudes is impressive and is politically significant given whites' status as the majority racial group in the United States. These changes, however, should not be taken as evidence that racism has disappeared from the American landscape. Extensive evidence shows that many white Americans hold racial beliefs like those of their counterparts in the past but express their negative attitudes using different explanations (Kinder and Sanders 1996; Sears, Sidanius, and Bobo 2000; Sniderman and Piazza 1993). But even though racial bias continues to exist, competing norms discourage openly discriminatory attitudes and behaviors. These norms have changed what attitudes can be expressed in public discourse, which is consequential to everyday intergroup interactions. In general, whites cannot be openly hostile or discriminatory toward nonwhite identities, and this norm creates a more inviting environment for the expression of multiracial identities.

Promotion of Diversity as a Desirable Social Feature

The second major shift in American values following the modern civil rights movement concerns "diversity" and "multiculturalism" (see Pellegrini 2013). Both of these concepts refer to the desire to recognize and include different voices, ideas, and people in public and private practices. Over the last half of the twentieth century, these concepts were increasingly framed as desirable societal attributes. Moreover, in contrast to historic discussions of diversity, primarily limited to academic writings, today we find not only the advocacy of diversity but also the implementation of policies that promote diversity, such as affirmative action and multicultural education.

America has always been a diverse nation among many dimensions, including religion, ethnicity, and social class,[20] yet a positive valence has not always been attached to racial diversity. This is not to say that there were not advocates of diversity prior to the mid-twentieth century. For example, Horace Kallen's (1970) original theory of cultural pluralism, published early in the twentieth century, advocated the idea that ethnic minorities could retain their distinctive cultures without weakening national unity.[21] At the same time, arguments in favor of diversity did not represent the dominant perspective, nor were they regularly adopted in practice (Rathner 1984). For example, anti-immigration policies, such as the national origins quota instituted in 1924, which sought to maintain the white, Protestant Anglo-Saxon majority of the nation, were passed in the midst of academic debates over diversity and assimilation (Rathner 1984; Tichenor 2002).

Today, concepts such as diversity and multiculturalism are not limited to scholarly circles but viewed positively by the general public. Public opinion polls report that Americans value diversity. A 2008 Pew study found that six in 10 Americans prefer to live in communities that are racially, religiously, politically, and economically diverse (Wang et al. 2008). The strength of this preference did vary across subpopulations, but overall, most Americans preferred diversity to homogeneity. Americans are also optimistic about the effects of diversity. A 2013 survey reported that 69% of Americans believed that a bigger, more diverse workforce will lead to more economic growth (Teixeira et al. 2013). In addition to diversity, Americans also value the practice of diverse cultures and religions. A 2013 Gallup poll found that over 70% of Americans believed it was important that Americans speak a second language (Gallup 2013). These public opinion studies show that support for diversity and multiculturalism is widespread across the American public.[22]

Most importantly, it is not just that there has been a changing orientation toward diversity, but many public policies since the 1960s have sought to produce diversity to rectify historical underrepresentation and inequalities in the United States. Peter Schuck posits that, since the 1960s, the "government in the United States has come to see diversity as an ideal that public law should not only protect (a familiar role for liberal governments) but *promote* in a variety of new ways" (2003, 16). A striking characteristic of policies passed during the civil rights movement is the activist stance taken by the federal government to ensure that states and localities would properly comply with policy directives (Graham 2000). The primary enforcement tool was economic incentives through various grants-in-aid programs sponsored by the federal government. In order for states, localities, or private businesses to receive federal aid for education, construction projects, and other social programs, they were required to demonstrate compliance with the antidiscrimination measures outlined by the 1964 Civil Rights Act as well as executive orders issued by the president. The active pursuit of proper representation was extended with the development of affirmative action programs that required hiring quotas or set-asides that allocated a particular share of government contracts to minority-owned businesses (Anderson 2004; Graham 2000).

Outside of governmental policy, we find the promotion of diversity in many other activities. One of the most prominent examples is in the American education system (Glaser 1998). "Multicultural" programs are now commonplace in American schools and universities. Practices that have developed out of this multicultural movement include instructional units that teach about the cultures, religions, and histories of particular social groups, the incorporation of textbooks authored by nonwhite writers in curriculums, and programs that promote recognition and public understanding of different social groups (Banks 1993). The goal of multicultural education is to promote the idea that all cultures and peoples are equal, and that every group plays an important role in American history and society. Multicultural programs in education also mean that valuing diversity is today a part of early childhood socialization. While there is opposition[23] to these multicultural programs, opposition to these policies is rooted in concerns about their implementation, not in a rejection of diversity.

Narratives that promote diversity and multiculturalism, coupled with government action that encourages more diverse and culturally sensitive environments, have made Americans more open to others with whom they do not share race, ethnicity, or religious or cultural values. Narratives that undercut the relevance of race, such as the need to be "color-blind" or the belief that the United States is "postracial" (Bonilla-Silva 2004; Gallagher 2015) do continue, and thus demonstrate that not all Americans embrace diversity. However, racism is framed as undesirable, and diversity and multiculturalism have been offered as more suitable values. This promoted openness to diversity helps shape environments in which individuals can publicly assert alternative racial identities, such as "multiracial."

Rise of Identity Politics

Finally, individuals today are encouraged to celebrate identities that in the past have been marginalized. Strategies and ideologies developed by minority groups as they mobilized during the civil rights movement created "identity politics" or "new social movements" (Pichardo 1997; Gitlin 1995; Gutmann 2003; Young 1990).[24] Two important ideas were embraced by racial minority groups over the course of the twentieth century and rose to prominence during the civil rights era. The first was the belief that racial minorities and other marginalized groups should have authority over the meanings attached to their identity. The second was the mobilization of racial group consciousness, a politicized variant of group identity in which group solidarity is connected to strategies for improving the group's inferior status. These two ideas articulated a sense of empowerment attached to one's racial identity and flourished in the new environment created by civil rights policies. As will be shown in the following chapter, the language articulating modern identity politics has been adopted by multiracial activists as they assert the right to define the meaning attached to their own multiracial identity.

The embrace of ethnic identity has been commonplace in US history. Shared national origin has been a social resource for incoming immigrants to rely on as they struggle to integrate into a new country (Dahl 1961; Wolfinger 1965). At the same time, there also existed a norm of assimilation in which successful integration into the United States would only occur when immigrants relinquished original attachments in favor of an "American" identity (Alba and Nee 2005; Gordon 1964). Inherent to this assimilation ideal is a belief that racial minority identities were inferior, undesirable, and disadvantageous. An important modern cultural development was to embrace difference and reframe racial minority identities as desirable bodies. Racial minorities began to express normative frames that connected positive difference with their identities. Examples in music, literature, and the arts reveal that racial minority groups sought to present their language, body types, and experiences in an aesthetically pleasing light, as a cause for celebration and respect (Young 1990). The assimilation ideal continues to be embraced by many Americans,[25] but today the embrace of racial difference exists as a counterargument.

In addition to associating respectability and beauty with nonwhite identities, racial minorities and Native American groups in the 1960s organized social movements that focused on their racialized status and the commonalities that arose from the discriminatory treatment they witnessed (Espiritu 1993; Morris 1986; Rosales and Rosales 1997; Wilkins 2002). A new ideology, then, aimed to direct public attention to oppression (Young 1990). In particular, nationalist political ideologies articulated the problems associated with oppression. Nationalism promotes the idea that those of a similar racial background share a common experience of racial subjugation and thus share a political interest in eradicating the constraints placed on them (Dawson 2001). Many black Americans have embraced some form of nationalism since the turn of the twentieth century. Black leaders such as Marcus Garvey and W. E. B. DuBois advocated for black self-determination and a reduced reliance on white social and political institutions. During the 1960s black nationalist ideologies again became prominent, with leaders demanding black political autonomy and asserting a distinctive black cultural and spiritual identity (Karenga 2010; Ture and Hamilton 1992). These nationalist ideologies were embraced by other minority groups, including Asians, Mexicans, Puerto Ricans, and Native Americans, who all sought to assert political, cultural, and social cohesion among their communities (Espiritu 1993; Johnson 2008; Rosales and Rosales 1997; Torres 1998)

Another important feature of identity politics was their orientation toward mainstream politics. After passage of voting rights legislation, the federal government created opportunities to incorporate excluded groups into democratic decision-making. This "politics of presence" (Phillips 1995) articulated the value of including a diverse and descriptively representative population in decision-making (see also Skrentny 2002). For example, central to the defense of congressional redistricting was the opportunity for racial minority groups to elect a "candidate of choice," assumed to be a candidate of the same race (Davidson and Grofman 1994). Advocates argue that descriptive representatives are more attuned to the problems of the racial or ethnic group of which the representative is a member (Dovi 2002; Mansbridge 1999; Phillips 1995). Over the long term, voting rights legislation created a new policy environment that enforces different forms of "presence": those who occupy seats in elected office must reflect the diversity of the adult citizen population. Consistent with past public policy models, voting rights reforms led to new legislative and legal strategies adopted by racial minority groups who sought to protect gains created by the Voting Rights Act (Skrentny 2002). Therefore, rather than asserting identities only in particular social circles, groups sought to have their identities incorporated in mainstream practices.

Finally, new generations of Americans are exposed to, if not socialized to embrace, modern identity politics through changes in the educational curriculum. One target of minority social movements was the educational system, in particular their representations of minorities in textbooks and academic curricula (Symcox 2002; Zimmerman 2004). Activists argued that standard educational programs presented history only from the perspective of white Americans. Activists sought to change the content of history and social studies textbooks so that non-Eurocentric views would be incorporated in the assessment of historical events (Banks 1993). Other efforts targeted scholarship and the educational curriculum on college campuses, which ultimately led to the creation of ethnic studies programs, which include African American or Africana studies, Asian American studies, and Latino studies (Yang 2000).[26] These programs became institutionalized as they spread across American universities.

Changing white racial attitudes and the positive orientation toward diversity and multiculturalism represent two societal-level phenomena that explain the development of a more accepting cultural environment for multiracial identities. In contrast, identity politics movements have offered a narrative and strategy that individuals can adopt in their own efforts to advocate for their preferred identities. As will be seen in chapter 3, some multiracial activists promote positive images and increased representation in the public sphere. Others seek to provide educational programs to socialize families on how to deal with multiracial or other forms of racial identity. In this way, the self-identified multiracial population is another group that falls into the identity politics paradigm.

Institutional Changes to the Practice of Racial Classification

In addition to the cultural shifts that have occurred since the civil rights period in the 1960s, there have also been changes in institutional practices of racial classification. Institutional theories in political science point to government structures and laws as central guiding features of individual behavior (Peters 1999). Institutions create certain rules that organize incentives and obstacles for certain forms of individual action. Accordingly, when institutions promote certain behaviors, citizens begin to conform to those expectations and a general public norm becomes established. Adopting this institutional perspective, I argue that two important changes in institutional approaches to racial classification have paved the way for multiracial identification: changes in data collection efforts to enumerate by race, and growing recognition of the race-ethnicity distinction. The belief that individuals can choose their own identities and embrace the unique qualities of being multiracial represents a logical extension of these two modern practices of racial classification.

Institutional Underpinning: Racial Enumeration on the US Census

One way of showing changes in racial practices is tracing how governing institutions have employed racial categories. In the United States, the institution that plays a critical role in the creation of racial categories is the decennial census (Anderson 1988; Nobles 2000; Prewitt 2013). A short review of the history will show that racial categories represented in the census reflect the social assumptions about race at a given time. At the same time, census changes can affect Americans' definitions of racial categories (Lee 2008). In this way, the shift from understanding race as an assigned classification to understanding it as a reporting of personal identity can be seen in how the census enumerates race.

It is first important to understand the census as a politically consequential institution. The Constitution requires that the federal government conduct a full enumeration of the population every ten years to determine representation. The decision to determine political representation in Congress on the basis of population created the need to count the number of individuals residing in designated districts. Because black slaves were to be counted as three-fifths of a person, officials could not rely on a simple head count but also needed to identify the status of each individual. Thus, identifying the size of racial populations became an essential task of the government (Anderson 1988). Of course, the original census counted the difference between free person and slaves, but given that the correspondence between race and slave status became stronger in every decade leading up to the Civil War, enumerating by race can be understood as a constitutional directive (Nobles 2000).

Although the census has always collected data on race, the types of categories and methods of defining race have evolved. For most of its history (until 2000), the census presented race as a set of discrete groups, and respondents were assigned to one category. This approach perfectly reflects the long-standing cultural practice of understanding race as a categorical variable. However, the labels for racial groupings have varied over time. For example, to enumerate blacks, the census has used the label "slave," "Negro," and "African American." In addition, the same racial groups have not always been represented on every census: "Hindu" appeared as a racial category on the 1930 census but is no longer recognized as racial grouping, while "Mexican" was a racial category in 1930 but today is subsumed under the Hispanic/Latino ethnic category. The changing labels and representation of groups demonstrates that the census reflects the norms about race at a given time. The one consistent feature is the presentation of race as discrete categories.

The shift from presenting race as an assigned trait to one that reflects personal identity was not a purposeful move made by the Census Bureau but rather, I argue, is the unanticipated outcome of an administrative change in how data are collected: the move from enumerator-assigned race to self-reported race. In the early days of the census, the head count and completion of forms were done by an enumerator. Racial categories were defined by the government, and enumerators followed the directions provided. Extensive notes about what constituted "black" or "white" were provided to enumerators. For example, in the 1940 census, enumerators were given the specific instructions for filling out the personal description of the respondent.[27] The directions stated that "Mexicans are to be regarded as white unless definitely of Indian or other non-white race." For "Negros," the directions stated that "a person of mixed white and negro blood should be returned as a Negro, no matter how small a percentage of Negro blood.... A person of mixed Indian and Negro blood should be returned as a Negro, unless the Indian blood very definitely predominates and he is universally accepted in the community as Indian."[28] So for the first 17 censuses collected, the Census Bureau dictated how a person's race was to be classified. Enumerators used their best judgment to complete the forms consistent with these directions.

Beginning with the 1960 census, officials collected data through a mail-in form sent to each residence (Anderson 1988). The decision to collect data through a mail-in form was related to the practical matter of collecting a head count of an increasingly large population. Simply put, the method of enumerating in person was becoming infeasible. The mail-in form gave

Americans the opportunity to self-report their characteristics, including their race. Although the government provided documentation defining racial categories, Americans had the liberty to report the racial category that they believedbest described their raceand the race of the members of their household.[29] This was a distinct change in how racial information was collected: race became a characteristic that individuals declared for themselves rather than one imposed by enumerators.[30] Although this was not the specific intent of the mail-in form, as Americans became used to declaring their own race for official records, a symbolic link developed between personal identification and race.

In 2000, the "mark one or more" option was added to the directions for reporting race on the census (Farley 2002; Nobles 2000). This change further broadened options because Americans could now report multiple races. This mark-one-or-more option is an example of how citizens can influence the representation of categories on the census.[31] In the 1990s a group of activists, largely parents who wanted the opportunity to so report their biracial and multiracial children, lobbied Congress to allow multiracial identification on the census (Williams 2006). As will be covered more extensively in the next chapter, these activists argued that the existing census rule, which allowed respondents to mark only one racial category, excluded a growing population who desired to recognize their diverse heritages. In the end, the Census Bureau decided to allow Americans to check multiple boxes for racial identification. The mark-one-or-more option was again offered in the 2010 census, suggesting that this practice may become standard. This addition solidifies the view that race is an identity and that, because it is an identity conceived by individuals, the Census Bureau should allow respondents wider latitude in reporting their race.

By integrating particular categories and procedures into data collection, the census influences how Americans conceive of race (Bailey 2008; Kertzer and Arel 2002). Taken together, the shift to self-reporting one's race and the most recent mark-one-or-more option represent the state-sanctioned view that race is not strictly an imposed classification. Although the future implications of the new option cannot yet be known,[32] self-reporting one's race is now second nature to most Americans: it is common for a person to be asked to report her racial background on daily forms ranging from healthcare to education and consumer preferences. The census does not offer freedom to declare any racial identity one wishes (the categories to choose from are still limited), and there are efforts to make the race question align further with patterns of self-identification. For example, proposed changes to the 2020 census include adding Middle Eastern North African (MENA) and Latino categories, on the basis that there are identities not offered in the census that deserve representation (Prewitt 2013).[33]

Conceiving Ethnicity: Emphasis on Identity and Group Distinctiveness

The creation of the conceptual distinction between "race" and "ethnicity" suggests how group identities and practices of identification can vary. Scholars have emphasized the distinction between race and ethnicity because important consequences follow from each concept, but the lack of institutional clarity on these concepts has muddled the differences for the general public. The average citizen may not distinguish between her race and her ethnicity, and this has created an opportunity to diversify racial categories. Narratives that historically have been used to justify white ethnic identities, particularly those that emphasize personal identity and individual distinctiveness, are now used to describe multiracial identification, even though "multiracial" is commonly treated as a racial identity.

Before the turn of the twentieth century, there was very little conceptual distinction between different forms of background: terms like "race," "nation," and "peoples" were often used interchangeably to designate the general concept of group difference (Roediger2005). This practice corresponded with the previously held belief that intrinsic differences existed between groups, and so words such as "race" and "peoples" generally communicated where basic group boundaries were drawn. Yet today, the federal government uses terms such as "race," "ethnicity," and "ancestry" in enumeration forms, and each indicates a different way of grouping people (Cornell and Hartmann 2007; Hattam 2007; Omi and Winant 1994).

Making a conceptual distinction between ethnicity and race was a project largely motivated by new European immigrants who entered during America's second major immigration wave midway through the nineteenth century. Roediger (2005) convincingly argues that the creation of the concept of "ethnicity" is a modern one that developed through a circuitous process in which European immigrants became, as it were, "white" (see also Hattam 2007; Jacobson 1998). His research shows that when they arrived to the U.S., European immigrant groups sought to establish unique cultural, language, and religious identities that corresponded to their distinctive nationality groups. Yet, given the political and material advantages American institutions gave to whiteness, such as citizenship and landholding, new European immigrants saw advantages of embracing a white racial classification over their distinctive cultural, linguistic, and religious identities.

Victoria Hattam's (2007) documentation of Jewish intellectual thought reveals how the concept of ethnicity became recognized as a distinct concept by the federal government. Hattam argues that state recognition of what we now understand as "ethnicity" began in 1910, when Jewish intellectuals convinced the Census Bureau to include a new question on one's "mother tongue." Jewish immigrants, who began arriving in mass at the turn of the twentieth century, challenged the notion that social distinctiveness could be defined by national origin or by race. Jews believed themselves to be a distinct and cohesive group, connected by a common religion and language, but not necessarily a common nationality or phenotype. To distinguish their group from others, Jewish elites sought to create a contrast between "race" and "ethnicity" by connecting the former with characteristics such as color and the latter with culture, language, or religion. The question on mother tongue required enumerators to account for the primary language spoken in the home and was asked separately from the race question. But, as Hattam notes, the key advantage in an ethnic distinction is that Jews could represent the distinctiveness of their group while at the same time being classified as "white" in order to maintain the privileges associated with that racial category.

The practice of white ethnicity we see today is often attributed to the implementation of national immigration restriction in 1924 (Gans 1979; Roediger 2005). With the halting of new immigration, the perceived distinctiveness of Southern and Eastern Europeans faded as these groups assimilated into the American mainstream (Jimenez 2010). The end to new immigration, along with the rise of Jim Crow, paved the way for Americans of Southern and Eastern European background to be classified as whites. The positive group distinctiveness that European immigrants had perceived upon their arrival now could flourish in this twentieth-century racial environment. European Americans openly identified as ethnic and emphasized their distinctive ancestral and cultural background. However, in contrast to their immigrant grandparents, third-generation and subsequent European Americans benefited from relatively higher levels of socioeconomic status and so practiced ethnicity largely as a form of identity. Instead of depending on one's ethnic group for survival, as did early European immigrants, later generations of European Americans could voluntarily evoke an ethnic identity during leisure activities. Herbert Gans (1979) called this process "symbolic ethnicity," and Mary Waters (1990) characterized white ethnic identities as products of personal choice.

In white ethnic identity practices, ethnicity is an attractive concept because it distinguish oneself from others based on practices that the individual can control.[34] Ethnic distinctiveness can be asserted when the individual chooses to embrace certain cultural practices. In other circumstances, when fitting in with the group is advantageous, ethnicity can be ignored by downplaying cultural difference. Ethnicity promotes the idea that social classification can be controlled by the individual, not by others. More importantly, ethnicity offers European ethnics the privilege of being classified as whitebut also of being recognized as a distinct subpopulation within the white racial category (Waters 1990).[35]

Ethnicity may be developing a different meaning today, given that since 1980 the federal government has designated Latino (or Hispanic) as an "ethnic" category.[36] Therefore, one can be ethnically Latino but racially white, black, Asian, Native American, or Pacific Islander. While federal classification as an ethnic group does offer Latinos choices for identification, this is an example of the general lack of clarity on race versus ethnicity in practice. While white ethnics advocated for ethnic categories in order to show cultural diversity within the white racial category, Latinos are defined as sharing an ethnicity but also racially diverse. Moreover, Latinos in practice are a marginalized group, and the federal government covers them as a legally protected group in redistributive policies, such as racial redistricting and affirmative action (de la Garza and DeSipio 1997; Garcia1994; Skretney 2002). They therefore do not have the same experiences with group difference as white ethnics.

Thus, while scholars have declared an important difference between ethnicity and race, in practice these concepts have not been consistently applied. In this way, it might be hard for some individuals to understand that the ethnic practices employed by whites are different from the experiences of difference among Asian Americans, blacks, or Latinos. This lack of clarity between race and ethnicity means that individuals may apply narratives of white ethnicity to the formation of nonwhite racial identities. Indeed, the features that explain white ethnic identities—the embrace personal identity, fluidity, and individual distinctiveness—all emphasize the primary role of personal agency. The idea that race is a reflection of personal identity corresponds to arguments that explain white ethnicity, which generally discount the role of external or structural constraints. This convergence, where narratives that used to explain white ethnicity are now being used to describe race, is another factor that has created opportunities for assertions of multiracial identities.

From Classification to Identification

This chapter traced the cultural movement from conceptualizing race as a product of assigned classification to considering it a product of personal identification. For most of American history, racial categories have been seen as rigid constructs, and strict segregation of the races was policed. This can be explained by the fact that race and citizenship became intertwined for the entire period leading up to the Civil War. Race justified the existing order of citizenship. Therefore, race could not be perceived as a fluid set of categories since doing so would threaten the existing status quo. As a result, race has been established largely as a classification system: individuals are sorted into racial categories based on the ruling definitions of a given time, and their placement in society is governed by their classification.

However, this chapter shows that American practices of race have changed over the course of the twentieth century. At a cultural level, new norms have been cultivated as a product of the political and social gains from the civil rights movement. Scholars have documented the public rejection of white supremacy since the second half of the twentieth century, and the public sees positive value in diversity and multiculturalism. At the institutional level, racial classification in the census has shifted, from having enumerators define a resident's race to having respondents self-report their race. The more recent implementation of the mark-one-or-more option offers Americans more ways to express their racial identity. These cultural and institutional changes indicate that race is increasingly seen as a form of personal identity. Many Americans today thus self-identify as multiracial because an inviting environment accepts these identities, and institutional venues allow the formal assertion of these identities.

At the same time, the shift to embracing race as personal identity has not challenged established practices of racial classification. Multiracial identities instead add an alternative to the existing set of discrete racial categories. As we will find in the next chapter, the embrace of identity choice by self-identified multiracial activists does not rely on a novel argument but is largely an extension of existing narratives. In particular, many of the frames that have been used to explain white ethnicity and the ideas generated from the identity politics of racial minority groups are integrated into claims made by multiracial activists. In this story of modern racial formation, we find that multiracial identities are a response to past practices of racial classification and thus cannot exist without the presence of the established racial categories of white, black, Asian, or Latino.

3 | Advocating for Choice

POLITICAL VIEWS OF MULTIRACIAL ACTIVISTS

THE POST-CIVIL RIGHTS ERA IS characterized as an encouraging environment for Americans to assert their racial and ethnic identities. Yet because multiracial identities are a distinct contrast to past racial norms that enforced identification with only one racial category, we should not assume that multiracial identities immediately come to mind for Americans. Rather, multiracial identities needed to be conceived and mobilized within the mass public. Today, activists dedicate time to generating public attention to multiracial identities (Dacosta 2007). In fact, the mark-one-or-more option for racial identification in the US census was a change made in response to lobbying efforts by parents of multiracial children (Williams 2006). The presence of these activists who lobby on behalf of multiracial identities represents a unique dimension of the modern multiracial population.

This chapter presents data from in-depth interviews with a sample of these activists to learn about the logics that explain why representation of multiracial identities is important. Because a large majority of the activists I spoke with self-identified as multiracial, these interviews allow me to explore why a person chooses multiracial identities over others. Some scholarship shows that social identities are largely symbolic in nature, motivated by simultaneous desires of belonging and individuality.[1] However, as their responses show, these activists had political reasons to adopt a multiracial identity. In fact, they view their multiracial identities as a response to everyday experiences of racialization. Activists reported their frustration with established practices of racial classification, which led them to advocate for the right to choose their racial identities. They contended that a person's racial classification and identification should be first determined by the individual, not by others who impose a particular racial classification on them. I thus find that activists adopted a unique approach to race: they highlight the primacy of individual agency and personal choice in racial classification.

The perspectives highlighted in this chapter represent a specific type of multiracial identifier: activists who have dedicated personal effort to promote multiracial identification. They are unique because they demonstrate not simply self-identification as multiracial but a politicized group consciousness: a connection between their group identity and a set of ideological beliefs about the status of their group and how to improve that status (Chong and Rogers 2005; Miller et al. 1981). Given this political ideology, the perspectives presented in this chapter are not necessarily representative of the larger self-identified multiracial population. At the same time, these interviews, which offer insight into the organizational structure and mobilization activities of these activists, suggest that their ideas are often communicated to self-identified multiracial individuals in the wider public. Since research has shown that the frames disseminated and promoted by elites or activists often influence the attitudes of average voters (see, for example, Stimson 2004), the narratives produced by multiracial activists may have substantial implications for trends in multiracial identification.

This chapter begins with a historical background to the social movement to change the racial identification question on the 2000 census. This background details the political agenda activists promoted and the political tensions that their agenda caused. The contestation over racial identity revealed the social and political consequences of increasing self-identification as multiracial. After this historical background, I outline the state of multiracial activism following the 2000 census change and present the key themes drawn from interviews with activists: the constraints of race, the proposed right to identity choice, and their continued status as nonwhite Americans.

Politics of Recognition: Lobbying for the Right to Identify as Multiracial

Those groups involved in the efforts to change the race question on the 2000 census did not organize at first with an aim towards political lobbying. Most of the initial organizations involved began as support groups for interracially married couples, and later their families, in the late-1970s and 1980s. When the Supreme Court struck down state antimiscegenation laws in 1967, the legal barrier to interracial marriage was eliminated, but the social stigma persisted. Therefore, interracial couples, primarily those with one white partner and one black partner, sought out accepting spaces in which to socialize (DaCosta 2007; Williams 2006). As these couples began to have children, concerns for their childrens' mixed race identitiesemerged in these groups. When their children enrolled in school, parents realized that schools failed to recognize children's diverse racial heritages. Parents were often forced to follow official racial practices, designating their child as only one race. Normally they had to follow the rule of hypodescent, classifying their children as black (or another nonwhite category).

In 1979, parents in Berkeley, California, founded Interracial and Intercultural Pride, later known as iPride, a group organized primarily to lobby for the right to report mixed racial heritages on records in the public school system (Brown and Douglas 2003). The group also sought to ensure that their children's multiracial identities were acknowledged and respected by teachers. Since the formation of iPride, other organized efforts were mobilized to lobby on behalf of multiracial identification in schools. Starting in the early 1990s, mothers—the vast majority of whom were white, living in states such as Ohio, Georgia, Michigan, Illinois, and Maryland— successfully lobbied their respective state legislatures to include a multiracial category on official state forms (Williams 2006). Many of those parenting organizations formed an umbrella organization, the Association of MultiEthnic Americans (AMEA), in 1988. At the national level, the AMEA sought to leverage its membership and geographic dispersion to advocate on behalf of interracial families and multiracial identities.

These activities served as the foundation for what Kim Williams (2006) labels the "multiracial movement," a newly formed network of leaders and organizations and a specific political agenda focused on ensuring the representation of mixed-race identities in governmental forms and record-keeping. Although local-level lobbying could resolve the immediate concerns of school enrollment, multiracial advocates quickly acknowledged that racial reporting takes place in most areas of public life, including healthcare and grant funding. Because state and local procedures in data collection follow federal guidelines outlined by the Office of Management and Budget, changes would have to be made at the federal level if they were to have national impact. The decennial census, the primary data collection tool used by the federal government, soon became the target of these multiracial advocates.

Originally, advocacy groups fought for a separate "multiracial" category on census questionnaires. They argued that marking only one racial background constrained people into inflexible categories. This system, they claimed, perpetuated the "one-drop rule" that historically was used to discriminate against blacks. However, the demand for a separate multiracial category mobilized unexpected advocates and opposition groups. Republicans in Congress were prominent in their support of a multiracial category. At a committee hearing in 1997, Republican Speaker of the House Newt Gingrich argued that a multiracial category would "be an important step toward transcending racial division and reflecting the melting pot which is America" (quoted in Williams 2006, 55). In opposition, civil rights groups, which included the National Association for the Advancement of Colored People, National Urban League, Mexican American Legal Defense Fund, National Asian Pacific American Legal Consortium, and National Congress of American Indians, fought against a multiracial category. They argued that a multiracial category could be used to reclassify minority individuals in the new group and thus dilute the size of federally protected minority populations (Nobles 2000; Williams 2006). They posited that many race-conscious public policies, such as affirmative action and racial redistricting, were originally created to increase representation of racial minorities in government, employment, and education and thus relied on racial group enumerations collected by the census. It would be more difficult to prosecute these policies if data needed to determine a violation were unavailable (Goldstein and Morning 2002; Persily 2002).

In the end, the Office of Management and Budget revised its Statistical Directive 15, the formal rules governing data collection procedures, to include a multiple box option, or the ability to "mark one or more," on racial classification questions on official data collection forms (Nobles 2000). Although many in the multiracial movement preferred a "multiracial" category, a mixed-race designation was still possible with the mark-one-or-more option since a respondent could designate a diverse racial background by checking multiple racial categories. The decision to allow a multiple-box option was largely attributed to the influence of civil rights organizations, which supported a multiple box option as long as the government continued to collect data on the primary racial categories (Williams 2006). As long as respondents are still required to check at least one established racial category, the federal government can continue to identify the size of black, Asian, and Latino populations.[2]

Kimberly DaCosta (2007) argues that by earning official representation of multiracial identities, the multiracial movement effectively "made" a modern multiracial population. In line with existing political theory, DaCosta points to the powerful role of activists in framing the parameters of a multiracial political agenda. These activists successfully lobbied for state recognition of multiracial identities and sought to implement an institutionalized option to assert a multiracial identity. If they choose, Americans today can self-identify as multiracial precisely because the option has been made available by activists. The narratives developed by these activists thus represent an important dimension for understanding why and how Americans choose to self-identify as multiracial.

Interviews with Multiracial Activists

Data and Methods

In 2006, after the initial distribution and analyses of 2000 census data had been conducted, I recruited a sample of multiracial activists to discuss the politics of multiracial identification and how things had changed since the implementation of the mark-one-or-more option. I began by contacting the organizations involved in the original movement to change the 2000 census. Williams's (2006) careful documentation of the movement allowed me to follow up with the three most prominent organizations that had organized the movement: the Association for MultiEthnic Americans, Project Race, and A Place For Us. In addition to these three organizations, I also contacted seven of the eight[3] groups organized by interracial parents that Williams identified as part of the multiracial movement. I found that many of the original activists involved in changing the census remained active in local groups. Given this continuity, I attempted to interview both the new leadership of these organizations and, if possible, those involved in the original movement to change the 2000 census.

Researching about multiracial advocacy as well as information obtained from early interviews revealed that new organizations existed in addition to those involved with the multiracial movement. In particular, two organizations, Mavin Foundation and Swirl, were extremely active in multiracial advocacy at the time I conducted these interviews. I was also fortunate to conduct interviews in the midst of a major lobbying effort in California. In the spring of 2006, State Senator Joe Simitian introduced SB 1615, the Ethnic Heritage Respect and Recognition Act, seeking to enforce federal standards of racial classification on all state forms in California. Although this was a policy specific to one state, the bill attracted the attention of multiracial advocacy groups across the country since it identified the next bureaucratic step toward ensuring representation of multiracial identities. In the end, the bill did not pass the state legislature, but the process did mobilize individuals and groups to take action. I included interviews with individuals involved in the push for passage of SB 1615.

In total, I identified 18 groups or nonprofit organizations for this study. For each organization that I was able to contact, I interviewed the current president or director and in some cases other leaders. In total, I conducted interviews with 28 respondents between June and August 2006. The interviews were semistructured, and I asked all interviewees about the goals of their organization and efforts, their reasons for involvement in issues related to multiracial identification, and their personal experiences with racial identity. I conducted interviews primarily over the phone; they lasted between 45 minutes and two hours. All interviews were tape-recorded and fully transcribed. Table A.1 in appendix A includes a list of the interview subjects and information about their background.

One challenge during these interviews was that many of the activists hesitated to offer "on the record" statements revealing their unfiltered opinions about past and present events. Given the political conflict that had occurred during the committee hearings to change the 2000 census, these activists had been subject to significant coverage in both the mainstream media and academic scholarship. They believed that their actions and statements were often misinterpreted or taken out of context. Therefore, in return for an open and frank conversation with these activists, I promised that I would not attach their names to any of the quotations presented.

Characteristics of Multiracial Organizations and Activists

Before turning to the interview data, I offer a portrait of the multiracial activists, the organizations they lead, and the activities they sponsored as of 2006, to show how the landscape had changed over the approximate span of a decade since the peak of the multiracial movement (Williams 2006).

First, the racial identification of activists can be categorized into two patterns: parents who identify with one established racial category who have multiracial children (10 out of 28 interviews) and individuals who self-identify as multiracial (18 out of 28 interviews). Interestingly, 11 out of 18 of the self-identified multiracial activists included Asian as one of their racial backgrounds. Given that I did not survey the membership of the groups led by these activists, I do not know whether the members' self-identification corresponds to the leaders'. In fact, the latter are quick to note the racial diversity of their membership. However, the overrepresentation among leaders of people of partial Asian descent is striking (see also Lee and Bean 2010). Among those who were parents, eight out of

10 respondents were white mothers with biracial children, and the other two self-identified as a monoracial minority. Consistent with Williams's (2006) findings on the demographic makeup of the multiracial movement, my research showed that white women continued to be active in multiracial advocacy in 2006. However, self-identified multiracial activists made up the majority of the respondents I spoke with.

Another striking characteristic of activists was their high level of education. Only four respondents had not earned a college degree, and all four had taken some college courses. Half of the respondents had taken graduate-level courses, and of those with graduate school experience, most had completed at least a master's degree. The interviewees often cited academic research as a justification for their viewpoint. Even those that did not hold postgraduate degrees often cited books or other scholarly sources that had influenced their views on racial identity. Since my target population included activists involved in organizations with some focus on public policy, the fact that most were highly educated was not surprising. Research in political behavior shows that personal resources, in particular education and income, are strong predictors of individual political activity (Verba, Schlozman, and Brady 1995). However, academic research does not predict that activists will integrate abstract academic theories in forming their viewpoints. At the same time, the predominance of postgraduate degrees is consistent with the arguments made by scholars who have posited a connection between the college experience and multiracial identification (Renn 2004; Dacosta 2007). University culture and ideas fostered in an academic setting could be seen as supportive conditions for multiracial identification. The two newest organizations in this study, Mavin Foundation and Swirl, were created as a result of the organizers' college experiences.

In terms of organizational characteristics, activists defined their targeted constituency as individuals of mixed racial heritage, interracial families, and families with a transracially adopted child. This was a distinct contrast to groups that made up the multiracial movement, who largely addressed the interests of interracial, primarily white-black, couples. Activists emphasized the existence of a more diverse multiracial community and believed that the three populations they identified as constituencies shared the experience of living outside the confines of the established racial system. Activists reported that since Americans practice race as a set of discrete categories, those with mixed racial backgrounds and racially diverse families were often viewed as abnormal. As a result, mixed-race individuals, interracial families, and families with transracially adopted children experienced similar reactions and thus felt a sense of shared community. While activists noted that we should not simply lump together these three populations, they believed that the three groups share the same basic concerns.

Related to the definition of the constituency, I learned that two primary populations were recruited by multiracial organizations: students on college campuses and individuals interested in joining an online community. Activists saw college students as those most open to multiraciality and most likely to self-identify as multiracial. Interviewees believed that many individuals who might self-identify as multiracial did not have a language for doing so. Thus, their organizations played a role in the socialization of college students. In addition to college students, activists perceived their constituency as largely a virtual community. Most leaders relied on their organization's website to recruit new members. Respondents reported that most new members had found their organization as a result of a web search, rather than through personal recruitment. Thus, their community was a global one. Many organizations rely on listservs to communicate with members so that they reach outside the United States. In fact, two of the major leaders in this study did not form an organization but rather sponsored websites dedicated to multiracial issues in an effort to mobilize a virtual community of interested persons.

Generally speaking, groups that were involved in the multiracial movement did not continue their political advocacy after the 2000 census. Most returned primarily to organizing social activities for interracial families. Groups that continued to be involved in politics tended to focus on promoting public awareness of interracial marriage and developing early childhood programs for interracial families. In contrast, groups that came into being after the 2000 census were more politically active. These new groups had largely taken over the political battle to ensure a multiracial identification option on official forms. Newer groups tended to focus on multiracial representation and offered fewer programs for interracial families. Therefore, although organizations targeted a diverse constituency, most focused on one issue: the needs of interracial families or representation of multiracial identities.

Finally, there appeared to be a legacy from the multiracial movement, given that most lobbying efforts focused on offering a mark-one-or-more option on state data collection forms. Although the racial identification question changed on the census form, other federal and state agencies had yet to follow the federal guidelinesu on racial classification. Activists believed that they needed to enforce consistency across other federal and state agencies. One example is the lobbying of the Department of Education to change the racial identification question on school forms.[4] In addition to lobbying for the mark-one-or-more option, multiracial organizations sought to generate public recognition of the *Loving* case, the 1967 Supreme Court decision that banned antimiscegenation laws. Outside of political activities, organizations' goals were raising awareness of and educating others about mixed-race families. Activists wanted to promote appropriate images of the multiracial community by organizing panels, distributing videos, and organizing youth- and college-level programs that foster multiracial identity development.

Promoting multiracial identification is a value for activists and likely does not characterize the activities of self-identified multiracial individuals in the mass public. At the same time, these activists have taken on leadership roles and actively promote multiracial identification by creating organizations that have broad reach within the mass public. Their strategy of recruiting college students and other young adults makes them an influential socializing force for newer generations. So although activists represent a unique subpopulation, their views likely influence those in the mass public.

Multiracial Identities according to Activists

The activists I spoke with had clear ideas about multiracial identities. As stated above, activists represented two categories of racial identities: the majority self-identified as multiracial, while a smaller group primarily identified as white mothers of multiracial children. For the first group, multiracial identification is a personal identity, but not so for the second. Given this difference, I did not analyze all respondents together and instead present the results for the two groups separately. First, I present interview data from those who self-identify as multiracial. Because the experiences of racialization were a common theme for them, I include the respondent's reported racial makeup. The final section presents data from interviews with white mothers.

Interviews with Self-Identified Multiracial Activists

Interviews with self-identified multiracial activists suggest they share similar experiences of race. Many of the respondents recounted frustration at being classified in a racial category that they felt was incorrect. As a response to these experiences, respondents had developed a narrative that promoted their belief that racial classification should originate from their own preferences and not be assigned by others. This "choice" is the primary opportunity activists believed they were fighting for.

Experiencing the Constraints of Race: Restrictiveness of the One-Drop Rule

All Americans experience the consequences of race in their everyday activities. Particularly illuminating in these interviews was that most of the self-identified multiracial activists shared frustrations over how race constrained their personal belief system and daily activities. The dominant narrative was that race was a process of "forced" categorization in which individuals are compelled to identify with one of the existing racial categories, regardless of how they prefer to be identified. As one respondent remarked, daily activities persistently require individuals to describe their race:

> Well I think one of the major problems that multiracial individuals face is constantly being forced, to you know, [say] something that they're not. So, I think it's a considerable amount of social pressure causes a lot of internal stress and trauma. [For example,] business applications you have to apply for grants and stuff, they want you to go to the Internet, you know they want to know what race you are, and when you look at all the options they do not list "choose more than one race." There is no reason why they cannot put that on there. There's no reason whatsoever, but that's the kind of social pressure that multiracial families and individuals face all the time: that you have no where to check. [Regardless of] what your family looks like, you got to be one or the other, but you can't be [multiracial]. Or, you get to be "other" where you're essentially not counted at all.
> —*Self-identifies as multiracial; racial makeup is black, white, and Native American*

The common social practice of identifying with one race was viewed asnot only limited but also upsetting because the complexity and distinctiveness of respondents' real identities were being silenced. Multiracial individuals often attempt to classify themselves outside of the typical racial categories but are rarely offered an opportunity to report their own conceptualization of their race. These barriers are not viewed as isolated but, rather, seen as extremely common.

Another common frustration was that, when race is brought up, multiracial respondents are often misclassified. Many respondents reported instances when others tried to guess their racial background by pointing out physical traits. One respondent reminisced about such an experience:

> When my youngest child was a baby, there were people would see him in all kinds of different groups—Latino or even Arab. We had one [of these experiences when] we were looking for cars and he was probably six months old, and the car salesmen thought we had adopted him in Saudi Arabia. He was enthusiastic about it, like, "Oh, we adopted a baby out of Saudi Arabia. That's my home." No, that's not quite what happened.
>
> *—Self-identifies as multiracial; racial makeup is white and Native American*

Misclassification of a multiracial person's racial background was sometimes reported in relatively harmless situations, such as at the car dealership. But many respondents emphasized that this experience happened to them often. Some recounted that their racial ambiguity encouraged discussions about racial classification even when the respondent did not want to discuss race. These experiences with racial ambiguity led respondents to want greater personal control over their racial classification.

Particularly problematic was that other people, in particular strangers, played a powerful role in deciding a person's racial identity. Many expressed aggravation over outsiders' right to exercise control over respondents' racial identity:

> We've got to be able to honor people's right to have an opinion different from our own. The only problem I have is when someone outside of my community was telling me who I was. You don't get to do that. If you're not paying my taxes and you're not living my life, then you have to accept my definition of me. And I think that's where a lot of multiracial people come from.
>
> *—Self-identifies as multiracial; racial makeup is black and white*

As this respondent's plea demonstrates, many multiracial individuals want to define themselves, but others impose a racial classification that does not match their personal identity. As many see it currently practiced, racial classification is policed by members of society and offers little opportunity for individuals to have their own agency in determining how they are racially classified.

In relation to the idea of "forced" classification, respondents reported that they were often confronted with stereotypes about mixed-race people.

One respondent summarized multiracial stereotypes as of two types. First, there is the "tragic mulatto" trope, whereby mixed-race people are assumed to have psychological difficulty adjusting to society, given that they are not part of one racial group. The second stereotype was labeled "the best of both worlds," according to which multiracial people were lucky to be able to practice more than one culture. Even though the second stereotype was framed as positive, this respondent saw these tropes as oversimplifying the multiracial experience. Respondents believed that stereotypes of multiracial people are inaccurate and can be used to form problematic assumptions about multiracial people. Their exposure to these stereotypes was one reason their race represented a salient feature in their everyday lives.

Respondents believed that the structural nature of race was vivid and consequential for multiracial people. Multiracial individuals do not fit into the established norm of race because they do not self-identify with only one racial category, yet most of their everyday experiences of race enforce the existing norm that they must identify with only one racial group. Given the saliency of race in the United States, respondents are made constantly aware of the problems associated with racial classification. It is this awareness that motivated many of the respondents to advocate on behalf of multiracial identities.

Expressing the Right of Personal Choice

Because race was understood as "forced" categorization, respondents saw the need to advocate for personal choice in those activities that collected information about a person's race. One of the primary problems respondents identified was that when a person attempts to assert a multiracial identity, that identity is often rejected by others. One respondent offered an example:

> Who else, you know like Barack Obama, the senator from Illinois, he mentions like, "oh, I'm half white," people were like, "oh black guy in denial," that kind of thing. Even when he accepts he's mixed race, he still puts forward this mono-racial character. And I think part of that is because, in the public we do things similar to [what we do in] private, in everyday life. You know, where it's just like you want to put people in one box. You want to make people kind of choose because if people are in the middle, it's kind of uncomfortable . . . overall, I would say that in society today, it is not okay to be multiracial.
>
> —*Self-identifies as multiracial; racial makeup is white and Japanese*

Promoting the right of personal choice, respondents wanted individuals to have the authority to define their own racial identities and have them respected by others. Many respondents cited the "Bill of Rights for Racially Mixed People," by Maria Root, one of the earliest writers on the modern multiracial experience. It includes rights "to identify myself differently than strangers expect me to identify," "to identify myself differently than how my parents identify me," "to create a vocabulary to communicate about being multiracial," and "to change my identity over my lifetime—and more than once" (Root 1996a, 7). Embracing similar sentiments, respondents commonly supported the right for a person to choose his or her identity. One respondent explained to me:

> There are going to be some people in the community that will not say they're multiracial and that's their prerogative, it was all about choices to be begin with. We wanted to have choice in the matter.
>
> —*Self-identifies as multiracial; racial makeup is black and white*

Respondents wanted many different racial choices. Most wanted the opportunity to declare a hybrid, multiracial identity. Some noted that, although they were frustrated when a monoracial category was imposed (for example, the insistence that a person of white and Asian descent is Asian), the imposed category was not insulting but rather an incomplete description of what they saw as their "true" identity. In fact, many emphasized that by asserting a multiracial identity, they were not trying to "run away" from their minority background, an accusation sometimes made against them by other racial minority groups. Rather, their frustration developed, again, from the fact that racial classification was forced on them.

Other respondents defined choice as the option to identify with their mother's race or their father's race. Respondents who wanted this form of choice recognized that it is atypical, since most Americans have parents of the same race. But even though they saw themselves as a small minority, they believed it was important that they be given the right to choose. Some respondents reported that they identified with only one of their racial identities if they believed that the political or social circumstances so warranted. For example:

> For me, whenever I'm told to check one, and I'm half Latino and I'm half Asian, sometimes [I'll say Asian], but because my last name is [Japanese sounding] and everybody can see through my name I'm Japanese, I tend to pick Latino because of that particular thing, and also there aren't a lot

of people at my education and income level statistically that are Latino. I want to beef up those numbers, so I'll check off, and I'll be basically 100% Latino for whatever survey I've taken.

—Self-identifies as multiracial; racial makeup is Japanese and Mexican

As this above respondent explained, multiracial individuals can make a strategic choice to emphasize one identity over another to serve a particular goal. I was surprised to find that the general preference was to use the more marginalized racial identity. Respondents often believed it was more politically valuable to represent the marginalized group.

The racial identity that was never framed as a choice was identifying as white. Perhaps in the post-civil rights era, the respondents did not believe it culturally or normatively appropriate to desire whiteness, and so it may be the case that respondents chose not to discuss it in a formal interview. While I cannot rule out the role of social desirability, respondents seemed not to recognize whiteness as an identity option (Dalmage 2004; Spickard 2003; Spencer 2010). A few respondents reported that they could visibly "pass" as a white person because of their phenotypic features. They recognized circumstances when others assumed they were white (see also Rockquemore and Arend 2002). In general, being identified as white was possible only when others assigned that racial category. It did not exist as a personal choice.

Even though the respondents wanted choices for themselves, most did not believe that the ultimate goal was to impose a racial identity on others. Many respondents were quick to acknowledge that a multiracial identity need not be embraced by all. Rather, they were staunchly committed to personal choice:

I think that, even [when events are] not explicitly about identity, like a discussion group about identity or something like that, our other events, like social events, can really provide a supportive place for people to feel like their identity is developing and supported. I also think that [our organization] supports choices and identity. So people might have a primary identity as a black person or a Asian person and a secondary identity as a mixed person; or primary identity as a mixed person and secondary identity as a black person or Asian, or whatever. Yeah, so I think that's really what we're about.

—Self-identifies as multiracial; racial makeup is Italian and Japanese

Activists also noted that they wanted the opportunity to embrace different identities at different times. As the following respondent articulates, choice can refer to changing one's racial identity at different times or in different contexts:

> You know it's funny because sometimes I would mark if they had Japanese or Asian; sometimes I would mark white; sometimes I would mark other. It really just depended on the time in my life and I think if you ask most mixed race people, that especially of our age generation, I'm sure they would say something very similar.
>
> —*Self-identifies as multiracial; racial makeup is Japanese and German*

Because their efforts focused on race as a complex and fluid construct, many multiracial activists viewed their race as a flexible identity and were not committed to any one category or identity. Racial identity is conceptualized as context-specific, and identity can be matched with the given circumstances (see also Rockquemore and Brunsma 2007; Renn 2004).

Given their awareness of the constraints imposed by racial classification, respondents recognized that identifying as multiracial challenges existing practices of race. As a result, respondents could see their identity as a small but significant act of resistance:

> I just check multiple boxes anyway. Like I said, I officially work in statistics, so in some ways, I feel kind of bad because I know what kind of havoc that is causing with whatever poor data-entry clerk they have. But, it's something I have to do for myself. . . . If they have an "other" or "mixed" box, I'd check that. But, if they don't really give you any options for me to choose one, [I check multiple boxes]. I just feel like in my life I've been forced to choose one so many times that, if can get away from choosing one, I'm just not going to do it.
>
> —*Self-identifies as multiracial; racial makeup is white and Japanese*

By advocating for choice, the self-identified multiracial respondents wanted to shift the authority of determining racial classification away from society and place it in the hands of the individual. Many saw a multiracial identity as the one that best reflected themselves, even though these identities were not commonly recognized as legitimate by others.

Multiracial Activists' Political Attitudes toward Race

Since activists' demands for choice and multiracial identification were direct responses to existing racial practices, I asked respondents to discuss their views on American race relations more broadly and how multiracial identification related to other racial identities. The majority of activists adopted a liberal or progressive stance on politics and believed that multiracial people could ally with other civil rights groups in efforts to reduce racial inequality. Even though these activists had been advocating for a distinctive multiracial identity, they were treated as a monoracial minority by society:

> Of course, yeah, I think that a lot of times I experience racial discrimination. I suspect that is because people think I'm Latino. So they follow me in stores, or I may get poor service, And I think that I also experience racial discrimination in kind of more subtle ways: certainly of being a person of color or mixed person in a predominately white class or things like that.
> —*Self-identifies as multiracial; racial makeup is Italian and Japanese*

This respondent reported to have one white parent and one Asian parent but often experienced situations in which others classified her as Latino. Because of this, she speculated that her experiences with racial discrimination did not occur because she is multiracial but rather because she was taken for a racial minority. She thus personally identifies with racial discrimination experienced by monoracial minority groups.

Nearly all of the self-identified multiracial respondents reported being treated as a nonwhite "other." In other words, they saw their racial background as a source of social exclusion, differential treatment, or sometimes blatant discrimination. But, surprisingly, respondents often did not attribute their experiences to fact that they were multiracial. Most often, respondents described forms of discrimination that were waged against all people of color:

> Those guys are not thinking that way, in terms of he's multiracial [or] he's African... No, they're just saying this guy has brown skin, I don't like him. You know, and they don't really care about what color brown skin, you know, got brown skin... if he's not white he's not pure, he should go back to wherever he came from. Forgetting, of course, that he came from somewhere else. No, I think racism doesn't go for the finer points
> —*Self-identifies as multiracial; racial makeup is black, white, and Native American*

Although respondents did report specific negative experiences due to their multiracial background, those more severe forms of racial discrimination were often connected with being a nonwhite minority. In this way, I found descriptions of racial discrimination to be similar to those often expressed by Asian Americans, blacks, and Latinos (see, for example, Garcia Bedolla 2005; Rogers 2006; Tuan 1998.

Given these experiences, the respondents emphasized a progressive and racially conscious stance toward politics. In fact, multiracial activists believed that, by advocating on behalf of multiracial identities, they were encouraging public awareness about racial discrimination more broadly:

> People say, oh, that we don't talk about mixed race issues, well we don't talk enough about race issues in general. In any sort of mixed race curriculum for parents, like the one we're developing right now, the first step is always teaching parents how to talk to their kids about race. Because even before you can talk to your kids to talk about mixed race, most parents just never talk to their kids about race.
>
> —*Self-identifies as multiracial; racial makeup is white and Japanese*

One respondent believed that mixed-race groups could be understood as another organization included in the existing coalition of groups that are aimed to promote civil rights:

> They probably never thought about, "oh, we should really confront the racism that is happening at the polling station, let's contact the mixed contingency." We're not really thought of as a political force at all, and I'm not saying we should be thought of as a force in of itself. I just think that for the most part mixed raced people are unseen, we're not really thought about too much when it comes to race. People still think in these very finite boxes. So part of it is really trying to get out there more, to lend a hand to all of these causes that matter to all of us.
>
> —*Self-identifies as multiracial; racial makeup is Jewish and Chinese*

At the same time, even though respondents often believed that their organizations sought to advance discourse about race, few had actually worked with other civil rights or minority organizations. Respondents believed that working with minority organizations was a good idea, but most had not investigated the option.[5] This is not to say that the multiracial organizations worked in isolation: multiracial activists reported collaborations with other multiracial organizations, church groups, other nonprofit groups, and social service agencies in their sponsored activities. It was often reported to me that civil rights organizations continued to perceive multiracial efforts as threatening, as had happened in the 1990s during efforts to change the 2000 census:

> I think in a lot of rhetoric in certain areas have equated the idea that a multiracial or mixed heritage experience with the idea that race is no longer important; it should be done away with; the idea that civil rights laws and collection of data on race that affirmative action is no longer important. So the minute we say that we work with mixed heritage communities, red flags go off.
>
> —*Self-identifies as multiracial; racial makeup is Latino and white*

Thus, while multiracial respondents believed themselves to be aligned with the politics of monoracial minority groups, they perceived continued tensions between these two groups.

Although most of the self-identified multiracial activists considered themselves to be aligned with the politics of monoracial minorities this was not the only viewpoint expressed by activists. A less common perspective was that multiracial identification can demonstrate the absurdity of racial categorization:

> I view multiracial category as something that all Americans could and eventually would migrate to. A large number of people, if not a majority in this country, would claim mixed ancestry. You know, at a certain point, if a majority people check the multiracial box, why should there be a need to maintain these categories at all?
>
> —*Self-identifies as multiracial; racial makeup is white, black, and American Indian*

Some of the activists believed that the problems associated with race stem from the continued emphasis on racial categorization.[6] Those who held this view believed that multiracial identification, or encouraging Americans to mark all boxes on the racial identification question, would help to make race a socially meaningless feature. This perspective was expressed by a small minority of multiracial activists.

Like any group, the multiracial activists I spoke with revealed different perspectives on politics and race relations in America. At the same time, I was struck that most of the multiracial respondents perceived themselves to be aligned with civil rights and racial minority groups. I had expected that respondents who opted to self-identify with a distinct multiracial identity chose to do so because they failed to see commonalities with other racial groups. Yet respondents appeared to be aware that they were treated like racial minority groups and subject to racial discrimination (sometimes due to the assumption that they were a monoracial minority). Multiracial activists might assert a distinct identity, but their treatment by society labeled them as a racial "other."

Interviews with White Mothers of Biracial Children

The role of monoracially identified parents, particularly white mothers, has been a key focal point of past research. DaCosta (2007) noted that an inherent connection between family and ethnic identity, since "expressions of an ethnic identity are often used to symbolize relations with family members and ethnic celebrations participated in as a means to preserve the family (2007, 16). I found that white mothers of multiracial children played a visible, albeit less dominant, role in multiracial organizations.

While self-identified multiracial activists commonly spoke about their experiences with being a racial "other," white mothers of biracial children reported different reasons for promoting multiracial identities. In particular, they saw racial identity as communicating family heritage and respect for parents. One white mother described how racial identity influences the extended family:

> You can say that it doesn't matter to you because you have a white family, but what if your children grows up and marries someone of a different race or ethnicity. So in a way, this does affect a lot of people, its not just the multiracial kids, it's the family the parents, grandparents, aunts and uncles. It's the whole family. So the multiracial movement is not just for multiracial people but also their family. More awareness around the whole family to be supportive is a good thing too.

As these comments demonstrate, white mothers believed that through racial identity an individual communicates his or her family heritage. This logic implies that the child's race should match that of both parents. For the most part, these mothers wanted representation of both parents in the description of their child's identity. One respondent explained that, given the rule of hypodescent, children are always racially classified in the same way as the minority parent, which diminishes the role of the white parent. Many white parents wanted their racial identities reflected in their children's identities.

Although the mothers equated racial identity with family heritage, they, like self-identified multiracial activists, asserted the importance of personal choice:

We're hoping that ... the schools will recognize and include biracial and multiracial students in their curriculum so that the kids will grow up being themselves and not have to choose whether which parent they are going to align with racially. Some multiracial and biracial kids do identify with one parent or the other, that's you know their choice, but that it is okay for kids to align with both parents if that's how they identify.

The combined narrative of family heritage and identity choice described by these white mothers is similar to the narratives Mary Waters (1990) found in her study on white ethnic identity. According to Waters, whites construct their ethnic identity based on their knowledge of their family background and ancestry. Therefore, when whites explain their ethnicity, they construct narratives that explain their family tree. At the same time, whites embrace the availability of identity options. Waters found that when respondents told stories about their identities, they often simplified their family tree by selectively reporting only one identity that they believed was more desirable or better fit the social context. By framing ethnic identities as products of choice and family heritage, whites largely understand ethnicity to be a positive attribute worth celebrating rather than a negative feature.

White parents applied the logics they use for understanding their own ethnic identities to the racial identities of their children. There are important similarities: many white Americans understand themselves to be multiethnic (of multiple European ethnicities) and so see the option to choose among many different European ethnicities when describing their ethnic identity. They see their multiracial children as individuals who also are of diverse family backgrounds and so believe that their children should have the option of choosing between multiple races. These perceived similarities make it possible to apply the logic for understanding white ethnicity to understanding a multiracial identity (see also Karis 2004).

Although the self-identified multiracial activists and white mothers differed on how they defined and understood race, they shared the objective of framing racial identity as a product of personal choice. The fact that multiracial advocacy is populated primarily by white mothers and self-identified multiracial individuals mean that there is an important family dimension to multiracial advocacy. One white mother described a sort of generational change of multiracial advocacy in which the self-identified multiracial children had taken over from their interracial parents. Since I originally entered into these interviews with the objective of understanding multiracial advocacy, I did not fully investigate the relationship between parents and their children. But interviews with white mothers who continued to be involved in multiracial advocacy led me to wonder how far parental influence (particularly of the white parent) is an explanatory factor for the decision to self-identify as multiracial.

Lessons from Activists

These interviews offered insight into why activists chose to adopt multiracial identities and why it is important for multiracial identification to exist as an option for Americans. Activists' multiracial identities were largely developed as a response to the perceived constraints of the current practice of racial classification. Because they personally saw that current practices of racial classification do not account for their own experiences, multiracial activists reported being persistently made aware that racial classification is a rigid social process that "forces" a racial identity onto individuals. They experience conflicts over racial classification regularly, even in everyday activities such as trips to the park or interactions with a new acquaintance. Most respondents reported that they publicly assert a multiracial identity because they believe that a multiracial identity better reflects how they understand their race.

What is particularly striking in these interviews is that both self-identified multiracial activists and white mothers adopted a viewpoint that embraced the power of personal choice and agency to determine a person's racial classification. There was a normative claim that racial identity should be created by the individual, not by others. Moreover, they believed that their identities could be a "choice": individuals should have multiple options for their racial identification, and they should be able to change their identity depending on the given context. This perspective about race has been informed by respondents' own experiences, but interviews with white mothers also suggest that parental influence plays a role. White parents who largely understand race through the lens of ethnicity apply these views to their promotion of multiracial identities.

At the same time, while self-identified multiracial activists embraced the right of choice, they also revealed the effort required to assert a multiracial identity. Self-identified multiracial activists report that multiracial identities are still not commonly understood or expressed by others. As a result, respondents must purposefully promote multiracial identities. For activists, their multiracial identities are not inconsequential but rather developed with clear intention. This shows that multiracial identity and the belief that one has identity choices are contingent on open and inviting environments for these practices. Although there are multiracial organizations across the country, most of my respondents were at the time living in large, metropolitan areas. Multiracial activists involved in what appeared to be the most active organizations within my study sample were originally from the West Coast or in the Northeast (see appendix A). Moreover, activists target college students because they are strategic in their efforts to identify populations that will be receptive to claims of multiracial identity.

Some scholars describe multiracial self-identification as an act of political resistance (Daniel 2002; Root 1996b). To be sure, many of the activists involved in the changes to the census racial identification question originally sought their own "multiracial" category, while others saw how multiracial identities disturbed existing assumptions. However, multiracial activists did not seek to challenge most existing racial practices (see also Spencer 2010). All of the multiracial activists I spoke with, including the white mothers of multiracial children, were blunt in their assessment that American practices of race were rigid and difficult to change. Most viewed "white" and "black" as dominant racial categories that serve as firm constructs for orienting interpersonal interactions. These activists revealed that they did not seek to change the use of established racial categories through their advocacy of multiracial identities. In fact, the self-identified multiracial activists continued to use existing racial categories, with some revealing that in past instances they had personally identified with only one racial category.

The contrast between the normative belief that individuals should have a right to choose their racial identity and the acknowledged reality that society continues to be structured by the long-standing racial order is a clear reflection of the tension between racial classification and racial identification that characterizes today's racial norms. As demonstrated by the historical analysis in the previous chapter, Americans interact in a racial environment that increasingly emphasizes the importance of self-identification. However, long-standing practices of race, such as the rule of hypodescent, continue to orient individual behavior and attitudes. Multiracial activists respond to this environment in a unique way by capitalizing on an opening created by the tension between racial identification and classification to make a case for their preferred multiracial identities. Activists want to add new racial categories, in particular multiracial categories, to the existing racial system. Their approach to race emphasizes the modern norm of privileging self-identification. However, multiracial activists articulate the desire to have multiracial identities recognized, not as acts of political resistance, but as legitimate racial constructs *alongside* other established racial categories.

4 | Declaring Race

UNDERSTANDING THE OPPORTUNITIES
TO SELF-IDENTIFY AS MULTIRACIAL

THE PAST TWO CHAPTERS OFFERED a story about changing racial norms in the United States, and highlighted the important shift from conceptualizing race as an assigned classification to emphasizing personal self-identification.[1] Yet when Americans commonly discuss racial demographics in the United States, they tend to frame change as growth in the size of a population. For example, in the 2000 census data there existed approximately 6.8 million multiracial individuals, representing 2.4% of all Americans. In 2010, the multiracial population grew to approximately 9 million, a 32% increase. This change suggests that, over the course of a decade, about 2.2 million new multiracial Americans were added to the population. However, this interpretation does not take into account the fact that social norms about race have also been changing over time and so are Americans' understandings of how they understand their race.

Taking changing racial norms into account, this chapter advocates that we take an *identity choice approach* when interpreting empirical patterns in racial demographics. In an era when race is understood to reflect personal identity, individuals *choose* to report their race based on their personal understanding of race and their own identity. More importantly, an individual asked to describe her race today has the option to assert one of the established racial categories or to assert a multiracial identity. Most Americans choose the former, but a growing number choose the latter. This means that, rather than accept race as a stable or objective feature of the individual, we should integrate a subjective or interpretive dimension to race. Factors such as motivation, preference, social context, and perceived norms explain why an individual chooses to describe her race using a particular category or label. As we learned in chapter 3, multiracial activists conceptualized their race as hybrid and, frustrated with "forced" racial classification, advocated for the personal choice to self-identify as multiracial. An identity choice framework can also explain identification as monoracial. As the data in this chapter will show, many Americans believe that they have racially diverse family backgrounds but self-identify as only one race. An identity choice approach pushes us to question the factors that explain each of these patterns of racial identification.

This chapter seeks to explain why individuals choose to self-identify as multiracial. In doing so, I offer an example of how to apply an identity choice approach in practice. Although an identity choice approach can be applied to any racial identity, multiracial identities are particularly useful cases because previous research has typically defined multiracial individuals as the children of interracial couples . To start, I discuss how an identity choice approach differs from the more typical outlooks on today's multiracial population. It challenges the assumption that children of interracial couples all share the same understanding of race and so would report their race to be multiracial when asked. I offer empirical evidence to show that how individuals report their race does not always align with other definitions of race, such as being a child of interracial marriage, or by the rule of hypodescent. Then, moving forward with the assumption that individuals have made identity choices, the second half of the chapter examines how individual-level factors and particular social contexts can explain the choice to self-identify as multiracial.

Assigned Race by the Researcher: Children of Interracial Marriage

Most of our knowledge about the contemporary multiracial population originates from the social science fields of sociology and demography, which primarily defined a multiracial population as children of interracial parents. The researcher assigned research subjects' race, and subjects were grouped together based on the researcher's definition of "multiracial." The findings on racial identity generated from this research offer insight into the developmental processes that occur within a specific type of family environment.

By defining multiraciality as a product of interracial coupling, research sought to show that multiracial individuals face different social challenges and experiences than those who have parents of the same race (Root 1992, 1996). Research focused on the challenges created by interracial marriage. To put this focus in context, we should recall that for most of American history, individuals of different races could not legally marry. Children of legal interracial marriages after 1967 were thus uncommon and so seen pejoratively as abnormal (Moran 2001). Early sociological theories proposed that because multiracial individuals straddled different racial groups, they would experience significant social exclusion, stress, and confusion about their identity (Park 1928; Stonequist 1937). Most modern scholars, however, rejected this theory and so sought to show the positive, but unique, family formation processes experienced by such children (Cheng and Powell 2007; Dacosta 2007; Dalmage 2000; Rockquemore and Lazloffy 2005).

Most of the early literature focused on specific types of interracial families: those headed by one white parent and one black parent. (for example, Brown 2001; Dalmage 2000; Daniel 2002; Funderburg 1994; Korgen 1998; Rockquemore and Brunsma 2001; Zack 1993). The other group that has been the topic of scholarly attention is the white-Asian population, also referred to as "hapas" (Bernstein and De la Cruz 2009; King-O'Riain 2006; Williams-Leon and Nakashima 2001).[2] Research on children of white-Asian couples was concerned with many issues similar to that drove research on children of white-black couples, but researchers also considered the effects of immigration, such as language use in the home (Iijima Hall and Cooke Turner 2001; Khanna 2001; Root 2001; Xie and Goyette 1997).[3]

One finding that is consistent across studies is the variance in forms of racial identification asserted by children of interracial couples. Children of interracial couples do not necessarily self-identify as biracial or multiracial but rather follow at least four different trends. In-depth interviews conducted by Rockquemore and Brunsma (2001) and by Renn (2004) found patterns including identifying as biracial, identifying with one parent's (mono)racial identity, asserting a fluid identity that changed depending on the social context, and choosing no racial identity at all (for example, identifying as "American"). Thus, although children of interracial marriage share a common family formation, they do not adopt the same form of racial identity (Rockquemore, Brunsma, and Delgado 2009). However, Shih and colleagues (2007) show that children of interracial couples are more likely than other Americans to view race as socially constructed rather than essential.

The research on interracial couples also examined how parents define the racial identities of their children. The races of the parents played a role in how they classified their child: white-black couples often labeled their child as black, while white-Asian couples tended to label their child as white (Brunsma 2005; Qian 2004). These same studies found that mothers define their child's race differently than fathers. Other studies have shown that parents born in the United States are more likely to identify the child as racial minority, but if one parent is foreign born, the child is more likely to be identified as white (Roth 2005; Xie and Goyette 1997). Finally, Bratter's (2007) analysis of 2000 census data found that parents who self-identify as multiracial are most likely to designate their child as multiracial. However, if one parent self-identifies as multiracial (for example, white and Asian) and shares one race with the partner (for example, Asian), then the child is more likely to be designated as the race shared by parents (child is identified as Asian).

Past research on multiracial individuals typically collects research subjects by first identifying interracial couples and then assigning a multiracial classification to their children. This research offers us important insights into families in the United States and the unique challenges related to race faced by interracial couples and their families. However, we should be aware of how scholars have defined a study population and be precise about what the findings tell us about being multiracial. Studies that assert that children of interracial couples are multiracial depend on racial classification by the researcher. The results from these studies are thus determined by a particular definition of multiraciality.

Outline of an Identity Choice Approach

In contrast to past studies that largely defined the multiracial person as a child of an interracial couple, the identity choice approach proposes that the multiracial population includes only those who *self-identify* as multiracial. Given this definition, the remainder of this book employs specific strategies for collecting and analyzing data.

In terms of data collection of a multiracial population, I follow two guidelines. First, since "multiracial" is defined as a form of self-identification, only empirical sources that allow respondents to personally report their race will be used to identify a multiracial population. This strategy does not severely limit available data because most large quantitative datasets primarily measure a respondent's racial self-identification. Today, most individual-level data are collected from a survey. In most surveys, respondents self-report their race, which means that respondents tell the interviewer how they conceive of their race. There exist other forms of data collection in which race is assigned to the respondent: in many face-to-face interviewers, the interviewer indicates the race of the respondent based on how the interviewer perceives it or based on the study's protocols.[4] How we measure race has consequences, since self-identification and assigned race produce different estimates of racial populations (Campbell and Troyer 2007; Saperstein 2006; Saperstein and Penner 2012 Smith 2001). Therefore, choosing the technique of race measurement is an important dimension of the identity choice approach.

Second, I will also rely only on sources that offer respondents the *opportunity* to designate themselves as multiracial. Depending on how data were collected, researchers can offer a set of racial categories to choose from, or they can give respondents more flexibility. When respondents have flexibility, they can declare themselves to be monoracial (white, black, Native American / Pacific Islander, Asian American, or Latino) or multiracial. The data in this book employ two different forms of opportunity: a survey question that allows respondents to report the belief that they are multiracial, and a question that asks respondents to report their race and offers a mark-one-or-more option, like the one on the 2000 and 2010 censuses.

Although I use two different measures in this book, I acknowledge that scholars increasingly employ the mark-one-or-more option[5] to account for multiracial identification. The fact that the multiple-races option is increasingly used demonstrates the government's influence over how Americans understand race. Today, guidelines outlined in Statistical Directive 15, published by the Office of Management and Budget, establish how federal officials will collect racial and ethnic data. These guidelines represent the rule of thumb that guides data collection practices and are justified by the seemingly nonnormative mission to maintain data consistency. But by setting a standard for collecting racial data, federal officials mold public perceptions of how to understand and operationalize race (Bailey 2008; Kertzer and Arel 2002; Nobles 2000). It is thus the case that the widespread adoption of the mark-one-or-more option is creating a particular culture of multiracial identification today. So, for the time being, if an American wants to designate herself as multiracial, she must declare multiple races when asked to report her race. But this practice is not set in stone. Therefore, the mark-one-or-more option reflects the cultural practice of multiracial identification as it is carried out at the beginning of the twenty-first century, but other strategies for identify as multiracial may come into being in the future.

In addition to specific data collection strategies, the identity choice approach assumes that there are reasons why individuals choose a particular racial identity or racial category when asked to report their race. Therefore, hypotheses need to be generated and then empirically tested so that we can identify the specific factors that explain racial reporting. Moreover, we cannot assume that the factors that explain multiracial identification are the same as those that explain monoracial identification. Multiracial identification is unique: census data tell us that the overwhelming majority of Americans identified with only one race in both 2000 and 2010: 97.6% in 2000 and 97.1% in 2010. One possible way of explaining the distinction between monoracial and multiracial self-identification is that the former follows historic practices that define the established racial categories and perceives utility in adopting an assigned classification based on historic norms. As we reviewed in chapter 2, many rules have been employed to racially classify Americans, ranging from the rule of hypodescent and ancestry, phenotype, "common knowledge," and evolving scientific thought. All of these norms have informed how Americans practice race, but the identity choice approach asserts that each American has likely adopted these norms to varying degrees. Those who self-identify as monoracial see the continued relevance of monoracial identification and so employ those categories. Some, like the activists in chapter 3, reject them and so identify as multiracial. In this way, there is an important need to study the factors that explain multiracial identification.

However, while I frame racial reporting as an exercise of choice, I do not assume that an individual's choice of racial classification is unconstrained by external forces. In fact, research on the racial identities adopted by children of interracial couples shows that it is important to live in inviting contexts and that there are privileges associated with having resources that foster multiracial identity. For example, the formative study by Harris and Sim (2002) found that racial identity for children of interracial marriages is strongly influenced by institutional contexts. Their study found that adolescents were more likely to identify themselves as multiracial at home with their parents, but identify with only one race at school. These scholars argue that social contexts create different sets of pressures on young children to identify in particular ways. Factors such as the racial makeup in the neighborhood or the presence of the child's parents in the room during the interview determined how a child chose to racially identify. Moreover, Brunsma (2006) argues that there are important differences in how individuals experience their private lives and their public lives: while multiracial people may feel more at ease at home, there are social and political concerns to be considered when asserting a racial identity in public.

In addition to constraints of context, resources offer opportunities for individuals to express their preferred identity. For example, a longitudinal study found that children with high self-esteem who are from families of higher socioeconomic status are more likely to demonstrate consistent multiracial identities over their lifetime than those from families of lower socioeconomic status (Hitlin, Brown, and Elder 2006). Relatedly, Fhagen Smith (2010) argues that middle-class values and culture provide narratives for more resourced families to support their child's multiracial identity . Therefore, models used to explain multiracial self-identification should incorporate the constraints associated with individuals' surrounding context and the resources they have at their disposal.

Understanding the Complexity of Multiracial Identification

With the identity choice approach laid out, the following two empirical sections establish the distinction between self-identification and the empirical strategies for identifying multiracial individuals that are more typically employed by researchers: being a child of an interracial couple, or having a racially diverse family heritage. A comparison between these empirical strategies allows me to examine the processes that lead individuals to self-identify as multiracial. The more typical strategies that define a multiracial person as either the child of an interracial couple or as a person who has a diverse family heritage are practices of assigned race by the researcher. After identifying respondents who are typically categorized as multiracial, I seek to identify those individuals who self-identify as multiracial and those who identify as monoracial. I then further apply an identity choice approach by assessing the individual-level and contextual factors that encourage multiracial self-identification over monoracial identification.

Correspondence between Multiracial Identification and Being the Child of an Interracial Couple

This first analysis considers the relationship between being the child of an interracial couple and the belief that one is of mixed race. I employ data from the *Washington Post* / Kaiser Family Foundation / Harvard University survey *Race and Ethnicity in 2001: Attitudes, Perceptions, and Experiences* (WKH 2001).[6] This survey is unique because it was designed to collect data from a diverse sample and targeted respondents classified as one of four racial groups: white, black, Latino, and Asian. Unlike previous studies on multiracial identification that first targeted interracial families and then assessed the nature of their racial identity, the survey data analyzed here include respondents who are randomly selected and then queried about their families. The WKH 2001 survey is particularly advantageous in that it includes multiple items on racial identification.[7] This allows me to compare and contrast how respondents report their race through different survey measures.

The WKH 2001 survey is ideal for this analysis because it allows respondents to self-report their own family backgrounds and does not rely on assignment by the researcher. At the same time, it was taken at a unique time in history when the federal government first began allowing individuals to declare multiple races when reporting their racial background on the census. One could argue that the mark-one-or-more option was not fully entrenched in everyday practice, as it is now, and so the data collected in this survey represent a conservative estimate of the number of respondents who are willing to report that they are multiracial. Longitudinal studies that include more recent samples of respondents will need to be assessed to see how the entrenched practice of the mark-one-or-more option has influenced respondents' willingness to say they are multiracial.

I employ two key measures for this analysis. The first, which I will call *Parental ancestry*, is created from two separate questions that ask respondents to report the racial backgrounds of their mother and of their father. The *Parental ancestry* measure is operationalized as a dichotomous measure that distinguishes respondents who report parents of two different races from those who report parents of the same race.[8] The second measure, *Self as mixed race*, asks if respondents consider themselves to be of mixed race. This second measure reflects how a respondent views her race, but does not require the respondent to choose a multiracial identity over the other established (mono)racial identities (which could have been documented using the mark-one-or-more option).[9] Given my emphasis on race measurement, I acknowledge that the *Self as mixed race* is a measure of multiracial identity that would likely produce different results than the mark-one-or-more strategy. However, this measure allows me to examine the primary objective for this section, which is to compare multiracial identification against being the child of interracial parents.

The basic summary statistics of these two measures quickly reveal an important pattern of responses. The *Self as mixed race* measure finds that 18% of the sample (317 out of 1,709 respondents) is multiracial. These responses show that a healthy share of Americans are willing to recognize a mixed racial background. Turning to *Parental ancestry*, the survey finds that 10% of respondents in the survey (169 out of 1,709) report that they have parents of two different races. Interestingly, there are nearly twice as many respondents who consider themselves to be mixed race as there are children of interracial couples. If I weight these numbers to predict the size of the multiracial population at the national level, the *Self as mixed race* method produces a multiracial population that is 13% of the national population, while the *Parental ancestry* method produces a multiracial population that is 7% of the population. I note that both of these numbers are larger than the 2.4% of the national population who checked two or more boxes on the 2000 census race question. The WKH survey shows how different strategies of measurement produce different estimates of the multiracial population.

Although the summary statistics show that respondents who have parents of two different races are not the same as those who believe themselves to be mixed race, it may still be the case that there is significant correlation between the two measures. If Americans see race as primarily a feature inherited from parents, then we might expect that respondents with parents of two different races largely overlap with those who consider themselves to be of mixed race. At the same time, we would expect that those who have parents of the same race would *not* consider themselves to be of mixed race. An identity choice approach argues that individuals choose their racial identities as a function of their responses to racial norms and being in inviting opportunities that encourage multiracial identification. However, if there exists a strong correspondence between parental ancestry and belief that one is of mixed race, then this would suggest that individuals have a more operational or straightforward definition of race: primarily as a function of one's parents' race.

Table 4.1 compares responses to the *Parental ancestry* and the *Self as mixed race* measures. The table confirms that parental ancestry informs how an individual conceives her own race. Having parents of two different races inclines an individual to say she is of mixed race. However, the correlation between responses to the two measures is not perfect. Interestingly, a sizable number of individuals with parents of two different races do not consider themselves to be of mixed race: 36% of those respondents who had parents of two different races did not say they were mixed race (60 out of 169). Moreover, of all those who believed themselves to be mixed race, there were more respondents who have parents of the same race ($n = 208$) than the number of respondents who have parents of two different races ($n = 109$).

Table 4.1 shows that Americans understand in different ways the relationship between their parental ancestry and their own racial identity. The

TABLE 4.1 Relationship between the *Parental Ancestry* and *Self as Mixed Race* Measures

PARENTAL ANCESTRY	ACKNOWLEDGE MIXED RACE		
	NO	YES	TOTAL
Parents of same race	1,329	208	1,537
Parents of two different races	60	109	169
Total	1,389	317	1,706

NOTE: Unweighted data. SOURCE: WKH 2001.

majority of respondents in this sample consider themselves to be monoracial and report having parents of the same race. The table also shows that, of those who have parents of two different races, the majority perceive themselves to be mixed race. This suggests a dominant cultural norm that Americans conceive of a person's own race as a trait inherited from parents. However, it is just as important to note that this is not the case of all respondents. Moreover, an in-depth examination of the data revealed that the dominant match between parental ancestry and mixed racial background is more complicated than is presented in table 4.1. When taking into account how the respondent described the race of her parents and her own race, I found that 4.6% of the sample ($n = 79$) reported having parents of the same race but self-identified with a different monoracial category than the parents (for example, respondents who declared two parents who are white but self-identified as monoracial black).

The finding that there is not a perfect correspondence between parental ancestry and a belief that one is of being mixed race demonstrates the nuances of racial identification. It is true that for many Americans, being multiracial corresponds with having parents of two different races. However, this is not how all individuals arrive at their understanding of being multiracial. Table 4.1 shows that there are respondents who believe themselves to be mixed race but have parents of the same race. Therefore, by approaching "multiracial" as a form of identity, we can better incorporate the diverse definitions Americans employ when they conceive of their race.

Differentiating Forms of Racial Identity

Table 4.1 also highlights the complexity in how Americans practice racial identity. This table demonstrates four different logics of racial identity: (A) those who have parents of the same race and see themselves as monoracial; (B) those who have parents of two different races and see themselves as mixed race; (C) those who have parents of two different races but see themselves as monoracial and (D) those who have parents of the same race but see themselves as mixed race.

Thinking about the substantive meaning of these four logics of racial identity, we can see that group A represents the majority of Americans who self-identify as monoracial and have parents of the same race. However, each of the other three groups, B, C, and D, represents a distinct strategie Americans can use to define multiracial identity. Group B conforms to a conventional notion of the multiracial: persons with parents of two different races. For ease of description, I will label this group *Conventional biracial* in the following analysis. Group C reflects those who adopt the established racial norm of hypodescent: even though an individual reports having parents of different racial backgrounds, she is classified as monoracial, typically the minority category. I will label this group *Follow hypodescent* in the following analysis. Group D is distinctive, since these individuals can be explained by different rationales. It could be the case that these individuals adopt a multiracial social identity that is not defined by their parental ancestry. But it could also be that these individuals have mixed-race ancestors in a generation earlier than their parents. However, regardless of their logic, this group represents those who believe themselves to be of mixed race even though their parents are the same race. I will label this group *Unconventional multiracial*.

The identity choice approach classifies two of the groups, *Conventional biracial* and *Unconventional multiracial*, as multiracial because both self-identify as multiracial. However, the *Follow hypodescent* group is excluded because they do not self-identify as multiracial. Since respondents who are *Conventional biracial* or *Unconventional multiracial* are included in my definition of multiracial, I investigated if systematic differences between these two exist. I also wanted to understand how those who self-identify as multiracial (*Conventional biracial* and *Unconventional multiracial*) differ from those who might be designated as multiracial by a researcher even though they do not identify as multiracial (*Follow hypodescent*).

Hypotheses can be formulated about the expected differences across these three groups. *Conventional biracial* and *Unconventional multiracial respondents* assert an identity choice as multiracial, which at the time this survey was taken was a relatively new identity. In contrast, the *Follow hypodescent* group follows long-standing norms of racial classification and could feel constrained from asserting a multiracial identity. Therefore, I expect that respondents who have relatively few resources, such as those with low socioeconomic status and those who live in rural or more racially homogenous areas, which are governed by stricter and more conservative racial and social norms, are more likely to be in the *Follow hypodescent* group rather than in the *Conventional biracial* or *Unconventional multiracial* group. I also expect there to be some differences between those who are *Conventional biracial* and those who are *Unconventional multiracial*. The *Unconventional multiracial* group is represented by individuals who are not typically understood by others to be multiracial (because they do not have parents of two different races). Given this, they likely need more effort when they declare themselves to be multiracial. Given the effort taken to assert this identity, I expect that individuals who have the most resources, such as being of high socioeconomic status, will more often assert a multiracial identity. Therefore, I expect that those in the *Unconventional multiracial* group will be a more resourced group than those in the *Conventional biracial* group.

For this analysis, I seek to identify the determinants that characterize the three logics of racial identity (*Conventional biracial, Unconventional multiracial, and Follow hypodescent*). The multivariate analysis will test the role of three dimensions of independent variables: individual-level resources, the surrounding social context, and attitudes about race. To account for resources, my model includes formal education, family income, and experienced financial hardship.[10] To account for social context, I consider urban residence[11] and perceived racial diversity of one's neighborhood.[12] To account for attitudes toward race, I include an index variable accounting for the respondent's perceived level of discrimination toward racial minorities and if the respondent experienced racial discrimination.[13] These two variables account for both perceptions of racial inequality and the actual experience of racial inequality. In addition to my three primary dimensions, I also control for the sociodemographic[14] variables of age and gender and include two relevant ideological dimensions: political ideology[15] and religiosity, which allow me to consider if there exist alternative ideological dimensions to multiracial identification.

To identify which of the above determinants are significantly related to each of the three logics of racial identity, I employ logit regression. Since these are nominal groups, the analysis will be comparative, making a contrast between two of the groups. Three models were thus specified: the first model predicts *Follow hypodescent* when compared to *Conventional biracial*, the second model predicts *Unconventional multiracial* when compared to *Conventional biracial*, and the final model predicts *Follow hypodescent* when compared to *Unconventional multiracial*. This comparative strategy will thus allow me to identify how each of these three groups differs from the others.

Table 4.2 presents the results for the three models. The first model includes all those who have parents of two different races and compares the *Follow hypodescent* group against the *Conventional biracial* group. The results reveal that there are not many significant factors that explain the differences between these two groups. I find that among respondents with parents of two different races, those who follow the rule of hypodescent are older and live in more rural areas than those who are conventionally biracial. These results are consistent with the practice of hypodescent: as a long-standing practice, we can expect the rule to be followed by older generations.

The second model includes all respondents who consider themselves mixed race and compares those who do not have parents of two different races against those who do have parents of two different races (*Unconventional multiracial* versus *Conventional biracial*). The identity choice approach offers one way to interpret these results. If we interpret the *Unconventional multiracial* group as having to exercise more effort to assert a multiracial identity than the *Conventional biracial* group (who reflect a more conventional form of multiracial identity), then these model results reveal the types of experiences and resources that encourage those in the *Unconventional multiracial* group to assert a multiracial identity. The results show that the *Unconventional multiracial* group is more likely to report that they experience racial discrimination than those in the *Conventional biracial* group. Those in the *Unconventional multiracial* group are also less likely to be experiencing financial hardship and are less likely to be politically conservative than those who are in the *Conventional biracial* group. These three findings support the hypotheses grounded in an identity choice approach by showing that particular resources and attitudes encourage individuals to assert a less conventional racial identity.

The third model in table 4.2 compares two very different groups: *Follow hypodescent* and *Unconventional multiracial*. This is an interesting comparison since it contrasts two groups that have developed the view that their race does not directly correspond with their parents' racial backgrounds: those in the *Follow hypodescent* group adopt long-standing racial practices and identify as monoracial, while those in the *Unconventional multiracial* group identify as multiracial even though they are not children of an interracial couple. The results in Model 3 show that those in the *Follow hypodescent* group are less likely to report the experience of racial discrimination than those in the *Unconventional multiracial* group. However, those in *Follow hypodescent* are more likely to have higher

TABLE 4.2 Differentiating Three Forms of Racial Identity

| | MODEL 1 | | MODEL 2 | | MODEL 3 | |
	FOLLOW HYPODESCENT VS. CONVENTIONAL BIRACIAL		UNCONVENTIONAL MULTIRACIAL VS. CONVENTIONAL BIRACIAL		FOLLOW HYPODESCENT VS. UNCONVENTIONAL MULTIRACIAL	
	B (S.E.)	PREDICT PROB.[A]	B (S.E.)	PREDICT PROB.[A]	B (S.E.)	PREDICT PROB.[A]
Resources						
Education	.13 (.13)	.16	−.06 (.09)	−.09	.12 (.12)	.11
Income	.03 (.07)	.06	−.07 (.05)	−.15	.14 (.07)**	.21
Financial hardship	−.11 (.20)	−.07	−.24 (.14)*	−.17	.15 (.20)	.08
Social context						
Suburban[b]	−.22 (.46)	−.05	−.13 (.34)	−.03	−.08 (.45)	−.01
Rural	1.16 (.68)*	.27	.23 (.57)	.05	.58 (.57)	.11
Diverse neighborhood	−.22 (.46)	−.05	.46 (.30)	.11	−.52 (.38)	−.09
Attitudes on race						
Experienced discrimination	.10 (.09)	.24	.26 (.07)**	.46	−.19 (.09)**	−.24
Perceive discrimination	−.05 (.10)	−.10	.06 (.08)	.12	−.13 (.10)	−.20

Sociodemographics	.03 (.01)**	.50	.01 (.01)	.09	.03 (.01)**	.41
Age	.03 (.01)**	.50	.01 (.01)	.09	.03 (.01)**	.41
Gender (female)	.47 (.42)	.10	-.02 (.29)	-.004	.19 (.38)	.03
Other ideology						
Religiosity	-.25 (.21)	-.16	.18 (.15)	.13	-.16 (.18)	-.08
Nonideology[c]	.75 (.54)	.17	.10 (.40)	.02	.28 (.48)	.05
Moderate	-.22 (.55)	-.05	-.64 (.40)	-.15	.27 (.53)	.05
Conservative	-.47 (.63)	-.09	**-.84 (.47)***	-.20	.18 (.63)	.03
Constant	-2.18 (1.45)		-.80 (1.04)		-1.64 (1.36)	
N	153		261		206	
Log likelihood	16.62		41.06		24.48	
Percent predict Correctly	.712		.713		.777	
Prop. reduction of error	.102		.279		.061	

NOTE: Unweighted data. Models calculated using logistic regression. Language of interview drops from model in logit, so excluded from mode. SOURCE: WKH 2001.
[a] Predicted probability calculated using Spost in Stata and reports the minimum to maximum change in predicted probability: the change in probability when moving from the lowest value on the independent variable to the maximum value on the independent variable (Long and Freese 2006).
[b] Living context was operationalized as a nominal variable. Suburban and Rural are compared to the excluded value of Urban.
[c] Political ideology was operationalized as a nominal variable, Nonideology, Moderate and Conservative are compared to the excluded value of Liberal.
*p < .10 **p < .05

incomes and are older than those in *Unconventional multiracial*. The hypotheses grounded in the identity choice approach suggest that greater resources offer the opportunity for individuals to assert a multiracial identity. However, the results in Model 3 do not confirm this hypothesis, since those in the *Follow hypodescent* group have higher incomes than those in the *Unconventional multiracial* group.

Summarizing the results from Models 1, 2, and 3, I found there to be some clear patterns, but other findings did not conform to the expected hypotheses. The *Unconventional multiracial* group was more likely to report experiencing racial discrimination than the other two groups. Moreover, the *Follow hypodescent* group was older than the other two groups, which is consistent with the fact that the rule of hypodescent had the greatest social and political consequence for older generations. However, I hypothesized that since those in the *Unconventional multiracial* group asserted greater effort to express their multiracial identity since they are not children of interracial couples, there would be more differences in the types of resources and contexts experienced by those in the *Unconventional multiracial* group than the other two groups. The analyses in this section did not find consistent results confirming this to be the case.

Constraints of Racial Classification

The analysis presented in table 4.2 shows that there are individual-level and contextual factors that differentiate the *Unconventional multiracial* group from those who follow the more conventional or long-standing definitions of race (*Follow hypodescent* and *Conventional biracial*). But the analyses did not offer an intuitive picture explaining why individuals report different logics to their racial identity. For example, why was it the case that those in the *Unconventional multiracial* group were significantly more likely to report experiencing racial discrimination than those in the other two groups?

One important factor not considered in the previous analysis was how individuals are commonly racialized in society. Indeed, even though I originally hypothesized that a person privileged by resources is more likely to assert a multiracial identity even if she is not the child of an interracial couple, this hypothesis failed to recognize that a person's identity choices are also constrained by how others view that person's race. For example, we know that those who are perceived to be black are subject to different racializing experiences than those who are perceived to be Asian. Regardless of one's individual-level resources or surrounding context, race may be the first and dominant factor informing one's willingness to acknowledge a mixed racial background.

There are many different ways to test the constraints of race. Some scholars examine the role of visual appearance, phenotype or skin color and have found that perceivers are influenced by visual cues or a lack of visual cues (for example: Halberstadt et al. 2011; MacLin and Malpass 2001; Peery and Bodenhausen 2008; Terkildesen 1993; Weaver 2012. The WKH 2001 survey offers a different way to test how a person's racialization in an existing monoracial category influences willingness to acknowledge a multiracial identity. Because the WKH 2001 was a telephone survey that collected a racially diverse sample, when respondents were first contacted by an interviewer, they were asked to report their race. Because the mark-one-or-more option was not yet an established practice, respondents were offered the opportunity to designate one monoracial category or declare Hispanic ethnicity. This process, which I will label the *Established method*, reflects the long-standing practice placing individuals in one existing racial category.[16] Although this is a self-reported measure of a respondent's monoracial classification, it offers the opportunity to see if the respondent's typical monoracial classification is systematically related to the respondent's reporting of parental ancestry and willingness to acknowledge being mixed race.

This analysis examines the extent to which classification in a monoracial category has any influence on a person's willingness to acknowledge being mixed race. History can help generate working hypotheses for how the results collected through the *Established method*, the *Parental ancestry* method, and the *Self as mixed race* method are related. The historical development of the rule of hypodescent and protection of the white racial category tells us that those typically classified as nonwhite are more likely to have parents of two different races. In particular, the rule of hypodescent dictated that those with any African ancestry would be classified as black, which means that a person with one black parent and one parent of another race would be identified as black. The rule of hypodescent applies most strongly to those of African ancestry, but sociologists note other historical processes that suggest some form of hypodescent often excluded those of partial Asian or partial Native American descent from the white racial category (Spickard 1986; Spickard 1991 Spruhan 2006). Beyond the rule of hypodescent, the racially diverse history of Latin America also suggests that Latinos are likely to recognize that they have parents of two different races and so may be more likely to see themselves as multiracial (Menchaca 2001; Rodriguez 2008).[17] From this, I expect that respondents who originally classified themselves as nonwhite in the *Established method* are more likely to report to having parents of two different races and acknowledge being mixed race.

To assess this, I first disaggregated respondents by how they were racially classified using the *Established method*. Once they were disaggregated into the four monoracial categories of white, black, Asian, and Latino, I compared their responses to the *Parental ancestry* and *Self as mixed race* measures. Table 4.3 presents the cross tabulation of responses

TABLE 4.3 Relationship between the *Parental Ancestry* and *Self as Mixed Race* Measures, Disaggregated by Race

ESTABLISHED METHOD: WHITE

PARENTAL ANCESTRY	SELF AS MIXED RACE		
	NO	YES	TOTAL
Parents of same race	718	33	*751*
Parents of two different races	9	7	*16*
Total	*727*	*40*	*767*

ESTABLISHED METHOD: BLACK

PARENTAL ANCESTRY	SELF AS MIXED RACE		
	NO	YES	TOTAL
Parents of same race	196	80	*276*
Parents of two different races	15	19	*34*
Total	*211*	*99*	*310*

ESTABLISHED METHOD: ASIAN

PARENTAL ANCESTRY	SELF AS MIXED RACE		
	NO	YES	TOTAL
Parents of same race	197	27	*224*
Parents of two different races	4	12	*16*
Total	*201*	*39*	*240*

ORIGINALLY CLASSIFIED AS LATINO

PARENTAL ANCESTRY	SELF AS MIXED RACE		
	NO	YES	TOTAL
Parents of same race	153	45	*198*
Parents of two different races	21	59	*80*
Total	*174*	*104*	*278*

NOTE: Unweighted data. SOURCE: WKH 2001.

to these two measures, disaggregated by the established monoracial category. The first two-by-two table at the top of table 4.3 presents responses to the *Parental ancestry* and *Self as mixed race* measures for respondents originally classified as white using the *Established method*. In this two-by-two table, we see that of the 767 respondents who were originally classified as white in the *Established method*, 5.2% (*n* = 40) reported themselves to be of mixed race.[18] Whites were much less likely to acknowledge being mixed race than were the racial minority groups. For example, as shown in the second two-by-two table, among those classified as black, 31.9% (*n* = 99) acknowledged being mixed race. The share of those willing to acknowledge being mixed race is actually highest among Latinos: 37.4% (*n* = 104). The share who acknowledge being mixed race among those classified as Asian (16.3%, *n* = 39) is smaller than that among blacks or Latinos but higher than that for whites.[19]

Turning to the *Parental ancestry* measure, we find that among those classified as white, only 16 out of a total of 767 respondents reported having parents of two different races. They make up only 2% of white respondents. The group that had the largest share of respondents reporting parents of two different races is Latinos: 28.8% of this group can be classified as multiracial by parental ancestry. The numbers of multiracial individuals by parental ancestry among those classified as either black or Asian American falls between whites and Latinos: 11% of those classified as black and 6.7% of those classified as Asian American reported having parents of two different races.

In addition to the racial differences in terms of willingness to acknowledge being of mixed racial and parental ancestry, this analysis also finds that the rate of inconsistent responses—for example, those who identify as multiracial but have parents of the same race or those who have parents of different races but self-identify as monoracial—also varies across racial group. The rate of inconsistent responses is highest among those originally classified as black; 30.6% of black respondents reported answers to the *Parental ancestry* and *Self as mixed race* questions that did not match. In contrast, those originally classified as white had the lowest rate of inconsistent answers (5.5%). Strikingly, among those originally classified as white, black, or Asian, the number of respondents who acknowledge being mixed race but have parents of the same race is larger than the number of respondents who acknowledge being mixed race but have parents of different races. However, among Latinos, the pattern is reverse: the number of respondents who acknowledge being mixed race but have parents of the same race is smaller than the number of respondents who acknowledge being mixed race but have parents of different races.[20]

Consistent with historically informed expectations, established practices of race inform the degree to which Americans are willing to acknowledge being mixed race and report having parents of two different races. The results in this section offer some explanation for why the multivariate results presented in table 4.2 did not show a consistent pattern of results. Overall, the racial biases identified in table 4.3 distinctly point to the structural forces that influence how Americans understand race. These results confirm that the existing racial hierarchy and historical norms applied to racial classification continue to inform respondents' willingness to acknowledge being mixed race and their reporting of parental ancestry. The white racial category has been historically understood as an exclusive group and has been framed as a category that reflects a racially homogenous family ancestry. Consistent with this, the evidence shows that those who are racially classified as white are least likely to acknowledge being mixed race or report having parents of two different races.

Alternatively, blacks and Latinos are much more willing to acknowledge being mixed race and having parents of two different races. This reflects the historical formation of the black and Latino categories.[21] Thus, because those who are typically classified as black or Latino fall into the *Unconventional multiracial* or *Conventional biracial* group, this helps explain why the analysis presented in table 4.2 found few significant predictors and why those in the *Unconventional multiracial* group are most likely to report racial discrimination. How individuals are typically classified in monoracial categories plays a more dominant role in explaining willingness to acknowledge being multiracial and likely mediates the effect of the other individual level factors.

Correspondence between the *Mark One or More* and *Self as Mixed Race* Measures

The WKH 2001 was collected immediately following implementation of the mark-one-or-more option and included a unique measure for multiracial identification, *Self as mixed race*. The WKH 2001 data therefore reflect identities and attitudes at a unique moment in history, before the option to self-identify as multiracial was not yet fully integrated into regular practices. Moreover, as discussed in the previous section, the *Self as mixed race* measure likely documents a different form of multiracial identity than the more typically employed racial reporting strategy that asks respondents to mark one or more categories when reporting one's race. The analysis in this section will take into account a period when multiracial identification represented a more entrenched practice and will assess the relationships between different multiracial identity measures.

The data employed come from a 2009 survey collected by Pew Research Center for the People and the Press entitled *Racial Attitudes in America II*.[22] This survey was ideal because of the time at which respondents were interviewed and because it included different multiracial identity measures. This analysis will evaluate the relationships between the *Self as mixed race* measure that was first employed in WKH 2001 and what has become the more common method of reporting a multiracial identity: offering the mark-one-or-more option as adopted by the Census Bureau (the *Mark one or more* measure).[23]

Table 4.4 presents the relationship between responses on these two multiracial identity measures. We can see that more respondents are willing to report being mixed race than are willing to mark two or more races when asked to report their race. For the *Mark one or more* measure, 2% of the respondents (58 out of a total of 2,884) opted to self-identify with multiple races. In contrast, 16.8% of the respondents (484 out of 2,884) reported being multiracial on the *Self as mixed race* measure. Of those who mark two or more boxes when asked about their race, 76% also acknowledge being mixed race. Interestingly, however, 24% (n = 14 out of 58) of those who check two or more boxes do not acknowledge being mixed race. More importantly, there is a share of respondents who check only one race but acknowledge being mixed race. Like the findings from the WKH 2001 survey, those who identify as a (mono)racial minority are more likely to acknowledge being mixed race

TABLE 4.4 Relationship between the *Mark One or More* and *Self as Mixed Race* Measures

MARK ONE OR MORE RACES	SELF AS MIXED RACE			
	NO	YES	DON'T KNOW	TOTAL
White (only)	1,339	93	12	1,444
Black (only)	663	138	6	807
Latino (only)	222	129	12	363
Asian (only)	64	14	1	79
Other race (only)	59	66	8	133
Two or more races	14	44	0	58
Total	2,361	484	39	2,884

NOTE: Unweighted data. Results may not add to 100% due to rounding. SOURCE: Pew Research Center 2009.

while a smaller share of those who identify as only white acknowledge being mixed race. Out of all monoracial groups, Latinos include the largest share (36%) who acknowledges being mixed race.

Why do some who acknowledge being mixed race report multiple races, while others report being monoracial? To identify the factors that differentiate these two groups, I turned to multivariate analysis. First, I restricted the current analysis to those who acknowledged being mixed race. The dependent variable for this analysis is a dichotomous variable designating those who self-identify as multiracial over those who identify as monoracial.

Like the analyses in the previous section, I test the role of three dimensions of independent variables: resources, surrounding social context, and attitudes about race. I attempted to specify the same independent variables that were used for the WKH 2001 analyses but was limited to using the measures included in the Pew study. To account for resources, I included variables for the respondent's education and family income level. To account for surrounding context, I considered whether the respondent lived primarily around those of the same race and a variable that accounts for the population size of the county in which the respondent lives as a proxy for urban living environments.[24] To account for attitudes about race, I included an index measure for the respondent's perceived racial discrimination against blacks, Latinos, and Asian Americans).[25] To correspond with the multivariate model used in the WKH analysis, I also included the additional sociodemographic variables of gender, age, and foreign-born status as well as ideological controls accounting for political ideology and religiosity.[26]

The analysis finds that among respondents who acknowledge being mixed race, only two significant factors differentiate those who self-identify as multiracial (report two or more races) and those who identify as monoracial (report one race). As the results in table 4.5 show, one dimension of resources, the respondent's level of education, primarily predicts multiracial self-identification over monoracial self-identification. This education finding can be interpreted in different ways. It could suggest that those with greater intellectual sophistication are more likely to match their knowledge of their diverse family heritage with their choice of racial identification. It could also be the case that education creates more racially tolerant attitudes that encourage multiracial identification. We can also interpret this finding to demonstrate that certain resources promote the opportunity to assert an identity as multiracial, as suggested by the identity choice approach. One other unanticipated factor, religiosity, also predicted multiracial identification: I found that those who regularly attended church are more likely to self-identify as multiracial rather than monoracial. However, in general, the analysis in table 4.5 shows that, among those who acknowledge being mixed race, there are not many factors that differentiate those who self-identify as multiracial from those who self-identify as monoracial.

One limitation of the analysis in table 4.5 is that it aggregates respondents and does not take into account the constraints of race. The initial results in table 4.4 showed that (mono)racial minorities were more likely

TABLE 4.5 Reporting as Multiracial (Rather Than Monoracial) among Those Who Acknowledge Being Mixed Race

	IDENTIFY AS MULTIRACIAL	
	B (S.E.)	PREDICT PROB.[a]
Resources		
Education	.45 (.20)**	.15
Income	.10 (.09)	.06
Social context		
Homogenous neighborhood	−.09 (.21)	−.02
Population density	.00 (.13)	.00
Attitudes on race		
Perceived discrimination	.03 (.10)	.02
Sociodemographics		
Gender (female)	.53 (.38)	.04
Age	−.01 (.01)	−.07
Foreign born	−.79 (.54)	−.05
Other ideology		
Religiosity	.33 (.14)**	.12
Ideology (liberal)	.13 (.20)	.04
Constant	−5.46 (1.51)**	
N	336	
Log likelihood	26.66	
Percent predict corr.	.893	
Prop. reduction of error	.027	

NOTE: Unweighted data. Models calculated using logistic regression. SOURCE: Pew Research Center 2009.
[a] Predicted probability calculated using Spost in Stata and reports the minimum to maximum change in predicted probability: the change in probability when moving from the lowest value on the independent variable to the maximum value on the independent variable (Long and Freese 2006).
*p < .10   **p < .05

to acknowledge being mixed race than were whites. In a second analysis, I limit my analysis to those who identify with a monoracial category and evaluate why they are willing to acknowledge being mixed race while others are not. Given the clear racial dimension demonstrated in table 4.4, I also disaggregated respondents by monoracial category. But, due to sample size, I could not analyze Asian Americans separately. So the analysis includes four models: one for whites, one for blacks, one for Latinos, and one for all other monoracially identified respondents, which I will label "Other race." The dependent variable for this analysis is acknowledgment of being mixed race. For independent variables, I employed the set of variables used in table 4.5.

As a general pattern for whites, blacks, and Latinos, those with lower incomes and those who do not live in neighborhoods made up of people of the same race are those who acknowledge being mixed race (see table 4.6). This tells us the importance of individual-level resources and surrounding context for understanding the choice *not* to self-identify as multiracial. Poorer individuals may know they are mixed race but face constraints associated with social class that encourage identification with a monoracial category. Moreover, the results suggest that living in more racially diverse areas—at least those in which one is not surrounded by others of the same race—encourages willingness to acknowledge being mixed race.

Taken together, the results from the Pew data show that while a sizable share of Americans acknowledge being mixed race, they do not necessarily declare a multiracial identity when asked to report their race, even when given the mark-one-or-more option. Therefore, the opportunity to declare two or more races when asked does not alone explain why some individuals assert a multiracial identity. Even though many see themselves as of mixed race, this analysis shows that those with lower incomes and those who live in same-race neighborhoods more often report being monoracial rather than multiracial. There are, other important opportunities need to be in place before an individual will declare a multiracial identity.

Summary of Results

Taking the results from both analyses, I find that multiracial identity represents a much more complex practice than is commonly believed. The evidence shows that there is not a perfect correspondence between factors typically believed to be connected: responses to having parents of two different races, acknowledging being mixed race, and reporting two or more races on the racial identification question are not perfectly aligned. Collectively, this analysis helps support the identity choice approach,

TABLE 4.6 Acknowledging Being Mixed Race but Reporting Being Monoracial

	WHITE		BLACK		LATINO		OTHER RACE	
	B (S.E.)	PREDICT PROB.[A]	B (S.E.)	PREDICT PROB.[A]	B (S.E.)	PREDICT PROB.[A]	B (S.E.)	PREDICT PROB.[A]
Resources								
Education	-.12 (.13)	-.02	.09 (.12)	.05	.21 (.15)	.20	-.13 (.21)	-.13
Income	**-.12 (.06)***	**-.05**	**-.12 (.06)****	**-.11**	**-.24 (.08)****	**-.40**	-.11 (.10)	-.20
Social context								
Homogenous neighbourhood	**-.55 (.15)****	**-.09**	**-.27 (.12)****	**-.10**	**-.34 (.15)****	**-.23**	.15 (.21)	.11
Population density	**-.29 (.10)****	**-.06**	.10 (.09)	0.05	-.04 (.10)	-.04	.23 (.15)	.20
Attitudes on race								
Perceived discrimination	-.08 (.07)	-.03	.001 (.07)	.001	.11 (.07)	.22	-.07 (.09)	-.15
Sociodemographics								
Gender (female)	-.30 (.28)	-.01	**-.48 (.24)****	**-.06**	-.41 (.28)	-.09	.16 (.41)	.04
Age	-.01 (.01)	-.02	.01 (.01)	.06	-.01 (.01)	-.10	-.01 (.01)	-.15
Foreign born	.69 (.56)	.04	-.22 (.56)	-.03	-.23 (.29)	-.05	**-1.30 (.46)****	-.29

(continued)

TABLE 4.6 (Cont.)

	WHITE		BLACK		LATINO		OTHER RACE	
	B (S.E.)	PREDICT PROB.[a]	B (S.E.)	PREDICT PROB.[a]	B (S.E.)	PREDICT PROB.[a]	B (S.E.)	PREDICT PROB.[a]
Other ideology								
Religiosity	−.08 (.09)	−.02	−.13 (.08)	−.09	−.09 (.10)	−.11	−.11 (.13)	−.13
Ideology (liberal)	−.03 (.14)	−.01	−.12 (.11)	−.06	−.27 (.16)	−.24	−.18 (.20)	−.17
Constant	1.94 (.97)**		−.36 (.93)		1.8 (1.18)		1.90 (1.55)	
N	1,058		604		247		126	
Log likelihood	37.68		19.08		19.14		15.54	
Percent predict corr.	.94		.844		.660		.683	
Prop. reduction of error	.00		.000		.097		.216	

NOTE: Unweighted data. Models calculated using logistic regression. SOURCE: Pew Research Center 2009.

[a] Predicted probability calculated using Spost in Stata and reports the minimum to maximum change in predicted probability: the change in probability when moving from the lowest value on the independent variable to the maximum value on the independent variable (Long and Freese 2006).

*p < .10 **p < .05

which frames "multiracial" as an identity that individuals arrive at, rather than an objective or standardized trait reported by the individual.

The findings in this section also emphasize the continued power of established racial categories and their role in providing the opportunity to self-identify as multiracial. I hypothesized that those with more resources and those who live in more inviting contexts would be more likely to declare some form of multiracial identity. Yet, in the multivariate analyses, I generally found many null results and inconsistent patterns. This suggested that hypotheses that highlighted the importance of individual agency were not the most appropriate way to approach multiracial identification. Once I took into account how respondents are typically classified into monoracial categories, I found that monoracial assignment as white, black, or Latino is the strongest predictor of multiracial identification. Those who are typically classified as a minority—in particular, black, or Latino—are most likely to acknowledge being mixed race. At the same time, even though blacks and Latinos acknowledge being mixed race, they report only one race on the racial reporting question. These findings suggest that established practices of racial classification continue to dictate who is able and willing to assert a multiracial identity. Therefore, historic practices of race represent a key factor that must be incorporated in hypotheses about identity choice.

Lessons from Census Data: Features of the Two-or-More-Races Population

It was the federal government that made the initial decision to employ the mark-one-or-more option and set in motion a particular strategy for how Americans report their race. Data collected by the Census Bureau are often turned to as our most authoritative source of information on the multiracial population (labeled the "Two or more races" population in most official documentation). Because the Census Bureau distributes details about the multiracial population that are commonly used as a reference point for most research on race in the United States, this final section reviews what the census tells us about the multiracial population. This analysis employs data from Summary File 1 of the 2000 and 2010 censuses.[27] More detailed analyses, particularly on education and income, were calculated from the 1 Percent Public-Use Microdata Sample (PUMS) of the 2000 census, a sample of 1% of those respondents who filled out the long-form census questionnaire.[28]

I present census data in a separate section because they represent an important source of information about multiracial identity. The previous sections in this chapter employed survey data and documented multiracial identities as self-reported by adult respondents. In contrast, census data are a household survey in which one person reports the race of every individual living in the household. For the respondent completing the survey, race is a self-reported feature and measure of her racial identity. However, the respondent assigns the race for all other individuals in the household. This makes the census a mixture of data that measure racial identity and data where race has been assigned to an individual.

Therefore, while the census does suggest that there are particular characteristics that distinguish the two-or-more-races population from other racial groups, I argue that these figures require greater interpretation than is commonly offered. Typically, census data are interpreted as "facts" about the population. However, the identity choice approach pushes us to be more precise about how data have been collected and how those strategies influence our interpretation of the results. If we embrace the identity choice approach, then we interpret census data differently. The objective of this section is to review results from the census and offer an identity choice interpretation of census data. Specifically, I argue that census patterns reveal that existing racial norms, the privileges enjoyed from high socioeconomic status, and certain social contexts offer the *opportunity* for certain individuals to be labeled as multiracial while discouraging others from being counted as such.

Racial Enumeration

If we focus on the two-or-more-races population, it is striking how many different racial combinations are reported in the census. There were 57 multiple race combinations reported in both 2000 and 2010. Certain racial combinations were dominant; for example, the most often reported was white and black, which accounted for 20% of the entire two-or-more-races population.

Looking at the racial combinations patterns presented in figure 4.1, one can see that there are racial biases in how Americans report multiple race combinations. As in the analyses conducted on the WKH and Pew studies, established cultural norms of race, particularly the rule of hypodescent, can be used to explain how Americans' report race. Within the two-or-more-races population, most are biracial and report a combination of white and a racial minority. This suggests that "multiracial" does not simply designate any form of racial mixture. Rather, those who want to report race as a

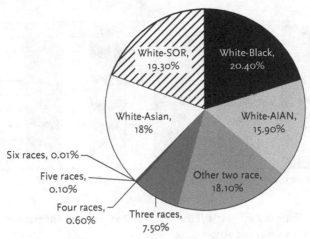

FIGURE 4.1 Racial Combinations of the Two-or-More-Races Population, Census 2012

combination of white and nonwhite are most likely to check two or more boxes on the racial identification question. This is a distinct alternative to the rule of hypodescent; instead of following historic cultural norms that would assign an individual to a racial minority category, respondents choose to designate themselves as partially white.

Shifting the analysis to how the mark-one-or-more option can change the enumeration of the traditional (mono)racial groups, figure 4.2 disaggregates the population by single race categories and adds to each the share of individuals who marked two or more races. The first important pattern revealed is that the two-or-more-races population results in the least change to the size of the white population. Of those who selected white as their race,[29] only 2.5% marked two or more races. In contrast, 52.5% of those who selected Native Hawaiian or other Pacific Islander marked two or more races. So even though "white" is most often included as a race among the two-or-more-races population, the effect of the mark-one-or-more option is most strongly seen in how we calculate minority populations. Interestingly, relative to other racial minority groups, the size of the black population is least affected by the inclusion of the two-or-more-races population: approximately 6.1% of blacks report themselves to be of two or more races.

Because Latinos are identified through a separate ethnicity question, there are complications to interpreting the two-or-more-races population among them. To clarify, since Latinos are officially considered an ethnic group, they may be of any race. In 2010, 53% of Latinos reported themselves white, 36.7% reported themselves "Some Other Race," and

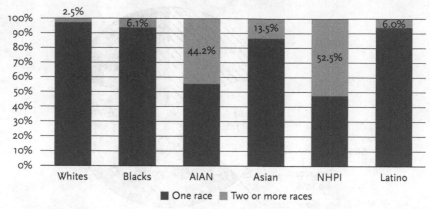

FIGURE 4.2 Share of Each Racial/Ethnic Group That Declared Themselves to Be of Two or More Races, Census 2012

the remainder reported one of the other racial categories.[30] Sonya Tafoya (2003) posits that Latinos' propensity to consider themselves "Some Other Race" demonstrates that they perceive their racial identities as falling outside the bounds of the official six-category racial spectrum provided by the census. She asserts that since 97% of those in the "Some Other Race" category also declared that they were of Latino ethnicity in 2000, the category represents a de facto Latino racial category.[31] Given some of the challenges presented by Latino identification, many scholars and the Census Bureau warn that the two-or-more-races population among Latinos may not reflect an identity similar to the rest of the population. However, census data show that, like other Americans, the overwhelming majority of Latinos (94%) report only one race. At the same time, Latinos are generally more likely to report two or more races than whites: 6% of Latinos marked two or more races.

Patterns of racial identification expose racial biases in Americans' understanding of race. Census data show that the sizes of the white and black populations, the two groups whose racial categories are defined by historic and persistent cultural norms, are least likely to be changed by the presence of the two-or-more-races population. In contrast, reporting two or more races is most dominant among indigenous populations such as American Indians and Pacific Islanders. Indigenous populations have long experienced forced and voluntary integration with other racial groups, and this history is revealed in how Americans report the American Indian and Pacific Islander races. Moreover, increased cultural openness to recognizing an indigenous family lineage among Americans (particularly white Americans) today is consistent with public willingness to designate American Indian as part of one's racial background.[32] Taken together, reporting of one's racial background continues to be consistent with the norms of the time: Americans report those racial identities that are deemed culturally or normatively amenable with existing social rules.

Age Structure

The two-or-more-races population is, on the whole, a young population. In 2000, its median age was 22.7 and dropped to 19.9 in 2010. This population is younger than the white, black, Asian, and Latino populations whose median ages in 2010 were 42, 32.7, 35.5, and 27.3 respectively.[33] At the same time, the age distribution varies depending on the racial combination. For example, those who selected white and black are the youngest multiracial population, with a median age of 11.8. The oldest biracial group is represented by those who selected white and American Indian or Alaska Native, with a median age of 31.4. The three-or-more-races population is also relatively young, with a median age of 18.6. If we disaggregate those who are Latino, the median age of Latinos who reported two or more races is 20.5.

The age structure of the two-or-more-races population suggests an important generational dimension to reporting multiracial identities. Consistent with the modern shift toward conceiving race as a primarily a product of self-identification, reporting two or more races is most prevalent among those Americans who were primarily socialized in the post-civil rights era. Older Americans who were socialized in a racial environment characterized by the existence of Jim Crow and more rigid rules of racial classification are more likely to designate themselves as monoracial than multiracial.

Most importantly, since the two-or-more-races population is on average so young, it is likely that those who are reported to be two or more races are not self-reporting. Is it more likely that a parent is reporting the race of a child. The decreasing median between 2000 and 2010 also shows that more parents are labeling their children as multiracial over time. As the research reviewed in the first section of this chapter demonstrates, certain types of parents are more likely to designate their children as multiracial (Bratter 2007; Roth 2005; Xie and Goyette 1997). Therefore, at least half of those reported to be two or more races were assigned that characteristic, which may not reflect self-identification. Only time will tell whether children designated as two or more races will later self-identify as multiracial.

The Role of Immigration

Immigration data reflect how the practice of racial reporting on the census is culturally specific to the United States. The two-or-more-races population is primarily native born: In 2010, only 9% of the two-or-more-races population reported themselves to be immigrants. This is actually a smaller percentage than reported ten years earlier. In 2000, 22.2% of the two-or-more-races population reported themselves to be immigrants. We can find more evidence of the idea that racial classification is a cultural product by examining the differences across different immigrant groups. Among Asian Americans, those who are native born are more likely to mark two or more races than those who are foreign born: 25% of the native born self-identify as multiracial, while only 2% of the foreign born do so. For Latinos and blacks, there is a difference across immigration status, but that difference is not as large as that demonstrated by Asian Americans. Among Latinos, 6% of the native born and 2% of foreign born report themselves to be two or more races, while among blacks, the share is 6% of the native born and 3% of the foreign born. In contrast, for whites, there does not appear to be an effect related to immigration: 2% of both native-born and foreign-born whites report themselves to be two or more races.

Socioeconomic Status

According to the 2000 census, education and family income levels for the two-or-more-races population rank in the middle of all racial groups.[34] But treating the two-or-more-races population as one group masks important socioeconomic variation. Once we disaggregate the population by racial combination, we see that declaring two or more races over declaring one race corresponds with socioeconomic status. As a general rule, those who reported to be two or more races have higher levels of income and education than their (monoracial) minority counterparts but lower levels than whites. There are many different racial combinations to analyze, but for the purposes of this discussion, I focus on three multiple-race groups—white-black, white-Asian, and Latinos reported to be two or more races—and compare these groups to their monoracial counterparts.

In terms of education, census data show that 26.1% of whites hold a college degree or more (see figure 4.3). In contrast, 14.3% of black adults have obtained a college degree. Yet 24.9% of those who declare themselves to be white-black hold a college degree. The educational attainment of those who report to be white-black thus falls in between

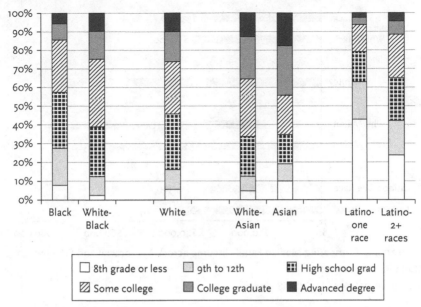

FIGURE 4.3 Comparing Educational Attainment across Monoracial and Selected Multiple-Race Groups

SOURCE: 2000 Census; 1% IPUMS Dataset

their monoracial counterparts, with the white-black population being more educated than the black population. A similar pattern is apparent for Latinos: 10.5% of Latinos who only declare one race have obtained a college degree, but 11.6% of Latinos who declare two or more races have obtained a high school degree. However, the results are different when comparing white-Asian individuals to their monoracial counterparts. Asian adults are the most educated, with 44.3% obtaining a college degree, while 35.5% of multiracial individuals who report to be white-Asians hold a college degree. In this case we find the reverse: those who report as white-Asian have lower college graduation rates than their minority counterparts.

Figure 4.4 compares median family income levels across racial groups and shows a pattern similar to that found for educational attainment. Those who declare themselves to be white-black have a median family income of $35,800, which is slightly higher than blacks ($33,600) but much lower than whites ($51,800). Latinos who report two or more races also have a higher median family income (of $37,400) than Latinos who report only one race ($35,470). Unlike the pattern for educational attainment, those who report themselves to be white-Asian have a median family income of $60,000, which is higher than the median family incomes of both whites

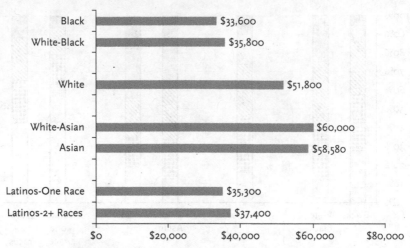

FIGURE 4.4 Comparing Median Family Income across Monoracial and Selected Multiple-Race Groups

SOURCE: 2000 Census; 1% IPUMS Dataset

and Asians. Taken together, in terms of socioeconomic status, those reported as white-Asian enjoy a high standard of living.

These comparisons across groups along the basic indicators of socio-economic status demonstrate the importance of individual-level resources when choosing to report two or more races. Those with more resources have more opportunity to assert two or more races. Moreover, the data show that the two-or-more-races population is, on average, wealthier and better educated than their (monoracial) minority counterparts. Thus reporting to be a single-race minority, particularly black or Latino, is correlated with lower socioeconomic status. The only exception to this pattern is when we compare those reported to be Asian, a group with the highest average educational attainment. Yet this should not distract us from the fact that those reported to be white-Asian represent one of the best-educated and wealthiest groups. At the same time, the contrast between those reported to be white-Asian and those reported to be white-black or Latino of two or more races shows that within the two-or-more-races population, certain racial combinations are associated with greater socioeconomic privilege.

Geography

The final striking pattern characterizing the two-or-more-races population is their geographic concentration in certain areas in the United States. In both 2000 and 2010, census data found a clear regional bias where the largest number (38%) of those who report to be two or more races lives in the West. Within this region, the largest number lived in California. In 2000, the Midwest had the smallest two-or-more-races population, but in 2010, the smallest population was in Northeast. If we disaggregate the two-or-more-races population by racial combinations, the 2010 census found that nearly half (47.4%) of those reported to be white-Asian and 42.6% of those reported to be white–Some Other Race (who are likely to be of Latino ethnicity) lived in the West. The largest share of those reported to be white-black (36%) lived in the South. Thus, the reporting of multiple race combinations appears to be influenced by the type of (mono)racial populations found in those regions.[35] Moreover, reporting two or more races is an urban phenomenon. The largest numbers of those who report two or more races live in the two largest cities in the United States: New York and Los Angeles are both home to over 150,000 individuals who report two or more races.[36]

The geographic concentration of the two-or-more-races population in the West and in urban areas suggests that an individual's surrounding social context does indeed foster willingness to declare multiple races. All else being equal, we should expect the two-or-more-races population to make up a similar share of the population in all regions. Yet the concentration of the two-or-more-races population in the West tells us that some contexts present more welcoming environments for multiracial identities, which, in turn, encourage individuals to declare multiple races.

In many ways, patterns reflected in census data align with the findings from the multivariate analyses presented in the first half of this chapter. Both census and survey data show that the assertion of multiracial identities is systematically related to particular features in American society. Even though census data do not depict patterns of self-identification only, the reporting of two or more races can still be seen to be constrained by historic social norms that define established monoracial categories and by opportunities created by individual-level resources and context.

Multiracial Identity Choice: Opportunities and Constraints

This chapter presents an example of how to apply an identity choice approach to the analysis of race data. This approach asserts that when Americans report their race today, they are communicating how they understand their identity. More specifically, this chapter emphasizes the claim that "multiracial" is an identity evoked when there are particular opportunities to do so. By framing "multiracial" people as an identity group, I embrace a definition of multiracial that differs from previous scholarship, which typically assigns a specific group of people (children of interracial marriages) to the category. I argue that an emphasis on identity allows us to better understand the patterns we find today.

If we view multiracial as an identity, then "inconsistent" patterns in the data can be understood in a more coherent way. For example, I found that there is not a perfect correspondence between parental ancestry and seeing oneself as mixed race or between seeing oneself as mixed race and reporting oneself to be two or more races. While some Americans see their multiracial identity as a product of being the child of interracial parents, there are others who see themselves as mixed race but choose not to designate themselves as multiple races when asked to declare their race. In this chapter, I focused on a specific set of logics that emphasized family heritage, but there are others, such as the role of phenotype, that Americans can also use to understand their race. But the general lesson in this chapter is that individuals rely on many different logics when they declare themselves to be multiracial. Because individuals rely on different logics, we find a number of different patterns in the relationships between parental ancestry, seeing oneself as mixed race, and reporting to be two or more races.

But while individuals rely on different logics to understand multiracial identities, the data show that ultimately declaring a multiracial identity is constrained by external factors. Most importantly, the long-standing norms that define how individuals are assigned to established (mono)racial categories continue to inform Americans' understandings of being mixed race and expressing multiracial identities. Established racial norms reaffirm the racial hierarchy that makes those classified as white the most privileged group and those classified as nonwhite less privileged. As a result, the white racial category is as an exclusive group with membership rules that are rigidly defined. It should be no surprise, then, that the data in this chapter show that those typically classified as black or Latino are most likely to acknowledge being mixed race. Those typically classified as black or Latino are also more likely to report having parents of two different races. So while race may be increasingly seen as a product of personal identity, historic norms that define assignment in racial categories continue to inform how Americans understand being of mixed race.

Moreover, the evidence suggests that not all individuals who see themselves as of mixed race or who might prefer a multiracial identity ultimately report being multiracial when asked about their race. The data confirm that multiracial identities are asserted when there are opportunities to do so. Multiracial identification is most often seen in individuals who have resources at their disposal (specifically high socioeconomic status) and who live in particular contexts that support multiracial identities. Census data reveal that those reported to be of two races, one of which is white, are more socioeconomically advantaged than their (mono)racial minority counterparts. Those who are reported to be white-Asian are among the most highly resourced in the nation. In contrast, those reported to be single-race blacks or Latino are the most socioeconomically disadvantaged. Integrating the option to declare oneself as multiracial therefore has not appeared to level the racial order but instead created a more variegated one in which those with more resources have the opportunity to declare themselves as multiracial rather than monoracial.

Of course, the data in this chapter offer broad patterns and do not allow me to rule out other possible ways of explaining these patterns. For example, the evidence presented here cannot tell us the extent to which personal self-interest is a driving force. It could also be the case that certain individuals perceive benefits from asserting identity choice. One explanation could be that racial minorities, who do not enjoy the social and political privileges associated with membership in the majority group, may be driven by self-interest to identify as multiracial since they have little to "lose" by choosing multiracial identities. However, those who normally enjoy the status affiliated with being white may intuitively understand the disadvantages of being nonwhite and so choose not to identify as multiracial. Yet, even in this scenario, it is clear that external pressures related to historic American racial traditions inform an individual's perceived self-interest in asserting particular types of racial identities.

In sum, the data suggest that there are distinctive processes that lead to multiracial identification compared to those that explain monoracial identification. Yet, at the same time, social norms that govern race continue to inform the racial identities of all Americans, including multiracial identities. With these ideas in mind, the following chapter considers one set of consequences attributed to multiracial self-identification: the development of political attitudes and views about American race relations.

5 | Implications of Racial Identity
COMPARING MONORACIAL AND MULTIRACIAL
POLITICAL ATTITUDES

I N A CONTEXT WHERE RACE is practiced as a set of discrete and homogenous categories, the rise of multiracial self-identification is, in and of itself, a significant social development.[1] Individuals who conceptualize race as personal identity and choose to describe their race as outside the established racial order reflect a distinctive direction in American racial formation. Yet, while these demographic patterns are striking and noteworthy, there may be other social or political consequences to multiracial identification. This chapter will consider one possible political consequence of multiracial identification by assessing to what extent multiracial identities are manifested in patterns of individual political attitudes, in particular racial attitudes.

As I will cover in the first section of this chapter, racial categorization and identity have been identified as key antecedents to political attitude formation. There exists a long-standing literature on the relationship between race and political behavior. This scholarship points to the unique attitudinal patterns demonstrated by African Americans and their persistent differences from whites' attitudes. Racial classification as nonwhite in the United States has clear implications for how a person perceives her individual and group interests, which are, in turn, reflected in a distinct pattern of political attitudes (see, for example, Dawson 1994; Fraga et al. 2010 Wong et al. 2011. If this is our baseline, then we can expect that racial identification, including the adoption of a multiracial identity, informs a person's politics.

Political attitude patterns are primarily documented for those Americans who identify as monoracial, and we cannot expect the same patterns among those with a multiracial identification. In the case of monoracial identities, scholars have pointed out an important distinction between racial group identification and racial group consciousness (Chong and Rogers 2005). Group identification primarily measures a person's sense of belonging in a group. However, one's perception of group membership may not represent what that person normatively thinks about that group or the degree of commitment to that group. Alternatively, the concept of group consciousness assumes not only that a person has adopted a group identity but that that identity is connected with a set of ideological beliefs. The difference between group identification and group consciousness is important because it helps explain why race strongly influences some individuals' political attitudes and behaviors, while for others the implications of racial identification are less apparent.

The interviews with activists presented in chapter 3 demonstrated that those with a multiracial group consciousness embraced an agency-driven view about race. These individuals believed that individuals should have the right to choose their racial identity rather than be constrained by a category imposed by others. As a result, activists' multiracial identities reflected a unique racial worldview, and responses demonstrated that their identity was connected to their political attitudes. On the other hand, evidence from the previous chapter demonstrated that, within the mass public, multiracial identification is contingent on many factors, in particular the continued role of racial classification. The conditional nature of multiracial identities could lead to the expectation that multiracial identification among average citizens may not always inform their political attitudes. The evidence presented in previous chapters thus leaves open a question as to how multiracial identification informs political attitude formation.

Although different empirical strategies can be used to assess the relationship between racial identification and individual political attitude formation, this chapter employs a comparative method and examines to what extent multiracial political attitudes systematically vary from those of other racial groups. First, using a variety of public opinion datasets that include a multiracial self-identification option, I examine how the political attitudes of self-identified multiracial individuals differ from those who identify with the established monoracial categories of white, black, Asian, or Latino. Because we learned in chapter 4 that existing monoracial categories inform multiracial identification, the second set of analyses in this chapter disaggregates the multiracial population by racial mixture and compares the attitudes of each multiracial subgroup with self-identified monoracial individuals of the same racial background. This analysis will be used to examine to what extent established racial categories inform multiracial political attitudes. Finally, I consider the extent to which multiracial individuals believe they live a distinctive multiracial experience. This final analysis explores initial evidence to determine the validity of the claim made by the activists in chapter 3 that multiracial individuals perceive a shared racialized experience.

Race and the Formation of Individual Political Attitudes

One of the most striking patterns in American public opinion is the consistent divide by race. Comparing opinion patterns for whites, blacks, Asian Americans, and Latinos, scholars have found that each racial group demonstrates a unique configuration of political interests. Thus, the relationship between race and political attitude formation is not uniform across all Americans. Rather, the meanings attached to each racial category lead to a particularized, group-based interests and worldviews. By reviewing the literatures on the political attitudes of each (mono)racial group, we can understand the complexity of the relationship between race and public opinion.

The basic and most prevalent divide in public opinion is that between whites and blacks, particularly on issues related to race and racially conscious policies, policies that seek to rectify racial inequality and discrimination, such as affirmative action, racial redistricting, and school busing. Scholarship in public opinion and political psychology shows that, even with decreased racial intolerance among white Americans since the modern civil rights movement, the topic of race continues to divide white and black attitudes (Schuman et al. 1997). Whites, who do not experience a subordinate position on the racial hierarchy, are less likely to view race as a force constraining life chances. As a result, whites see contradictions between solving racial inequality and liberal democratic thought, which embraces individualism and meritorious behavior. This perceived tension leads whites to give low levels of support to government redistribution programs aimed at alleviating racial inequality (Bobo 2000; Sidanius and Pratto 1999; Sidanius et al. 2000; Sniderman and Piazza 1993). In contrast, blacks, who directly and personally experience their subordinate racial status, are more likely to view race as the cause of significant social problems and so are supportive of race-based policy solutions (Dawson 1994, 2001). For blacks, racial considerations are always cognitively accessible, while for whites, racial considerations are more latent and typically must be primed by political communication strategies (Mendelberg 2001; White 2007).

Blacks are much more likely to consider the interests of their racial group and support group-based strategies in politics than are whites. In general, individual agency and self-interest are key motives that drive white political attitudes. Theories emphasizing the role of political ideology, rational action, and personal threat are commonly employed to explain white racial attitudes (Bobo, Kluegel, and Smith 1997; Kinder and Sanders 1996; Sidanius and Pratto 1999; Sniderman and Piazza 1993). However, analysis suggests that white racial attitudes are not uniform and vary across educational and ideological lines (Huber and Lapinski 2006 Sniderman and Piazza 1993). Alternatively, blacks tend to use group-based interests or racial group cues in determining their personal interests. Michael Dawson (1994) argued that because blacks believe that their race dictates how they will be treated by society, blacks perceive a sense of "linked fate" or the belief that one's individual fate is connected to the fate of the racial group. Perceptions of linked fate lead blacks to take considerations about their general racial group into account when forming their individual political preferences (see also Tate 1994). Blacks are thus more likely to act as a collective group, hold relatively more homogenous political attitudes, and rely on a racial group consciousness in the formation of their individual political attitudes (Chong and Rogers 2005; Shingles 1981).

White and black attitudes thus provide opposite cases of how race informs individual political attitudes. Whites are less likely to believe race is a politically consequential factor or to rely on a collective racial group consciousness, and more likely to rely on their own individual interests, while blacks perceive the persistent consequences of race and are more likely to rely on group-based interests in development of their individual political attitudes.

Research on Asian American and Latino public opinion shows that the patterns demonstrated by whites and blacks are not generalizable across all groups (de la Garza et al. 1992; Fraga et al. 2010; Lien Conway and Wong 2004; Wong et al. 2011). In general, Asian American and Latino public opinion do not mirror white or black patterns; rather, each group demonstrates its own unique pattern. Asian Americans and Latinos are more likely to see race as a problem than whites but less likely than blacks. Accordingly, Asian American and Latino attitudes tend to fall between the political attitude scores reported by whites and blacks.

Different theories have been proposed to explain Asian American and Latino attitude patterns. Chong and Kim (2006) posit that when these two groups experience increased social mobility, they feel less reliant on their race and so are less likely to rely on racial considerations when forming their political opinions. Implicit in this argument is the claim that because Asian Americans and Latinos are more socially mobile than blacks, they are less likely to believe their race matters. However, Kim (2000) argues that embracing a status as a more successful or model minority is a reflection of how clearly individuals perceive the importance of their race and how they understand their place in the racial order. Other theories have emphasized the fact that Asian Americans and Latinos are more likely to be new immigrants, and so factors related to their social incorporation act as intervening variables in attitude formation (Cho 1999; Hajnal and Lee 2011; Ramakrishnan 2005; Wong 2006). As newcomers to society, immigrants may be less likely to understand American race relations, and so it cannot be expected that these groups would rely on racial considerations to determine their individual interests. Furthermore, both the Asian American and Latino categories are panethnic, which means that each category encompasses multiple national origin groups who may not share interests and goals (DeSipio 1996; Lien 2001).

While Asian American and Latino attitudes do not directly mirror the patterns demonstrated by blacks, this should not be taken as evidence that they fail to use race as a salient political consideration. Both Asian Americans and Latinos respond to group-based cues and perceive the existence of racial discrimination (Barreto 2010; Junn and Masuoka 2008; Sanchez 2006; Wong et al. 2011). However, their racial group identities are generally more latent than blacks'. Race is less likely to be automatically accessible for Asian Americans and Latinos, and so reliance on group identities may be contingent on mobilization strategies that offer connections between their racial status and their political interests (Junn and Masuoka 2008; Perez 2012). Furthermore, there are important differences between Asian Americans' and Latinos' attitude patterns: Latinos are generally more likely to support redistribution policies than are Asian Americans (Bowler and Segura 2012).

One of the weaknesses in the literature is that studies on white, black, Asian American, and Latino public opinion have generally focused on the content of each group's political preferences rather than explaining *how* and *why* racial differences persist. However, a comparison of attitude patterns across racial groups helps to develop a general theory on the relationship (see Masuoka and Junn 2013). The patterns across the four groups point to the powerful and structural role of race. Racial categorization serves an important function because it designates social status to groups within a society. Race, then, creates the social context in which individuals live. Individuals respond and develop their political interests based on their social position created by the racial hierarchy. Because Americans practice race as discrete categories, the circumstances surrounding each racial category are distinct, which means each racial group is subject to its own particular configuration of opportunities and constraints. Those classified in marginalized racial categories live in a world in which their race constrains individual opportunity and advancement. In contrast, those who are classified in more privileged racial categories do not experience disadvantages associated with their racial status and so are less likely to be aware of the role of race. Taken together, the more likely it is that members of a racial group experience constraints of race, the stronger the racial group identification and reliance on race-based considerations (see also Sidanius and Pratto 1999).

Testing Three Theories on Political Attitude Formation

Throughout this book I have argued that self-identified multiracial individuals represent a distinct group because they assert an identity that falls outside the established racial spectrum. However, the general novelty of multiracial self-identification also makes it difficult to rely on an existing literature for drawing expectations about multiracial identity and political attitude formation. Moreover, while the above review of the literature demonstrates that there exists a general understanding that racial categorization informs individual and group interests, this understanding is based on attitudinal patterns held by those who adhere to and identify with existing (mono)racial categories.

Given these constraints, what will be conducted in this chapter is an exploratory data analysis to determine to what extent we can identify a link between multiracial identification and political attitude formation in the first decade of the twenty-first century. The analyses in this chapter were guided by three different theories that have often been applied to racial and ethnic identification in the United States: assimilation theory, racial formation theory, and group identity theory. Although these theories were not originally developed to explain multiracial political attitudes, they provide a useful set of hypotheses for how we can compare multiracial political attitudes with those of other racial groups.

The classic theories on assimilation examine processes of immigrant incorporation in the United States. Generally, assimilation theories identified diminishing ethnic attachments and generally a smooth integration of new immigrants into mainstream society (Alba and Nee 2005 Dahl 1961; Gordon 1964). These theories reported that over generations, descendants of immigrants have weakening attachments to their ethnicity or national origin backgrounds. Because early assimilation studies focused on early European immigrants, these studies also showed that, along with the loss of immigrant ethnic attachments, there was also a strengthening racial identification with the privileged white racial category (Jacobson 1998; Roediger 1991). Typically, assimilation theories have been applied to longitudinal data: studies track immigrant populations over the number of generations they have lived in the United States (see, for example, Dahl 1961). However, I will argue here that one can also apply assimilation theory to cross-sectional data. I contend that multiracial populations can be used as an outcome of assimilation. In the original scholarship, researchers pointed to interracial marriage and intimate racial group interaction as key indicators that a group has assimilated into mainstream society (Gordon 1964). Accordingly, if you characterize multiracial individuals as a product of racial intermarriage, multiracial individuals can be empirically used to represent groups that have reached a late stage of the assimilation process.

Assuming this, one hypothesis that can be generated from assimilation theory is that multiracial identification reflects a symbolic identity. That is, we expect multiracial identity to be a characteristic individuals use to describe themselves but does not inform their politics. In this way, there is a correspondence between the identities of multiracial individuals and the ethnic identities embraced by white Americans. Empirical research has found that white Americans not only continue to assert their ethnic identities but also believe that their ethnic identity is an important marker of the self (Gans 1979; Waters 1990). Early theories on immigrant ethnic identification such as the "Hansen's Law" speculate that while marginalized immigrants wanted to shed their ethnic markers in order to be accepted as American, assimilated grandchildren of immigrants desired to reclaim their ethnic identity labels (Hansen 1928. At the same time, Waters (1990) pointed out that white Americans typically assert ethnic identities only asserted in leisure activities, but unless these identities are perceived to offer some social or political advantage, they are not emphasized in other, more consequential interactions. Therefore, ethnic identities have weak influence on white political attitude formation. Instead, white political attitudes are influenced more strongly by other individual-level characteristics such as socioeconomic status, gender, and ideology (see, for example,

Campbell et al. 1960).[2] If multiracials reflect symbolic identities as do white ethnics, then we will expect self-identified multiracial individuals to have a pattern of political attitudes similar to whites'.

In contrast to assimilation theories, theories on racial formation posit that racial classification as nonwhite has negative consequences for one's individual life chances in the United States. Racial formation theorists argue that because "white" is a socially privileged category, those not classified as such witness social disadvantage through their out-group status (see, for example, Omi and Winant 1994; Masuoka and Junn 2013; Sidanius and Pratto 1999). What is most distinctive about racial formation theories is that they generally challenge the argument by assimilation theorists that the disadvantages associated with ethnic difference diminish as groups become more established in the United States. One can point to African Americans, most of whom have families that have long resided in the United States, as a case in which assimilation theories fail to apply. African Americans continue to be stereotyped in society as a deviant group and are subject to many forms of discrimination (Dawson 1994; Tate 1994). However, African Americans are not the only group used to understand the persistence of the racial order: others have argued that all those classified as nonwhite also experience racial disadvantage that informs their politics (Hero 1992; Kim 2000). Therefore, the salience of race leads nonwhite Americans to adopt group attachments to their racial category because it plays a dominant role in their individual life chances. If one assumes that multiracial individuals are nonwhite, then racial formation theories would hypothesize that, at a minimum, self-identified multiracial individuals will not adopt a pattern of political attitudes like that of white Americans.

While racial classification as nonwhite has important consequences, Asian Americans, blacks, and Latinos do not all demonstrate the same pattern of political attitudes. As reviewed above, the political attitudes among these three groups are quite distinct. It has also been argued that the unique racial tropes and stereotypes assigned to each racial category create a distinct set of constraints and opportunities for each group. Therefore, a second, more specific hypothesis can be drawn from racial formation theories: the pattern of multiracial political attitudes will correspond with those of the same nonwhite racial category. For example, the political attitudes of a respondent who self-identifies as white and black will correspond more closely with black political attitudes than those of whites.[3] In a way, this second hypothesis applies the long-standing rule of hypodescent to multiracial political attitude formation.

Finally, we can apply a third set of theories, which I label group identity theories, to explain multiracial political attitudes. This category includes theories from social psychology that claim that individuals develop immediate and strong attachments with members of one's in-group (Tajfel and Turner 1979; Tajfel 1981). Building from these theories, one can pose that multiracial individuals perceive a cohesive group identity with other multiracial individuals. One hypothesis developed from this assumption is that multiracial identities will function like all other ethnic identities, and so multiracial individuals will perceive that all multiracial individuals constitute a collective group. If this hypothesis is true, then we should expect that multiracial individuals will demonstrate positive biases toward others in the in-group and believe that multiracial individuals share a common culture, history, and experience in the United States. It could be argued that multiracial individuals see themselves as a distinctive racial group because multiracial identities have been legitimized by the state. Just as importantly, because scholars have documented a rise of multiracial social and civic organizations among young adults, we can expect that this has helped create a more stable and widespread multiracial community across the nation (DaCosta 2007; Renn 2004).

Two other expectations can also be specified if one assumes a collective multiracial identity exists. First, political attitudes will be relatively uniform within the self-identified multiracial population. Specifically, we should expect that a perceived shared experience of being multiracial is not contingent on a certain racial combination (such as white and black or white and Asian). Political attitudes of multiracials should be similar regardless of the racial combination reported. Second, multiracial attitudes will not simply vary from whites but will reflect a unique pattern of attitudes distinct from all other monoracial minority groups.

Comparing Attitudes across Multiracial and Monoracial Groups

With these theories in mind, this first set of analyses will test the first two: the assimilation hypothesis and the racial formation hypothesis. To do this, I will compare the political attitudes of multiracial individuals with those of monoracial groups: whites, blacks, Asians, and Latinos. By comparing multiracial political attitudes to those of monoracial groups, we can see whether self-identified multiracial individuals develop attitudes similar to whites' or attitudes like those held by persons who share their racial minority identity.

Three Dimensions of Dependent Variables

For this analysis, I have limited the dependent variables to political issues that have been documented to have racial undertones and have consistently shown differences across racial groups (see also Bowler and Segura 2012). The dependent variables in this analysis can be classified into three distinctive dimensions: racial attitudes, politics, and support for public policies.

The racial attitudes dimension includes the individual's perceptions about other racial groups and the perceived role of race in determining the life chances of racial minorities. The most common measure of racial attitudes for white Americans is the racial resentment index, which has been developed to account for modern forms of white racism against blacks (Kinder and Sanders 1996).[4] The racial resentment index is often most appropriately applied to a very specific relationship between whites and blacks and has primarily been tested on white public opinion rather than minority public opinion (see, for example, Feldman and Huddy 2005; Tesler and Sears 2010). To account for this limitation, I also included perceptions of discrimination against each of the four monoracial groups (white, blacks, Asian Americans, and Latinos). Perceived discrimination is a more relevant measure for capturing views about race among racial minority groups and is a common measure employed in studies on minority public opinion (see, for example, Chong and Kim 2006; Conover 1988; Sanchez 2006; Schildkraut 2011).

The politics dimension is represented in this analysis by party identification. Party politics has been documented to have racial undertones, in which the Democratic platform supports more causes on behalf of racial minorities, while the Republican platform is understood to generally reject those causes (Carmines and Stimson 1981 Frymer 1999).

Finally, the public policy dimension includes survey items that measure support levels on public policies that seek to rectify racial inequality. I include a measure on general levels of support for government involvement to reduce racial inequality: whether the respondent believes government should ensure that blacks get fair treatment in jobs. I also include a survey item that measures support for a specific policy: affirmative action. Finally, I include attitudes toward a racialized policy area that is not directly framed in terms of white-black racial conflict: immigration policy. Immigration policy today has led to growing Asian American and Latino populations. Open immigration thus advantages these two racial minority groups since it leads to their population growth and thus is often seen as a racial policy targeting Asian Americans and Latinos (Chavez 2008; Masuoka and Junn 2013; Perez 2010).[5]

Expected Attitudinal Differences by Racial Group

Evidence from previous studies suggests that if we were to visualize an attitudinal scale, from support to opposition, on each of these three dependent variables, we would find that each of the four monoracial groups occupies a specific position on this scale, which is depicted in figure 5.1. Conceptually, we can order the four monoracial groups along this scale by the degree of reliance on racial group considerations and preference for maintaining the status quo. With the exception of attitudes toward immigration, whites and blacks occupy opposite positions on all of these measures. In general, whites are least likely to report the existence of racial discrimination and most likely to believe historic racial problems are lessening over time. However, whites do protect racial group interests by supporting maintenance of the status quo, and so is the group most likely to reject redistributive policies that attempt to reduce racial inequality (Sidanius et al. 2000; Sniderman and Piazza 1993). Given that the political party that is currently framed to support maintenance of this status quo is the Republican Party, whites today represent the majority voting bloc for this party. In contrast, because their race plays a determinative role in their individual lives, blacks report the highest awareness of racial inequality and discrimination in society (Dawson 1994, 2001). Because blacks witness the direct effects of racial marginalization, they are the most supportive of redistributive policies that seek to change how society functions. The political party that is currently understood to support these redistributive efforts is the Democratic Party (Frymer 1999). Today, blacks overwhelmingly identify as Democrats.

Between the two diverging attitudes occupied by whites and blacks on these measures, we can place the positions of Asian Americans and Latinos. Research suggests that Asian Americans' attitudes on all three dimensions of the dependent variable are closer to whites', while Latinos' attitudes on all three dimensions are closer to blacks' (Bowler and Segura 2012). But because there are large immigrant subpopulations within both the Asian American and the Latino communities, scholars believe that their political attitudes may be less stable than those of whites and blacks

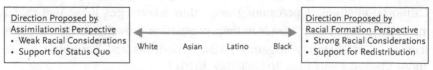

FIGURE 5.1 Conceptual Placement of Monoracial Groups on Attitudinal Scale

(Tam Cho 1999; Hajnal and Lee 2011. Thus, while Asian Americans and Latinos normally occupy the middle range on this scale, we should expect that their exact positions will vary depending on the survey question at hand and the context in which they are surveyed. However, the one exception to this rule is found on attitudes toward immigration policy. Both Asian American and Latino respondents have been consistently supportive of open and inclusive immigration policies (Masuoka and Junn 2013).

With the position of the four monoracial groups in mind, the analysis here will attempt to determine the placement of multiracial individuals on this scale. If assimilation theories are correct, then we should expect that attitudes for multiracial individuals will be like those for whites. Theories on racial formation predict that multiracial individuals will develop a racialized identity. If this perspective is correct, then we should expect that the attitudes of multiracial individuals will be significantly different from those of whites. Moreover, at minimum, the difference in scores between whites and multiracial individuals should be as large as that demonstrated by Asian Americans, the group that most often ranks in attitudes closest to whites.

Data Analysis

For this analysis, I employ data from the American National Election Study 2008 time series study[6] (hereafter referred to as "ANES") and the 2009 Pew, which was analyzed in the previous chapter. Both studies include extensive batteries on political and racial attitudes, and both identify multiracial respondents using the mark-one-or-more measure.[7] Because the ANES and Pew use a similar measure for multiracial identification, we can assume relative comparability across multiracial respondents.[8] One weakness of both datasets, however, is that they include representative samples only of whites, blacks, and Latinos. Asian Americans are thus excluded from the analysis in this section.

To make direct comparisons, I calculate the average scores for each monoracial group on each of the selected dependent variables. When comparing mean scores across monoracial groups, I expect to find the same patterns predicted in the hypothesized conceptual scale just described. I will then calculate the mean scores on each dependent variable for multiracial individuals and determine how the average score for multiracial respondents compares to the average scores for each of the four monoracial groups. Tests of statistical significance will be performed in order to determine if the differences across scores represent valid differences or if those differences are due to random biases related to sampling.

Starting with the first dimension of racial attitudes, I assess racial group differences on the racial resentment measure. For this analysis, the racial resentment index was coded on a 0 to 1 scale with respondents who score a value of 1 reflecting high levels of racial resentment toward blacks. Figure 5.2 compares the mean score for each monoracial group and multiracial individuals on the racial resentment index. The mean scores of monoracial groups reflect the expected pattern of attitudes and can be ordered as hypothesized along the conceptual scale. Whites' mean score on the racial resentment index is the highest and blacks' the lowest. Latinos' mean score ranks between whites' and blacks'.[9] Comparing the mean score of multiracial individuals against those for the three monoracial groups, I find that multiracial individuals report about the same level of racial resentment as blacks. Difference-of-means tests reveal that multiracial individuals' mean racial resentment score is statistically indistinguishable from both blacks and Latinos. Moreover, multiracial individuals' mean racial resentment score is significantly lower than that of whites ($p < .01$).

The second set of survey items used to measure racial attitudes is perceptions of discrimination. The Pew study asked respondents to rate the level of discrimination against each of the four monoracial groups. Measures for these questions were coded on a scale of 0 to 1, in which a value of 1 represented respondents who believed that "a lot" of discrimination was experienced by the listed racial group. Table 5.1 presents the mean scores on

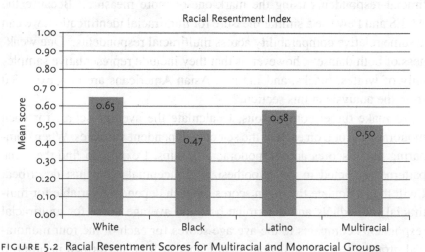

FIGURE 5.2 Racial Resentment Scores for Multiracial and Monoracial Groups

NOTE: Data are weighted to reflect the national population. SOURCE: American National Election Study 2008: Pre- and Post-Election Survey. Index is coded on a 0 to 1 scale with 1 designating high resentment.

TABLE 5.1 Mean Scores on Perception of Racial Discrimination: Comparing
Multiracial and Monoracial Groups

| | PERCEIVED DISCRIMINATION AGAINST | | | | |
RACE OF RESPONDENT	BLACKS	LATINOS	ASIANS	WHITES	N
White	.60 (.01)	.65 (.01)	.49 (.01)	.49 (.01)	1,444
Black	.76 (.01)	.70 (.01)	.56 (.01)	.43 (.01)	807
Latino	.53 (.02)	.57 (.03)	.42 (.02)	.31 (.02)	363
Multiracial	.64 (.06)	.64 (.05)	.48 (.05)	.41 (.05)	58

NOTE: Measures are coded on a 0 to 1 scale with 1 designating perceptions of "a lot" of
discrimination. Data are weighted to reflect the national population. Standard errors in parentheses.
SOURCE: Pew Research Center 2009.

each of the four perceived discrimination measures.[10] Strikingly, respondents of all races are in general agreement over which racial groups experience the most discrimination and which racial groups experience the least
discrimination. Respondents of all races perceive that blacks and Latinos
are subject to more discrimination than Asian Americans or whites. Racial
minority respondents believe whites experience the least racial discrimination, but white respondents believe Asians and whites experience the least
discrimination. At the same time, the respondent's race does influence the
perceived amount of discrimination each racial group experiences: black
respondents overall report the highest rates of discrimination (mean scores
are the highest in ratings of discrimination against racial minority groups).
Contrary to expectations, even though Latinos perceive that racial minorities experience more discrimination than whites, they report the lowest
mean scores on all the discrimination questions. While this does not conform to my anticipated conceptual scale (which expected whites to report
the lowest mean scores), this finding does reflect the existing expectation
that Latino attitudinal patterns are inconsistent across surveys.

At first glance, multiracial respondents' mean scores on the discrimination measures are closer to those of white respondents than those of black
respondents. Moreover, because of the wide variance reported by multiracial respondents on these measures, many of the differences shown in
table 5.1 are not statistically significant. Interestingly, the largest number
of statistically significant differences is found on the perceived discrimination against blacks measure. Multiracial individuals' mean rating on
perceived discrimination against blacks is statistically indistinguishable
from whites but is significantly lower than blacks and higher than Latinos.

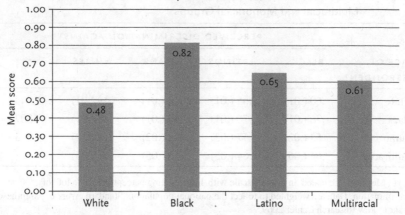

Party Identification: Democrat

FIGURE 5.3 Party Identification of Multiracial and Monoracial Groups

SOURCE: American National Election Study 2008: Pre- and Post-Election Survey. Party identification is coded on a 0 (Strong Republican) to 1 (Strong Democrat) scale. Data are weighted to reflect the national population.

Multiracial respondents are also significantly more likely to believe that whites experience discrimination than Latino respondents believe. Taken together, multiracial individuals' ratings on the discrimination measures suggest that they perceive only moderate levels of discrimination.

With respect to the second dimension of dependent variables, politics, figure 5.3 presents the degree to which respondents identify as strongly Democrat. Party identification was coded on a 0 to 1 scale with a score of 0 representing those who strongly identify as Republican and 1 representing those who strongly identify as Democrat. The middle value of .5 reflects those who identify as independent and do not lean toward either party. Whites' mean score on the party identification variable reflects a slight leaning toward the Republican Party, while blacks' mean score reflects their overwhelming support of the Democratic Party. Latinos also lean toward the Democrat Party but are not as strongly Democratic as blacks.[11] Multiracial respondents also strongly lean toward the Democrat Party and have a mean score that is statistically indistinguishable from that of Latinos. Difference-of-means tests confirm that multiracial respondents are not as strongly Democratic as blacks but significantly more Democratic than whites. This pattern on the party identification variable suggests that multiracial individuals could be included in the coalition of racial minorities who strongly support the Democratic Party.

Finally, table 5.2 compares support for racialized public policies. Like the other analyses, all variables were coded on a 0 to 1 scale with

TABLE 5.2 Mean Scores on Public Policy Items: Comparing
Multiracial and Monoracial Groups

RACE OF RESPONDENT	GOVT. ENSURES BLACKS JOBS	IMMIGRATION INCREASED	AFFIRMATIVE ACTION	N
White	.46 (.01)	.36 (.01)	.15 (.01)	1,177
Black	.77 (.02)	.37 (.01)	.57 (.02)	558
Latino	.57 (.02)	.49 (.01)	.30 (.02)	427
Multiracial	.77 (.06)	.40 (.04)	.30 (.07)	48

NOTE: Measures are coded on a 0 to 1 scale with 1 designating support of policy.
Data are weighted to reflect the national population. Standard errors in parentheses.
SOURCE: American National Election Study 2008: Pre- and Post-Election Survey.

1 representing those who support the given policy. Comparing mean scores across monoracial groups, I find that on the two policies that primarily address white-black racial conflict—government intervention to ensure blacks receive fair treatment in jobs and affirmative action—black respondents report the highest levels of support. As anticipated, white respondents' mean scores on these two measures are the lowest of all three monoracial groups. Latino respondents' mean score rank between those reported for whites and blacks.[12] In contrast, on immigration policy, Latinos report the strongest support for increased immigration of the three monoracial groups. Whites and blacks report similar scores on the immigration measure.[13]

Comparing multiracial respondents' scores with monoracial groups, I find different patterns across the public policy dependent variables. On the government intervention variable, multiracial respondents report one of the highest average scores of all racial groups. Difference-of-means tests confirm that multiracial respondents are significantly more likely to support government intervention than both whites and Latinos ($p < .01$). On the other two measures, multiracial respondents' mean scores rank in the middle of those reported by monoracial groups. Multiracial respondents' level of support for affirmative action is the same as that reported by Latino respondents. At the same time, multiracial respondents are significantly more supportive of affirmative action than whites but significantly less supportive than blacks. On immigration policy, multiracial respondents are significantly less likely to support increased immigration than Latinos, but their mean score is no different from that reported by white or black respondents.

Some Evidence for the Racial Formation Hypothesis

Given the large number of dependent variables, a summary table of all results in this section is outlined in table 5.3. This table allows easy comparison of statistically significant differences between multiracial respondents and each of the three monoracial groups. This analysis has shown that on many items multiracial respondents hold attitudes that are distinctive from monoracial groups'. This is particularly revealing given that although the sample size of multiracial respondents is relatively small, I still find statistically significant differences between multiracial respondents and monoracial groups. At the same time, multiracial respondents do not reveal an obvious pattern of attitudes. The analysis offered in this section aligns with previous studies in that there were consistently and an expected pattern of political attitudes across the three monoracial groups. But across dependent variables, the mean score of multiracial respondents did not consistently occupy the same place on the conceptual scale of attitudes.

TABLE 5.3 Summary Table of Results: Comparing Multiracial and Monoracial Groups

	COMPARED TO SELF-IDENTIFIED MULTIRACIALS, MONORACIAL ATTITUDES ARE		
	WHITES	BLACKS	LATINOS
Racial resentment	Hold higher resentment		
Perceived discrimination: blacks		Perceive more discrimination	Perceive less discrimination
Perceived discrimination: Latinos			
Perceived discrimination: Asians			
Perceived discrimination: whites			Perceive less discrimination
Party identification	More Republican	More Democrat	
Govt. ensures jobs for blacks	Want less govt.		Want less govt.
Immigration increased			Support increase
Support affirmative action	Less support	More support	

NOTE: Only those differences that reach statistical significance (at least $p < .10$) are shown in the table. Blank cells reveal that there was no significant difference between multiracial and monoracial respondents.

Some of the evidence supports the assimilation hypothesis because on some measures, particularly the perceived discrimination measures, multiracial attitudes are no different from whites'. However, on other survey items, multiracial political attitudes differ from those of whites, thus supporting the racial formation hypothesis. The position of multiracial respondents on racial resentment is similar to that of blacks and Latinos. Multiracial respondents also clearly lean Democratic and report more support for government intervention than whites. Therefore, the evidence does not conclusively support one theory over the other.

Considering the Implications of Established Racial Categories

The first analysis above analyzed multiracial respondents as one collective group. However, combining all multiracial individuals in one group may mask important racial differences within this subpopulation. In fact, the pattern of results in the previous section could be due precisely to significant diversity within the multiracial group. In other words, while the preceding analysis tested to what extent the assimilation hypothesis applies to multiracial political attitudes, I did not fully test hypotheses informed by racial formation theories. In particular, the second hypothesis proposed by racial formation theories predicted that multiracial political attitudes would be informed by the specific racial background of the individual. One way to examine the influence of racial background is to disaggregate multiracial respondents by racial combination and then compare attitudinal patterns.

Strategy for Analysis

In order to do this analysis, I return to the dataset employed in the previous chapter, the *Washington Post* / Kaiser Family Foundation / Harvard University *Race and Ethnicity in 2001: Attitudes, Perceptions, and Experiences Survey* (WKH 2001). Unfortunately, data from the ANES and Pew, which employ the mark-one-or-more method, generated a relatively small sample (less than 100) of multiracial respondents. This sample did not offer the statistical leverage to disaggregate multiracial respondents into more detailed racial combinations. However, as demonstrated in chapter 4, the acknowledge mixed-race measure identifies a significantly larger sample of self-identified multiracial respondents. In addition, the WKH 2001 also offered a follow-up question that asked self-identified multiracial respondents to describe their racial background. While chapter 4 found that those who see themselves as mixed race are not the same population as identified by the mark-one-or-more method, analyses of WKH 2001 data will at least generate some findings about the role of racial background in multiracial attitudes.

Given the two-part question on multiracial background in the WKH 2001 dataset, I can disaggregate all respondents in the survey into eight different racial groupings. The first four groupings represent those in monoracial categories: white, black, Latino,[14] and Asian. The second four represent multiracial individuals of different racial combinations: those who checked white as one of their races, those who checked black as one of their races, those who checked Asian as one of their races, and those who checked Latino as one of their races (hereafter labeled respectively as multiracial-white, multiracial-black, multiracial-Asian, and multiracial-Latino).[15] Because of the data limitations, I could not disaggregate these multiracial respondents into specific combinations (for example white-Asian, white-black, black-Latino, etc.). So, for example, the multiracial-Asian group includes all multiracial individuals who list "Asian" as one of their racial backgrounds and includes those who list themselves as Asian-white, Asian-black, or Asian-Latino. Coding multiracial respondents in this way does result in overlapping groups since, for example, a respondent who self-identifies as multiracial and claims to be black and Asian is coded as both multiracial-black and multiracial-Asian.[16] Because there are overlapping groups, I will not be able to empirically compare attitudes across multiracial groups. I will only compare one multiracial group against the monoracial group that shares attachment to the same racial category (so multiracial-Asian vs. Asian). The strategy employed here allows me to determine if individuals who report the same racial category hold similar or different attitudes.[17]

For the dependent variables, I again employ the same three dimensions of political attitudes analyzed in the previous section: racial attitudes, politics, and support for public policies. The WKH 2001 survey includes survey measures similar to those analyzed in the previous section. However, the WKH 2001 did not include items for the racial resentment index or questions on immigration policy, so these dependent variables are not included in this analysis.[18] Each of the three measures was again coded on a 0 to 1 scale with a score of 1 indicating positions reflecting strong awareness of race. I calculated the average response scores for each of their eight racial groups on the three dimensions of dependent variables. I then compared average scores between multiracial respondents and monoracial respondents of the same racial background. If racial background does indeed influence multiracial political attitudes, there should be no significant difference in the scores between these two groups.

Data Analysis

Table 5.4 compares mean scores on perceptions of discrimination. Consistent with the previous analysis, respondents of all races in the WKH 2001 generally believe that both blacks and Latinos are likely subject to discrimination and that Asian Americans and whites are less likely to be subject to discrimination. Black respondents report the highest mean scores on perceived discrimination against minority groups, and these means are significantly higher than those reported by white respondents ($p < .01$). Latino respondents in the WKH 2001 perceive more discrimination against minority groups than that found in the previous analysis. However, the differences between Latinos' scores and those of other monoracial groups are not always statistically significant. Of those significant differences, I find that Latinos in the WKH 2001 report significantly more discrimination against Latinos than other monoracial groups. Although Asian Americans' raw mean scores on perceived discrimination against minority groups are the lowest of all four monoracial groups, many of these differences are not significant. But strikingly, white, black, and Latino respondents are all

TABLE 5.4 Mean Scores on Discrimination Items: Comparisons across Racial Background

	PERCEIVED DISCRIMINATION AGAINST				
RACE OF RESPONDENT	BLACKS	LATINOS	ASIANS	WHITES	N
White	.62 (.01)	.57 (.01)	.50 (.01)	.44 (.01)	730
Multiracial white	.69 (.03)	.63 (.03)	.55 (.03)	.46 (.03)	168
Black	.78 (.02)	.70 (.02)	.57 (.02)	.37 (.02)	218
Multiracial black	.80 (.03)	.64 (.04)	.51 (.03)	.39 (.05)	91
Asian	.61 (.03)	.55 (.03)	.51 (.03)	.32 (.04)	209
Multiracial Asian	.65 (.06)	.62 (.05)	.57 (.07)	.50 (.09)	38
Latino	.66 (.02)	.67 (.02)	.54 (.03)	.34 (.03)	198
Multiracial Latino	.76 (.03)	.74 (.03)	.66 (.03)	.38 (.04)	102

NOTE: Measures are coded on a 0 to 1 scale with 1 designating perceptions of "a lot" of discrimination. Data are weighted to reflect the national population. Standard errors in parentheses. SOURCE: WKH 2001.

more likely to perceive discrimination against their own racial group than Asian American respondents ($p < .01$).[19]

The mean scores for multiracial groups on perceptions of discrimination do vary when sorting multiracial respondents by racial background. Multiracial-white respondents are significantly more likely to believe blacks experience discrimination than are monoracial whites ($p < .05$). Multiracial-Latino respondents are also significantly more likely to believe blacks experience discrimination than are monoracial Latinos ($p < .01$). Thus, among those who could be racially classified as either white or Latino, multiracial identification leads to stronger perceptions of racial discrimination against blacks. Multiracial-black respondents report the highest raw mean score on the discrimination against blacks measure, but their attitudes do not vary significantly from their monoracial black counterparts. Although Asian respondents report the lowest mean score of all groups on the discrimination against blacks measure, this analysis also finds that there is no significant difference between multiracial-Asian and monoracial Asian respondents.

Turning to the other discrimination measures, both multiracial-white and multiracial-Asian respondents report moderately high levels of discrimination against whites. Among those who would be classified as white, monoracial and multiracial respondents report similar levels of discrimination against whites: there is no significant difference between scores. But the difference between multiracial and monoracial Asian respondents' scores on the discrimination against whites measure is significant. However, multiracial-white respondents perceive significantly more discrimination against whites than do monoracial black, Asian American, and Latino respondents. In contrast, multiracial-Latino respondents perceive significantly more discrimination waged against Asian Americans than do monoracial Latinos. Multiracial Latinos also perceived more discrimination waged against Latinos than do monoracial whites.

Although the results presented in table 5.4 do not offer a clear pattern, I do find evidence to suggest that racial background influences the formation of multiracial political attitudes. Taken together, multiracial identification seems to encourage stronger racial considerations among those racially categorized as white or Latino. Multiracial-white respondents perceive more racial discrimination against all three racial minority groups than their monoracial white counterparts. Multiracial-Latino respondents also perceive significantly more discrimination against other racial minority groups than their monoracial Latino counterparts perceive. In contrast, there were no significant differences between multiracial and monoracial blacks on any of the discrimination measures. At the same time, both multiracial and monoracial blacks reported some of the highest mean scores on discrimination against racial minorities, and there were also no significant differences between multiracial-Asian and monoracial Asian respondents.

Table 5.5 compares mean scores on the politics and public policy dependent variables. In the results on party identification, responses in the WKH 2001 data generally conform to the expected pattern outlined by the conceptual scale of political attitudes: monoracial blacks report the strongest preferences for Democrats, while monoracial whites lean slightly Republican.[20] Both monoracial Asian Americans' and Latinos' scores on party identification fall between those of monoracial whites and blacks. When comparing multiracial respondents with their monoracial counterparts, I find a similar pattern of results as was found on the perceptions of discrimination items above. The most important finding identified is that, in contrast to their monoracial counterparts, multiracial-white respondents lean Democrat on the party identification scale. A difference-of-means test tells us that there are no statistically significant differences between multiracial individuals who report being partially black, Asian, or Latino and their monoracial counterparts.

In contrast, there were many significant differences in how multiracial and monoracial groups view government intervention to ensure racial equality.[21] In general, all three monoracial minority groups report stronger support for government intervention to ensure racial equality than whites ($p < .01$). Both multiracial-black and multiracial-Latino respondents also

TABLE 5.5 Mean Scores on Politics and Policy Items: Comparisons across Racial Background

RACE OF RESPONDENT	PARTY ID (DEMOCRAT)	AFFIRMATIVE ACTION	GOVT. INTERVENTION	N
White	.46 (.02)	.53 (.02)	.59 (.02)	730
Multiracial white	.60 (.05)	.65 (.05)	.71 (.04)	168
Black	.86 (.02)	.79 (.03)	.86 (.02)	218
Multiracial black	.82 (.04)	.81 (.06)	.90 (.03)	91
Asian	.64 (.05)	.71 (.04)	.78 (.03)	209
Multiracial Asian	.52 (.13)	.48 (.13)	.50 (.11)	38
Latino	.64 (.04)	.67 (.04)	.78 (.03)	198
Multiracial Latino	.63 (.05)	.56 (.07)	.82 (.03)	102

NOTE: Measures are coded on a 0 to 1 scale with 1 designating the liberal position. Data are weighted to reflect the national population. Standard errors in parentheses. SOURCE: WKH 2001.

strongly support government intervention and hold statistically indistinct scores from their monoracial counterparts. Interestingly, multiracial-white respondents also strongly support government intervention and hold significantly different attitudes than do their monoracial counterparts. However, the pattern is distinct for those racially classified as Asian. Multiracial Asians are significantly less likely to support government intervention than monoracial blacks, Latinos, and Asian Americans. Rather, multiracial Asians have levels of support for government intervention similar to that of monoracial whites.

However, I did not find the pattern when examining responses to the affirmative action question. While multiracial-white respondents report relatively strong support for affirmative action, the raw mean scores for multiracial-Asians and multiracial-Latino respondents were relatively low. However, the difference between multiracial and monoracial Asians is not statistically significant, nor is the difference between multiracial and monoracial Latinos. In general there is a high amount of variance in support for affirmative action within each of the multiracial groupings (as demonstrated by high standard errors), which tells us that multiracial positions on affirmative action are quite diverse.[22]

Evidence Suggests Race Continues to Matter

The analysis in this section suggests that racial minority background does continue to influence political attitude formation among multiracial respondents. However, the effects of racial background are not uniform across multiracial groups. A summary of results is presented in table 5.6. The evidence suggests that two multiracial groups—multiracial-white and multiracial-Latino respondents—adopt more racially conscious political attitudes than their monoracial counterparts. The finding that multiracial-white respondents demonstrate more racially conscious attitudes than their monoracial counterparts leads us to disconfirm the assimilation hypothesis and accept the first racial formation hypothesis. If we focus just on those who report a white racial background, the evidence shows that multiracial-white respondents report more racially conscious attitudes and do not mirror the attitudes of monoracial whites.

The analysis also confirms that there are no differences in political attitudes between multiracial-black and monoracial black respondents. Indeed, the evidence shows that the racial formation hypothesis strongly applies to multiracial respondents who see themselves as partially black. Interestingly, among Latinos, those who say they are multiracial are more

TABLE 5.6 Summary Table of Results: Does Race Matter?

| | COMPARED TO MONORACIAL COUNTERPARTS, MULTIRACIAL ATTITUDES ARE | | | |
	MULTIRACIAL WHITE	MULTIRACIAL BLACK	MULTIRACIAL LATINO	MULTIRACIAL ASIAN
Perceived discrimination: blacks	Perceives more discrimination		Perceives more discrimination	
Perceived discrimination: Latinos	Perceives more discrimination			
Perceived discrimination: Asians	Perceives more discrimination		Perceives more discrimination	
Perceived discrimination: whites				Perceives more discrimination
Party identification	More Democratic			
Govt. ensures jobs for blacks	More govt			Less govt.
Support affirmative action	More support			

NOTE: Only those differences that reach statistical significance (at least $p < .10$) are shown in the table. Blank cells reveal no significant difference between multiracial and monoracial respondents.

aware of racial discrimination than those who say they are monoracial. On the perceived discrimination items, multiracial Latinos also perceived the existence of even more discrimination against blacks and Asian Americans than do their monoracial counterparts. Therefore, the racial formation hypothesis also applies to multiracial respondents who report being partially Latino.

The one outlier group in this analysis is multiracial-Asian respondents. In contrast to the comparisons across those who identify as black or Latino, multiracial-Asian respondents report weakening racial considerations, as compared to their monoracial counterparts. Although there were many measures where there were no significant differences between multiracial and monoracial Asian respondents, the analysis did find that multiracial-Asian respondents support less government intervention to rectify racial problems and, interestingly, perceive more discrimination against the most privileged racial group, whites, than do all other minority groups. Thus, in contrast to multiracial-black and multiracial-Latino respondents, who can be explained by the racial formation hypothesis, multiracial Asians' attitudes may be explained by the assimilation hypothesis.

Perceptions on a Unique Multiracial Experience

The final set of hypotheses to be tested are those developed from group identity theories. Specifically, I examine whether multiracial respondents perceive a unique racialized experience as "multiracial." Although the previous section demonstrated that monoracial categories of white, black, Asian, and Latino influence the formation of attitudes for multiracial respondents, this does not rule out the possibility that multiracial individuals are also developing a unique multiracial group identity. It is possible that multiracial individuals believe that they share racialized experiences with monoracial minorities but also share experiences with one another. Multiracial individuals can collectively share a similar set of challenges or experiences that result from their identity choices, and these shared experiences may drive their desire to assert a multiracial identity.

There are indeed many different aspects of life that multiracial individuals could believe they share. These common experiences could range from the reflections of unique patterns of family formation to lifestyle choices. The data allow me to examine one particular shared experience: a similar experience of racialization. The activists in chapter 3 demonstrated that multiracial individuals can see themselves as racial "others." Their choice of multiracial identity was rooted in their belief that their racial experiences are distinct from other racial groups. Many spoke of their racially ambiguous features and that they were subject to persistent questioning to define their racial status. Activists argued that these common experiences that marked multiracial individuals as racially distinctive were shared by those who identified as multiracial.

One way to understand how individuals perceive their racialization is through the experience of racial discrimination. The formation of racial group consciousness among racial minorities is rooted in the shared belief that the group faces persistent and institutionalized forms of discrimination that largely explain their group's disadvantaged status (Chong and Rogers 2005; Dawson 1994). To investigate this view, this analysis will examine two questions about discrimination against multiracial individuals that were included in the WKH 2001 survey. The first measure asks: "How much discrimination do you think there is against multiracial Americans in our society today?" The second question asks: "Do you think multi-racial children face more problems or fewer problems growing up than children of a single race do, or isn't there much difference?"

By highlighting these two survey items on racial discrimination experi-enced by multiracial individuals, I seek evidence to determine if multira-cial individuals believe that they are a racially marginalized group. It may be the case that being multiracial is associated with negative racial experi-ences, and, if so, then multiracial respondents will perceive their group to be subject to racial discrimination. I recognize that group identities are not always formed from negative experiences, and it is possible that multira-cial individuals view their race as an advantage rather than a disadvantage. If this is the case, then it is possible that group identity theories still apply to multiracial individuals, but I would not find attitudinal differences on the discrimination measures. I acknowledge that this section tests only one particular form of group identity, a marginalized racial identity, and so these analyses represent a preliminary assessment of the group identity hypotheses posed above.

First, if we group together all respondents who believe themselves to be mixed race, a sizable share of multiracial respondents, 30%, believe that multiracial individuals face "a lot" of discrimination. The mean score for multiracial respondents on the discrimination item was .67 on a scale of 0 to 1. This score was significantly higher ($p < .01$) than the mean scores of monoracial whites, Asian Americans and Latinos (whose mean scores were .56, .49, and .52 respectively). However, multiracial respondents' score on the discrimination item was not higher than that of monoracial blacks, whose mean score was also .67. On the survey item asking about multiracial children, 29% of multiracial respondents believed multiracial children experience "a lot more" problems than single-race children. The mean score for multiracial respondents on this question was .70. Multiracial respondents' mean response on this question was not significantly differ-ent from that of monoracial white, black, or Latino respondents.

Given the previous analysis, which shows that the racial combination of multiracial respondents influenced political attitudes, the group means for multiracial respondents may mask some important differences within this group. As the previous analysis showed, perceptions of discrimination might be attributed to having a minority background, not to being multiracial. To determine if there are differences across the multiracial sample by racial background, I use the same eight groups as in the previous analysis (white, black, Asian, Latino, multiracial-white, multiracial-black, multiracial-Asian, and multiracial-Latino) and compare responses between monoracial

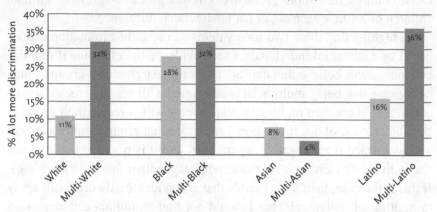

FIGURE 5.4 Perception of "a Lot" of Discrimination against Multiracial Individuals: Comparisons by Racial Background

SOURCE: WKH 2001. Data are weighted to reflect the national population.

and multiracial respondents who report sharing the same monoracial category. By disaggregating multiracial respondents, I can make some inferences about whether multiracial respondents all perceive there to be similar racialized experiences, regardless of their racial combination.

Figure 5.4 shows the percentage of respondents in each of the eight racial group categories who report "a lot" of discrimination against multiracial individuals. As seen in this figure, over one-third of multiracial-white, multiracial-black, and multiracial Latino respondents believe multiracial individuals are subject to "a lot" of discrimination. In contrast, only 4% of multiracial-Asian respondents believe multiracial individuals are subject to "a lot" of discrimination. Difference-of-means tests confirm that multiracial-whites, multiracial-blacks, and multiracial-Latinos perceive significantly more discrimination against multiracial individuals than do their respective monoracial counterparts. At the same time, monoracial blacks perceive high rates of discrimination against multiracial individuals. Thus, a collective multiracial identity may not be the primary driver of responses to the discrimination question. Rather, those groups more likely to perceive discrimination overall are more likely to believe multiracial individuals experience "a lot" of discrimination.

Figure 5.5 presents the share of each of the eight racial groupings who believe that multiracial children face "more" problems than single race children. As with the discrimination item, multiracial-white, multiracial-black, and multiracial-Latino respondents do appear to report similar

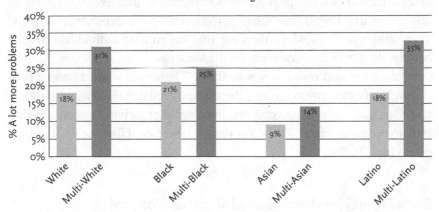

FIGURE 5.5 Perception That Multiracial Children Face More Problems Than Single-Race Children: Attitudes by Racial Background

SOURCE: WKH 2001. Data are weighted to reflect the national population.

means on this question. For these three multiracial groups, over one-quarter of respondents perceive that multiracial children face a lot more problems than single-race children. In contrast, only 14% of multiracial-Asian respondents believe multiracial children face more problems than single-race children. However, unlike the results for the discrimination question, there are fewer significant differences between multiracial and monoracial groups. Interestingly, the differences that do reach statistical significance are comparisons between multiracial and monoracial Asian respondents and between multiracial and monoracial Latino respondents.

Comparing across measures, we see that these results offer mixed findings regarding a perceived racialized experience among multiracial individuals. Although those acknowledge being mixed race may recognize that they are subject to discriminatory treatment, these perceptions vary depending on the respondent's reported racial combination. The data again suggest that multiracial-Asian respondents are an outlier group that does not perceive significant discrimination against multiracial individuals, in contrast to the other multiracial groups, who are more likely to perceive discrimination. These racial differences on the issue of discrimination suggest that multiracial individuals do not all view their multiracial identity as a source of marginalization. Taken together with the analyses in the previous two sections, this suggests that although multiracial individuals' political views appear to embrace their nonwhite status, these perceptions are likely driven by their monoracial minority background rather than their choice to identify as multiracial.

At the same time, this analysis does not exhaustively prove that multiracial individuals fail to perceive a common shared experience; rather this shows that they do not share perceptions on the experience of racial discrimination. It could be the case that multiracial individuals instead believe there exists a common family experience or another social circumstance not addressed in this analysis. Therefore, while I cannot conclusively say that group identity theory best explains multiracial political attitudes, this analysis suggests that in terms of perceiving a shared racialized experience, racial formation theory better explains the results than group identity theory.

Racial Considerations and Multiracial Political Attitude Formation

In the beginning of this chapter, I outlined three general theories—assimilation, racial formation, and group identity—each of which offered hypotheses on how multiracial political attitudes would compare with those of monoracial groups. In general, the data do not offer a simple conclusion about multiracial political attitude formation: one can look at the findings and see many different patterns. The first set of analyses, which analyzed multiracial individuals as one group, showed that on some measures, multiracial individuals hold attitudes similar to whites', while on other measures multiracial individuals hold attitudes similar to other racial minorities'. However, on the whole, the data suggest that multiracial political attitudes are better explained by racial formation theories.

The evidence offered a clearer picture once I disaggregated multiracial respondents by their racial background. The findings here are consistent with the findings in chapter 4 and so I continue to find that established racial categories must be considered when conducting analyses of the self-identified multiracial population. In this chapter, I found that the pattern of political attitudes among multiracial respondents varied by racial background. This suggests that scholars should not classify all multiracial individuals in one group when conducting analyses on political attitudes. Moreover, because I found different patterns across multiracial respondents once the group was disaggregated by racial background, I concluded that we cannot use only one theory to explain multiracial political attitudes. Rather I found that racial formation theories apply to some groups, while the assimilation theory applies to others.

More specifically, the data suggested that racial formation theories best explain political attitudes for multiracial respondents who reported a black or a Latino background. However, there were differences, when comparing multiracial and monoracial black respondents, from the comparison between multiracial and monoracial Latino respondents. Overall, the results comparing multiracial and monoracial blacks were the most consistent: there were very few significant differences between these two groups, which suggests that a racial identity as black influences the political attitudes of multiracial and monoracial identified respondents in similar ways. In contrast, for those who reported themselves to be Latino, those who saw themselves as mixed race demonstrated a stronger awareness than those who reported themselves to be monoracial. On the census, nearly half of Latinos racially identify as white, while the other largest group of Latinos racially identifies as "some other race." The results in this chapter could be related to the complex ways Latinos express their racial identities.

In contrast, I found some evidence to suggest that assimilation theories might increasingly explain political attitude formation of multiracial-Asian respondents. The pattern of multiracial-Asian political attitudes suggests that these respondents may not see themselves as marginalized. This corresponds with other evidence on multiracial individuals who claim to be of Asian descent. Census data on the white-Asian population show that this is an advantaged group, while scholars such as Nishime (2014) argue that multiracial individuals of partial Asian descent are often portrayed by the media as deracialized subjects. At the same time, the political attitude patterns for monoracial Asian respondents also reflect a group that does not see itself as being as marginalized as other racial minorities: mean scores for Asian respondents are typically lower than for blacks and sometimes for Latinos. I am also cautious about asserting generalizations about the findings presented in this chapter since the number of multiracial-Asian respondents in the WKH 2001 survey was less than 40. I thus do not think these findings should be used to make universal generalizations about Asian Americans, such asoffer an answer to the long-standing debate over whether Asian Americans are more assimilable into the white mainstream than other racial groups. More analyses will be needed before we can offer firm conclusions about multiracial-Asian respondents.

Finally, this chapter considered to what extent multiracial respondents reflect a group identity as multiracial. I focused on perceptions of discrimination that could indicate that multiracial respondents perceive a shared racialized experience. The evidence in this analysis was mixed but did not offer strong support for the theory that multiracial individuals are forming a unique group identity. Since the evidence showed that racial backgrounds of multiracial respondents are still a relevant factor, there may not be only *one* multiracial collective identity but rather multiple multiracial identities by racial combination. For example, some research has shown that multiracial individuals of mixed Asian descent organize as a group separate from other multiracial groups (Bernstein and De la Cruz 2009). Yet, since I only assessed experiences of discrimination, other forms of group identity will need to be examined before we can make any conclusive statements about the formation of a collective multiracial group identity.

The data used in this chapter were collected during the first decade of the twenty-first century when multiracial identities represented relatively new racial identities for Americans. The findings therefore reflect a specific moment in history but serve as a foundation for longitudinal studies on multiracial political attitudes. As multiracial identities have become more widespread, many new surveys[23] will be collected on the multiracial population that will give us more knowledge of how the pattern of multiracial attitudes, particularly as they compare to monoracial attitudes, will change over time.

6 | In the Eye of the Beholder

AMERICAN PERCEPTIONS OF OBAMA'S RACE

> I stand here today, grateful for the diversity of my heritage, aware that my parents' dreams live on in my precious daughters. I stand here knowing that my story is part of the larger American story, that I owe a debt to all of those who came before me, and that, in no other country on earth, is my story even possible.
>
> —*Senator Barack Obama, 2004*

FOR THE PAST THREE CHAPTERS, this book has sought to unveil the characteristics and consequences of multiracial identities. But, of course, no study that seeks to catalog the political implications of multiracial identification can ignore the momentous election of Barack Obama as president of the United States and the American electorate that supported his path to office. President Obama is an important figure for understanding the future direction of multiracial identification given that the family narratives he employed in his 2008 presidential campaign emphasized his interracial background. Obama's unique personal story as a child of an African immigrant and a white mother from Kansas was a common narrative evoked throughout most of the 2008 election cycle. But, just as importantly, Obama is labeled America's first "black" president and racially self-identifies as (only) black (Roberts and Baker 2010). This complex set of identity and family ancestry narratives expressed by Obama and his presidential campaign stirred a great deal of debate about his racial classification and serves as an illuminating case for exploring how the American public responded to these narratives.

President Obama represents a different outcome of identity choice from the racial identities embraced by the self-identified multiracial activists who were interviewed in chapter 3. The activists promoted the belief that individuals should have choices in their racial identity and advocated for the use of multiracial identities. However, as was documented in chapter 4, many Americans who are children of interracial couples self-identify with only one established racial category. Indeed, Obama could have self-identified as "biracial" or another multiracial label because he was the child of an interracial marriage. Yet Obama was clear that he racially identifies as black and, in public interviews, highlighted his racialized experiences living as a black man in the United States. The contrast between these two identity choices captures how individuals often respond differently to the constraints they perceive from norms of racial classification and the openness they believe exists as a result of those norms emphasizing self-identification. In reality, the American public witnesses many different racial identity choices, some of which the public finds to make perfect sense and some of which it finds confusing.

How the American public responds to identity choices is the focus of this chapter. Thus, this chapter pivots our attention away from the identities and political attitudes of self-identified multiracial individuals and considers how Americans assign race to others. Specifically, this chapter focuses on attitudes of monoracially identified Americans following the historic 2008 election and examines how they chose to racially classify President Obama. Survey data in this chapter will show that Americans do differ in how they perceive Obama's race: some view Obama as racially "black" while others view him as "mixed race." In the first half of the chapter, I will review the discourse surrounding, what was perceived by many, not to be a straightforward fact: Obama's racial identity. In fact, how Americans should understand Obama's race was a topic of contention throughout his bid for the presidency. The second half of the chapter builds from the existing literature in political science and examines the relationship between how a respondent racially classifies President Obama and the respondent's evaluation of his job performance.

I recognize that views about Obama represent a special case given that a citizen's attitudes about the president are not solely influenced by personal beliefs but are also by other factors such as partisan cues and information provided by the media. At the same time, the 2008 election represents a real political event in which a type of identity choice frame was used to mobilize voters. Perceptions of Obama's race are also the most politically consequential given that, as president, Obama ranked as the most powerful political leader in the country. Thus, while this is a special case, it is at the same time a real example of a national campaign where American voters were confronted with identity choices and a case in which these perceptions could have had real political consequences.

2008 Presidential Election and the Racial Classification of Barack Obama

Although the news media hailed the election of Barack Obama as evidence that America had entered a new "postracial" era, the persistent attention to Obama's race throughout the 2008 election demonstrated just how central race was to the outcome of the election. One of the striking debates that gained traction in media portrayals of Obama's candidacy is challenges to the authenticity of Obama's "blackness," as well as those questioning his true racial group loyalties (see also Frasure 2010; Jolivette 2012; Spencer 2010). Interestingly, for a society that had emphasized discrete racial categories over the course of the twentieth century, it was apparent in 2008 that Americans were fully capable of deliberating on the complications of race and racial classification in the context of Obama's candidacy for president. To begin this chapter, I first offer some discussion about the many competing statements that were expressed about Obama's racial identity during the election in order to contextualize Americans' different perceptions about Obama's race.

As in other modern campaigns for president, Obama's personal background was provided as information for the electorate to use when deciding how to vote. Given that Americans had not yet previously elected a nonwhite president, it was predictable that Obama's race and the political leanings that were assumed to be influenced by race were discussed by pundits, the media, and academics (Frasure 2010; Jolivette 2012; Spencer 2010). Obama's own campaign strategically promoted what I would label a *frame of multiraciality*: a narrative that emphasized the diversity of Obama's racial identity and background. To be sure, repeated references about his white mother and grandparents were offered throughout the campaign, and Obama's 2004 best-selling memoir was often used as a reference when pundits dissecting Obama's identity and political background. At the same time, a frame of multiraciality contrasted with the fact that Obama himself did not self-identify as biracial but as (only) black. Obama consistently offered the same narrative about his identity as African American. In a 2007 CBS interview, Obama stated: "I think if you look African American in this society, you're treated as an African American."[1] In this quote, Obama indirectly cites the one-drop rule as the basis for his identification as African American and over his tenure as president, he did not change his racial identification. After being elected president, Obama checked his race as "black" when filling out his family's census form (Roberts and Baker 2010).

This is the unique case of identity choice presented by President Obama: he self-identifies as African American but promotes his interracial background. Self-identification as a racial minority, in Obama's case as "African American," is not normally understood as an example of identity choice given the historic precedent of hypodescent. To be sure, Obama's racial identification as African American follows established norms of racial classification. Obama's own explanation for why he self-identifies as black conveys an understanding that one's race is not a choice but imposed on individuals. However, the decision to assert both a black racial identity and a mixed racial family background is an intentional strategy to frame racial classification as a more fluid and complex process and thus presents an important case of identity choice.

In this way, the 2008 election serves as a unique context in which to understand how competing messages about racial identity and family background are understood by voters. Most importantly, the voting public was asked to consider a much more complicated case of racial identity in 2008 than in a past national election.[2] Comments about Obama's racial identity offered by political leaders and pundits in the mainstream media provided a revealing glimpse into how Americans discussed Obama's race. Some individuals chose to recognize Obama as African American, while others designated him as not "fully" African American, citing his biracial background. For example:

At the 2004 Democratic National Convention, the then-Senator Obama spoke of one American family. He said: "There is not a black America and a white America and Latino America and Asian America." And yet in filling out the census form as he did, the president unequivocally declared himself part of black America In effect he disowned his white mother, and by extension, his maternal grandparents who acted as surrogate parents for much of his boyhood. Mr. Obama had hardly ever laid eyes on his father, but that absent parent shaped his own sense of identity.

—*Abigail Thernstrom*[3]

After all, Obama's mother is of white U.S. stock. His father is black Kenyan. Other than color, Obama did not—does not—share a heritage with the majority of black Americans, who are descendants of plantation slaves.... So when black Americans refer to Obama as "one of us," I do not know what they are talking about. In his new book, "The Audacity of Hope," Obama makes it clear that, while he has experienced some light versions of typical stereotypes, he cannot claim those problems as his own—nor has he lived the life of a black American.

—Stanley Crouch[4]

Mr. Obama, at the same time, has given us a more inclusive, broader reach into the needs and aspirations of our people. He's crossing lines—ethnic lines, racial lines, generational lines.

—Colin Powell[5]

Just because you are our color doesn't make you our kind.

—Rev. Al Sharpton[6]

America today is a world away from cruel and prideful bigotry of that time. There is no better evidence of this than the election of an African American to the presidency of the United States.

—John McCain[7]

As the range of opinions in these quotations suggest, even though Obama self-identifies as (only) African American, the frames of Obama's multiraciality that his campaign offered to the public were distinctively integrated into how Americans chose to describe Obama's race. Obama's racial identity was not seen by all as a straightforward characteristic; rather it was a feature that merited discussion and deliberation. What was also apparent was how normative American deliberations about racial categorization can be. In the above opinions, beliefs about how Obama *should be* racially identified drive each individual's evaluation. From this, we can see that race is not simply an objective demographic category but rather is understood to be a politically consequential statement about the self that implies particular values and attitudes toward American race relations.

These reactions to Obama's racial identity allow us to derive two general observations about how Americans responded to the Obama campaign's frame of multiraciality. First, Americans did not all interpret Obama's racial identity in the same way. This is because Americans do not necessarily agree on the meaning and impact of how multiraciality influences American race relations: multiracial identities can be assumed as either normatively positive or negative. Those who view multiraciality as a positive development contend that multiraciality moves us in the direction where racial boundaries hold less resonance and there is a diminishing tension between the races. Alternatively, those who are relatively more skeptical argue that multiraciality distracts from the fact that traditional racial categories continue to have an indelible hold on American society. While I do not want to promote the idea that discussions about Obama's racial identity can be distilled into two simple dimensions, the point here is that individuals very much diverged in how they viewed Obama's race, and the frames of multiraciality that were often used to describe his background were interpreted in different ways.

The second observation is that views on multiraciality are often intertwined with a person's normative views about race and personal background. Because racial groups view race and the normative implications of race very differently, the race of the perceiver likely informs how a person deciphers frames of multiraciality. As I argued in the previous chapter, since race in the United States structures experiences, how individuals are racially classified influences the formation of their racial identity and attitudes, such as prejudice, views on intergroup conflict, and support for racialized public policies. If we group the quotations presented above by the source's racial background, we find that black and white speakers discuss Obama's race in different ways. For example, the black public figures consider Obama's frame of multiraciality a source of inauthenticity as truly "black." Alternatively, Abigail Thernstrom regards being the child of an interracial couple as a valuable distinction that should allow Obama to recognize both his white mother and African father. These racial differences are consistent with Dawson's (2001) argument that one's race shapes one's political worldview. Dawson writes, "Since racial groups do not hold a shared understanding of commonly experienced political events, blacks and other [racial groups] could reach very different conclusions and trigger different political responses" (2001, 3).

American Perceptions of Obama's Race

Given public deliberations over Obama's background as well as the competing messages of racial identification offered by both President Obama himself and his 2008 campaign, we cannot assume that all Americans racially classify Obama in the same manner. Moreover, given that President Obama served two terms in office, we also have the ability to assess if he was increasingly racialized—in other words, the president became more connected with black stereotypes or was perceived to be only a representative of black people—in Americans' eyes over the course of his presidency.

As experts on presidential politics have documented, American views of the president always change over the course of a president's term (Brace and Hinckley 1991; Gronke and Newman 2003). Obama was elected to office running on the two campaign themes of "hope" and "change" with media narratives of a postracial politics prominent after the election. Given this, we might hypothesize that American views about Obama's race might be framed in a more positive light at the beginning of the Obama presidency than later in his term. At the same time, past research suggests other expectations. Research in social psychology suggests that as an individual becomes more familiar with another person, that individual is less likely to apply racial stereotypes or take other racial cues (Ball and Cantor 1974; Hamm, Baum, and Nikels 1975; Zebrowitz, Brondstad, and Lee 2007). If we build a hypothesis from this research, then we can argue that fewer Americans would perceive Obama as prototypically black over time. In contrast, opposition to public policies sponsored by the Obama administration, such as the Affordable Care Act, could lead citizens to emphasize Obama's blackness. For example, Tesler (2012) finds that positions on the Affordable Care Act were increasingly explained by white racial resentment.

To investigate how Americans perceive Obama's race and how their perceptions of his race might have changed over the course of his presidency, I compare data from two surveys. To capture American attitudes immediately following Obama's inauguration, I return to the 2009 *Racial Attitudes in America II* survey sponsored by the Pew Research Center. I also employ survey data collected at the end of Obama's first term in 2012 using the *2010–2012 Evaluations of Government and Society Study* (EGSS), a survey collected the American National Election Study.[8] Both of these surveys include questions on respondent's perceptions of Obama's race. They also include large samples of black and Latino respondents that allow researchers to study the political attitudes of all Americans. These two surveys were collected separately, and so we cannot draw firm causal conclusions because we are not tracing the same group of individuals over time. However, given that both are nationally representative and ask similar questions about Obama's race, they give us some insight into the nature of American attitudes at the beginning and at the end of Obama's first term.

Figure 6.1 presents American perceptions of Obama's race at the beginning of Obama's term in 2009. The Pew question asked, "Do you mostly think of Obama as: a black person or a person of mixed race?"[9] The figure

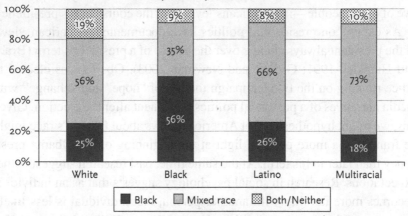

Do you mostly think of Obama as:

FIGURE 6.1 Perceptions of Obama's Race in 2009

SOURCE: Pew Research Center 2009. Results are weighted to reflect the national population.

reflects three possible answers because 14% of the total sample respondents did not take a firm position and said either that Obama was both black and mixed race or that Obama was neither. There was also a small share of respondents (4%) who chose not to answer this question and so were excluded from these analyses. Interestingly, the Pew data show that white respondents were the least likely racially classify Obama into one racial category , with nearly a quarter of whites either refusing to answer or saying Obama is both black and mixed race. Conversely, black respondents were the most likely to racially classify Obama. The sizable proportion of respondents who were unwilling to take a firm position on Obama's racial identity is surprising given the media focus on Obama's racial identity throughout the 2008 campaign.

Among respondents who took a clear position on Obama's racial identity there were differences in how racial groups racially classified Obama. Of those who reported being monoracial, Latinos had the largest share of respondents (66%) who classified Obama as mixed race. At the same time, the Pew survey identified a small sample of self-identified multiracial respondents ($n = 58$). Of them, 73% perceived Obama as mixed race. Whites were the next most likely (56%) to classify Obama as mixed race. Alternatively, over half (56%) of black respondents identified Obama as black. Thus, black respondents were not only most likely to take a firm position on Obama's race but also more likely to classify Obama in an established monoracial category than other groups. Chi-square tests confirm that these differences across racial groups are statistically significant ($p < .01$).

In 2012 the EGSS used a slightly different question to document American perceptions of Obama's race: "How would you describe Obama's race? Mark all that apply: 1) white; 2) black; 3) Hispanic; 4) Mixed Race; 5) Asian or 6) other race." In this question, respondents were offered greater freedom to describe Obama's race. Given that respondents were given racial choices, the responses were more complex than in the Pew survey. Table 6.1 disaggregates respondents by race but excludes

TABLE 6.1 Perceptions of Obama's Race in 2012

OBAMA'S RACE IS	WHITES		BLACKS		LATINOS	
	N	%	N	%	N	%
Black	252	24.28%	40	42.55%	34	29.82%
Mixed race	649	62.52%	39	41.49%	56	49.12%
Other race	14	1.35%			1	0.88%
White	1	0.10%				
Asian, black	1	0.10%				
Asian, mixed race	1	0.10%				
Black, white	5	0.48%			1	0.88%
Black, mixed race	50	4.82%	5	5.32%	8	7.02%
Mixed race, other race	1	0.10%				
Black, mixed race, white	11	1.06%	3	3.19%	1	0.88%
Black, mixed race, other race						
Black, Latino, mixed race, other race	1	0.10%				
Asian, black, Latino, Mixed race, other race, white	1	0.10%				
Did not respond	51	4.91%	7	7.45%	13	11.40%
Total N	1038	100%	94	100%	114	100%

SOURCE: *2010–2012 Evaluations of Government and Society Study*, unweighted results.

self-identified multiracial respondents since the sample was too small (n = 29) to offer reliable results.

One of the more striking characteristics of the results presented in table 6.1 is the wide variety of racial combinations reported by respondents, particularly by white respondents. Moreover, respondents tended to emphasize Obama as black or mixed race, rather than as white. Only one respondent reported Obama's race to be white, which reveals the continued influence of the one-drop rule on how Americans understand race. But even with the more complex racial options, there are many similarities with the results reported in 2009. The overwhelming majority of all respondents said that Obama was mixed race or two or more races, while only a small minority said he was black. Like the Pew survey, the EGSS reports that a larger proportion of black respondents perceived Obama to be black than white or Latino respondents. However, when weighted to reflect the national population, the 2012 survey estimated that approximately 45% of blacks perceived Obama to be black, while the 2009 survey (presented in figure 6.1) estimated that approximately 56% of blacks perceived Obama to be black. In contrast, the estimates for whites and Latinos were more similar between the two studies (in 2012, weighted results report that 26% of whites and 30% of Latinos perceived Obama's race as black). Therefore, if there was a change in American perceptions of Obama's race over time, it occurred primarily among black Americans.

Unfortunately, neither the Pew survey nor the EGSS recruited enough Asian American respondents to conduct a reliable analysis of public opinion.

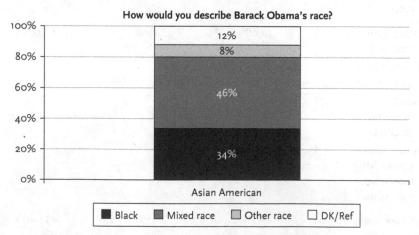

FIGURE 6.2 Asian American Perceptions of Obama's Race in 2012

SOURCE: Asian American Election Eve Poll, 2012. Results are weighted to reflect the national population.

To offer a glimpse, however, I present survey data from the Asian American Election Eve Poll–2012 Election (AAEE), a nationally representative survey of Asian American registered voters in 2012.[10] In the AAEE poll, the question asked: "How would you describe Barack Obama's race? Do you consider him to be African American, White, of mixed race or something else?" As what is shown in figure 6.2, the largest share of Asian American respondents (46%) described Obama as mixed race. However, the share of Asian American respondents who described Obama as black was closer in size to the share of respondents who described Obama as mixed race. Moreover, a sizable share of Asian American respondents (12%) chose not to take a clear position. Interestingly, among the 8% of Asian American respondents who classified Obama as a race other than black or mixed race, 3% said Obama was white. This survey shows that more Asian American respondents said Obama was white than respondents in the EGSS. These results offer some insight into how Asian Americans perceived Obama's race, but, unfortunately, an analysis of Asian American perceptions is limited to this figure.

What is striking about the responses in these surveys is that the American public does not share the perceptions about Obama's race and that there are clear differences across racial groups. Moreover, the survey responses also suggest that, while Obama self-identifies as African American, much of the public labels him as mixed race. This pattern appears to have remained unchanged in 2012, suggesting that—with the possible exception of African Americans—the American public did not shift in its perception of Obama's race over the course of this first term.

Factors Explaining Perceptions of Obama's Race

Public opinion data show that a respondent's racial background influences how that person racially classifies Obama, but I also wondered if other individual-level characteristics influence respondents' perceptions of Obama's race. We can hypothesize that there exist specific individual-level factors—such as a person's cognitive sophistication, information about President Obama, and interpersonal networks—that determine how an individual applies racial categories. Moreover, there also exists partisan or ideological variation within each racial group, particularly within the white population. I originally anticipated that partisanship or ideology guided whites' perceptions of Obama's race. Studies on white public opinion have showed that levels of racial resentment vary across white liberals and conservatives (Kinder and Sanders 1996. Moreover, Tesler and Sears (2013) demonstrated that racial resentment was a particularly strong factor influencing white conservatives' opposition to Obama. Therefore, based on what we know about white racial attitudes, I hypothesized that Republicans were more likely to racialize Obama—that is, classify him as black—than Democrats.

To identify what factors determine whether a respondent classifies President Obama as black or mixed race, I turn to multivariate regression analysis. For this exploratory analysis, I tested five dimensions of independent variables that could be expected to influence how individuals process racial categories. When running multivariate models, I was careful to choose similar variables to make the models for the 2009 and 2012 datasets as close as possible. The first dimension included the basic demographic variables: age, education level, yearly family income, gender, and nativity. The second dimension of independent variables accounted for political factors: party identification and being a registered voter. The third dimension of independent variables accounted for the respondent's media exposure and awareness about public affairs. The fourth dimension of independent variables reflects the racial attitudes of the respondent. For the 2009 dataset, I included perceptions of discrimination against racial minorities and perceptions about the state of racial equality in America. For the 2012 dataset, I included perceptions of discrimination against racial minorities, the racial resentment index, and racial group-linked fate. Finally, I accounted for the respondent's surrounding social context, specifically living in environments supportive of multiracial identities. For both datasets, I included living in the West. The models using the 2009 dataset also included living in a racially homogenous neighborhood and if the respondent had a multiracial child.

For the 2009 Pew data, I employed multinominal logit models with perceptions of Obama's race as the dependent variable.[11] I ran separate models for whites, blacks, and Latinos to allow for the possibility that different factors explain perceptions of Obama's race within each racial group. Unfortunately, because the small sample size prevented multivariate analyses, self-identified multiracial respondents will be excluded for the remainder of this analysis.

Even though I used an analytical strategy that allowed for the most variation across respondents, I found very few significant predictors ($p < .05$) that explain perceptions of Obama's race across all groups (results not shown; see appendix D, table D2). Most importantly, while

I had anticipated that party identification would explain perceptions of Obama's race, there was no significant effect of party identification for all three racial groups.[12] Of the few significant predictors identified in the 2009 data, there were some illuminating results: I found that among whites, those with higher levels of education were more likely to perceive Obama as black rather than as mixed race. Among black respondents, those who perceived a lot of discrimination against minority groups were more likely to perceive Obama as black rather than as mixed race. Among Latinos, registered voters were more likely to see Obama as black rather than as mixed race.

A similar pattern of null findings was demonstrated by the multivariate models using the 2012 survey (results not shown; see appendix E, table E2). For the 2012 data, I constructed a model used to explain perceptions of Obama as black rather than as mixed race or of two or more races. The analysis of the 2012 dataset revealed only one significant result for one racial group: Latinos with higher levels of racial group-linked fate were less likely to perceive Obama as black. Interestingly, neither racial group-linked fate nor racial resentment was a significant predictor for white or black respondents. Moreover, like the results found in the 2009 dataset, there were no significant differences between Democrats or Republicans for any of the three racial groups.

Although I had originally surmised that there could be specific factors that explained why an individual perceived Obama as black rather than as mixed race or of two or more races, the results in both 2009 and 2012 show that few factors systematically predict perceptions of Obama's race. Moreover, factors that explained perceptions of Obama's race in the 2009 data were not replicated in the 2012 data. For example, highly educated white respondents were more likely to perceive Obama as black rather than as mixed race in 2009, but there was no effect of education for white respondents in 2012. This suggests that there are many processes that explain how and why individuals apply racial categories to others and these processes cannot be explained by typical factors such as socioeconomic status, political factors, or even perceptions of discrimination. Perhaps those factors that are more difficult to measure—such as personality, implicit racial attitudes, and family socialization—that were not included in the models I tested best explain how people apply racial categories to others. But based on this analysis, I was unable to determine if there were, other than a person's race, systematic patterns explaining how individuals apply racial categories to the Obama.

Political Implications of Racial Classification

While it is difficult to explain why some classify Obama as black while others classify him as mixed race, important social and political consequences may follow from how an individual perceives race. Indeed, individuals sort others into racial categories because, historically, race has served as an important social proxy for how an individual should engage in interpersonal and intergroup interactions. The most obvious examples of this are instances when a person discriminates against those of a different race. While racial discrimination today is no longer socially acceptable, current research in the social sciences shows the many, oftentimes unintentional ways race mediates interpersonal and intergroup interactions. Indeed, studies in psychology show that we find more subtle shifts in behavior when a person is interacting with another who is perceived to be a member of a racial out-group. For example, a study by Norton et al. (2006) showed that, when asked to play a game that matched faces, white participants were less likely to use racial descriptions of the faces when paired with a black partner than when paired with a white partner (see also Goff, Steele, and Davies 2008; Plant and Devine 2003). Thus, beyond simply how individuals "see" others, research emphasizes that there are behavioral and attitudinal implications to racial classification.

In electoral politics, one of the long-standing concerns is whether or not a voter would be willing to support a political candidate who is of a different race. In particular, historical accounts have documented elections when white voters failed to support black candidates running for office (Reeves 1997). Although recent studies show that white voters are supportive and willing to vote for black candidates (Hajnal 2001; Highton 2004), research continues to highlight how voters of all races use the candidate's race to make judgments about that candidate.

Studies have shown that voters rely on a political leader or candidate's race to make assumptions about that candidate and that candidate's group-based loyalties (Feldman and Conover 1984 Huddy and Terkildsen 1993; McGraw 2003). Ethnicity, in particular, has long been identified as a strong mobilizing cue that activates group-based loyalties and so is used as a proxy for voters to identify shared interests with a political candidate. For example, studies on immigrant politics at the turn of the twentieth century found that immigrants are more likely to vote for coethnics (Dahl 1961; Wolfinger 1965; Parenti 1967). More recent literature on racial minority voting suggests that blacks and Latinos are also more likely to turn out to vote when a member of their own racial group is on the ballot (Barreto 2010; Tate 1994). Thus, race can foster voter affinity with a candidate by priming a shared group identity and a perceived belief that the candidate will support her own ethnic/racial group once elected into office.

Other research shows that voters rely on political stereotypes, such as assuming a link between a person's racial background and certain political characteristics like partisanship. For example, one consistent stereotype is that blacks are Democratic. To be sure, over the second half of the twentieth century, black voters have overwhelmingly supported the Democratic Party (Tate 1994). However, research shows that this stereotype leads whites to perceive greater political extremity among black candidates and leaders. For example, Lerman and Sadin (2016) show that white respondents stereotype hypothetical black candidates as more liberal than hypothetical white candidates. In contrast, they found that the assumed political stereotypes about black candidates encouraged black respondents to think that they shared a political ideology with the hypothetical black candidate. Other research, such as the study by Schneider and Bos (2011), shows that white respondents stereotype black leaders as more liberal than blacks who are not in politics.

Past studies assume that the race of the candidate or elected official is obvious to the voter. However, what happens when the race of the candidate is not so evident to the voter? Given the above findings that showed Americans vary in how they view Obama's race, I wondered whether respondents who perceive Obama as black evaluate the president differently than those respondents who perceive Obama as mixed race. Building from the evidence generated by past research, we can identify certain expectations of how individuals would evaluate Obama if they racially classified him as black. As reviewed above, early research suggests that white respondents find black leaders (or candidates) less desirable, particularly when compared to white leaders. White respondents are also more likely to apply political stereotypes to black candidates and believe that black candidates are more loyal to black constituents. This would all suggest that respondents who perceive Obama as black would follow patterns established by past research. However, past research also shows that evaluations of leaders depend on the race of the perceiver. If the perceiver is black and perceives Obama as black, we would expect her see him as an in-group member and a leader who would represent her group.

Research offers less insight on how voters will perceive the meaning of asserting an interracial background. Most of the research assumes that political leaders are either white or black, and so we do not have as much evidence to draw conclusions about how candidates of other races are perceived or stereotyped. However, one theory that can be tested is a form of the *deracialization* hypothesis. McCormick and Jones define a deracialized campaign as one "conducted in a stylistic fashion that defuses the polarizing effects of race by avoiding explicit reference to race-specific issues, while at the same time emphasizing those issues which are racially transcendent" (1993, 76; see also Stout 2010). Given the concern that race mediates how voters evaluate a candidate, a deracializing strategy may be implemented as an attempt to de-emphasize the candidate's racial background in the minds of the voters and, in effect, downplay the assumption that the candidate would favor a particular racial group.[13] It is argued that by campaigning with a more universal agenda, the candidate is more appealing to voters who do not share the candidate's racial background (Perry 1991).

Although most of the scholarship on deracialized strategies has focused on how a candidate frames his or her substantive policy agenda, I argue that frames describing the candidate's background characteristics can be strategically employed to promote a deracialized image. It could be the case that candidate strategies that promote an alternative racial identity such as "multiracial" prime voters to believe that the candidate does not have specific racial loyalties. In this way, it is possible that a candidate who frames him- or herself as multiracial is attempting to create social distance from established racial categories and the stereotypes attached to them.

I could argue that in 2008, Obama's mixed-race family background offered him the opportunity to frame himself as distinct from the stereotypical black candidate. If the deracialization hypothesis applies, then we would expect that white respondents who view Obama as mixed race will give more positive evaluations of him than those who view him as black. At the same time, the concept of deracialization is typically applied to a black candidate who is attempting to generate stronger support among a white voting public. It may thus not be the case that a deracialization strategy has the same effect on black and other racial minority voters as it does on whites. Since a deracialization strategy is often understood as one that attempts to de-emphasize the candidate's loyalties to his or her own racial group, a strategy that deracializes a black candidate may not generate high levels of support among black voters. To be sure, the reason why descriptive representation is perceived as valuable to minority voters is the assumption that their shared racial background with a candidate implies shared values and interests. If a candidate's deracialized image attempts to negate a shared racial status, then we may not expect minority voters to support that deracialized candidate. Therefore, I expect that black respondents who view Obama as black will offer more positive evaluations of the president than black respondents who view him as mixed race. Application of the deracialization hypothesis on Latino evaluations of Obama are less certain since it is unclear if Latinos feel political unity with blacks (Hero and Preuhs 2013; Telles, Sawyer, and Rivera-Salgado 2011).

Examining Evaluations of the President

To determine if perceptions of Obama's race have political consequences, I examine if respondents who view Obama as black evaluate the him and his policies differently than respondents who view Obama as mixed race (or of two or more races). In the 2009 dataset, I assess four different dependent variables that account for different evaluations of the president. For the first dependent variable, I use the typical favorability question asked by surveys to get a sense of voters' evaluation of the president: "Please tell me if you have a favorable or unfavorable opinion of each person. First, Barack Obama, would you say your overall opinion of Barack Obama is very favorable, mostly favorable, mostly unfavorable or very unfavorable?" The second dependent variable is a more direct test of the deracialization hypothesis and asks voters to assess the extent to which Obama favors too much attention to blacks. The last two dependent variables are used to measure how respondents see the relationship between Obama's election and American race relations: the extent to which the respondent believed the Obama's election as president improved race relations in America and the extent to which the respondent believes race explains opposition to President Obama's policies.

The first major pattern to note is that regardless of how respondents racially classify Obama, there are distinct racial differences in how respondents evaluate him. For example, on the favorability question, black respondents overwhelmingly give high favorability scores. In contrast, whites' favorability mean fell at nearly the center of the possible scale, denoting only a slightly favorable assessment. Latino respondents' favorability scores fell between those of whites and blacks. This same racial pattern is consistent across the other three dependent variables: whites and blacks hold opposing positions and Latino mean scores fall between those for whites and for blacks. Given this pattern, in the remainder of the analysis, I always disaggregate respondents by racial background.

Table 6.2 compares mean scores of those who view Obama as black against those who view Obama as mixed race for each of the four dependent variables. Difference-of-means tests show that that, for white and Latino respondents, those who view Obama as black do not systematically differ in their evaluations from those who view Obama as mixed race. In fact, perceptions of Obama's race influenced only the evaluations of black respondents on the favorability question: those blacks who perceived Obama as mixed race were less favorable about Obama than blacks who perceived him as black ($p < .10$). Therefore, consistent with the literature, black respondents who view Obama as a member of their racial group offer positive evaluations of him. However, blacks' perceptions of Obama's race did not have an effect on all forms of evaluation. There was no significant effect of blacks' perceptions of Obama's race on the other three dependent variables.

The mean scores depicted in table 6.2 do not take into account the important partisan variation that exists across respondents. One of the reasons often proposed for white respondents' lower evaluations of Obama is that whites are less likely to share his political views. Therefore, there may be an important interaction between respondents' party identification and how they perceive Obama's race. To investigate this, I disaggregated

TABLE 6.2 Mean Scores on Evaluations of President in 2009

	MEAN FAVORABILITY	TOO MUCH ATTENTION TO BLACKS	BETTER RACE RELATIONS	PEOPLE OPPOSE POLICIES BECAUSE OF OBAMA'S RACE
Whites: Obama as black	.51 (.03)	.54 (.02)	.58 (.02)	.40 (.02)
Whites: Obama as mixed race	.55 (.02)	.53 (.01)	.60 (.02)	.37 (.02)
Blacks: Obama as black	**.93 (.01)**	.43 (.01)	.76 (.02)	.71 (.02)
Blacks: Obama as mixed race	**.89 (.02)**	.43 (.02)	.71 (.03)	.65 (.03)
Latino: Obama as black	.79 (.05)	.59 (.04)	.68 (.05)	.58 (.05)
Latino: Obama as mixed race	.76 (.03)	.51 (.03)	.69 (.03)	.51 (.04)

NOTE: All variables are on a 0 to 1 scale. Standard errors in parentheses. Bolded cells designate statistically significant differences ($p < .10$). Results are weighted to reflect the national population.
SOURCE: Pew Research Center 2009.

whites and Latinos by partisan identification and conducted a series of difference-of-means tests across the four dependent variables. Given the lack of partisan variation within the black sample (the overwhelming majority of black respondents identified as Democrats), I did not analyze the interaction between partisanship and perceptions of Obama's race for black respondents.

Once accounting for partisanship, I found that perceptions of Obama's race explain some of the variation in how respondents evaluate him. However, although past research has shown race to strongly influence white public opinion, again I found few significant differences across white partisan groups. The main finding for whites were found among Democrats: white Democrats who perceived Obama as black where more likely to believe race was a reason people opposed the president's policies than white Democrats who viewed Obama as mixed race (see table 6.3; full results in appendix D, table D3). This partially supports the theory that perceiving Obama as mixed race can have a deracializing effect for whites. There were no significant differences across white Republicans or white independents.

In contrast, I found a stronger effect of the interaction between partisanship and perceptions of Obama's race among Latino respondents. Latino Democrats who viewed Obama as black were more likely to believe that Obama's election as president improved American race relations than Latino Democrats who viewed Obama as mixed race (see table 6.3; full results in appendix D, table D3). Additionally, Latino Republicans who viewed Obama as black were more likely to think that race was a reason people opposed Obama's policies than Latino Republicans who viewed Obama as mixed race. Controlling to socioeconomic status, age, gender, and nativity, I found that Latino Republicans who viewed Obama as mixed race were more likely to believe that Obama's election improved race relations than Latino Republicans who viewed Obama as black. The effect of perceiving Obama as mixed race was the opposite on the improving race relations variable for Latino independents. Therefore, for Latino Republicans, perceiving Obama as mixed race was deracializing, but Latino Democrats and independents who saw Obama as black were more optimistic about race relations. While the results are not consistent across all dependent variables, these patterns suggest that for Latinos there existed an interactive effect between partisanship and perceptions of Obama's race in 2009.

Turning to an analysis of 2012 data, I used four dependent variables different from those used for analysis of the 2009 data. Since the 2012 survey was collected at the end of the term, I was able to assess a wider variety of evaluations of the president. To measure assessments of Obama's job

TABLE 6.3 Mean Scores on Evaluations of the President, Taking into Account Party Identification in 2009

PRESIDENT OBAMA'S ELECTION LED TO BETTER RACE RELATIONS

	WHITES	LATINOS
Dem: Obama as black	.77 (.04)	**.86 (.05)**
Dem: Obama as mixed race	.75 (.03)	**.70 (.04)**
Indep: Obama as black	.58 (.05)	.77 (.07)
Indep: Obama as mixed race	.60 (.03)	.72 (.07)
Rep: Obama as black	.45 (.04)	.44 (.13)
Rep: Obama as mixed race	.43 (.03)	.46 (.11)

RACE IS A MAJOR REASON PEOPLE OPPOSE OBAMA'S POLICIES

	WHITES	LATINOS
Dem: Obama as black	**.55 (.04)**	.55 (.11)
Dem: Obama as mixed race	**.45 (.04)**	.54 (.06)
Indep: Obama as black	.37 (.05)	.59 (.09)
Indep: Obama as mixed race	.37 (.03)	.55 (.06)
Rep: Obama as black	.30 (.04)	**.51 (.05)**
Rep: Obama as mixed race	.28 (.03)	**.27 (.08)**

NOTE: All variables are on a 0 to 1 scale. Standard errors in parentheses. Bolded cells designate statistically significant differences ($p < .10$). Results are weighted to reflect the national population. SOURCE: Pew Research Center 2009.

performance, I used two different items: a feeling thermometer measure, which asks respondents to rate how warm they feel toward the president and a direct question that asks the respondents to rate their approval of Obama's job performance. Throughout Obama's first term there were also a number of erroneous rumors about Obama's background—such as the claim that Obama is not a natural-born citizen or that he is Muslim rather than Christian—which many different sectors of the population believed to be true. This was a process of framing the president as an undesirable "other" and has been found to be influenced by racial resentment (Tesler and Sears 2013).[14] As a test of the racialization hypothesis (particularly for white respondents), I include a measure that accounted for the respondent's belief that Obama is Muslim, since those who see Obama as black might be more likely to associate other perceived undesirable qualities with him. The final measure analyzed from the 2012 dataset was a question that asked if respondents believed Obama placed too much emphasis on race and gender when making official appointments. This fourth measure also offered a test of the deracializing hypothesis, since it takes into account the belief that Obama is more loyal to minority populations than to all Americans.

In the 2012 dataset, respondents assigned many different types of racial identities to the president. Since the group that is most atypical is those who perceived Obama as only black, the main comparison made in this analysis is between them and the rest of the respondents, who perceived Obama to be mixed race or other, which includes two or more races, white, or something else (for the purposes of brevity, this group will be labeled hereafter as those who perceive "Obama as mixed race").

Difference-of-means tests conducted across the four dependent variables show that, as with the 2009 data, there were minimal differences in evaluation scores between those who perceived Obama as black and those who perceived Obama as mixed race (see table 6.4). Also consistent with the 2009 results, in 2012 blacks who viewed Obama as black reported a higher thermometer score than blacks who viewed Obama as mixed race. Therefore, for black respondents, perceiving a shared race encourages more positive evaluations of leaders. In addition, this analysis found that whites who perceived Obama as black were more likely to adopt the erroneous belief that Obama is Muslim than whites who viewed Obama

TABLE 6.4 Mean Scores on Evaluations of President by Race of Respondent and Perceptions of Obama's Race in 2012

	FEELING THERM.	JOB APPROVAL	OBAMA IS MUSLIM	TOO MUCH FOCUS ON RACE AND GENDER
Whites: Obama as black	.39 (.03)	.33 (.02)	**.37 (.04)**	.60 (.02)
Whites: Obama as mixed race / other	.43 (.02)	.37 (.02)	**.25 (.02)**	.57 (.01)
Blacks: Obama as black	**.95 (.02)**	.86 (.04)	.09 (.06)	.48 (.03)
Blacks: Obama as mixed race / other	**.88 (.03)**	.81 (.05)	.04 (.03)	.43 (.02)
Latino: Obama as black	.60 (.08)	.59 (.05)	.36 (.11)	.51 (.04)
Latino: Obama as mixed race / other	.56 (.05)	.52 (.06)	.22 (.07)	.48 (.04)

NOTE: All variables are on a 0 to 1 scale. Standard errors in parentheses. Bolded cells designate statistically significant differences ($p < .10$). Results are weighted to reflect the national population. SOURCE: *2010–2012 Evaluations of Government and Society Study*.

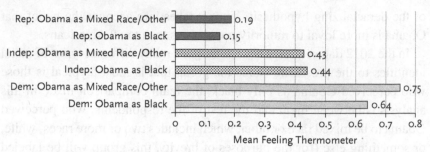

FIGURE 6.3 White Respondents' Mean Thermometer Ratings of Obama in 2012

SOURCE: 2010–2012 Evaluations of Government and Society Study. Variable is on a 0 to 1 scale. Results are weighted to reflect the national population. Significant differences only found for white Democrats at $p < .05$.

as mixed race. This supports the claim that for whites, perceiving Obama as black is racializing and encourages whites to attach more racial stereotypes and undesirable features to him. These results show that whites who saw Obama as more prototypically black were more likely to adopt false rumors about the president.

Given the findings from the 2009 dataset, which identified some interactive effects between partisanship and perceptions of Obama's race on evaluations of the president, I conducted a similar analysis taking into account partisan identification for the 2012 dataset (full results not shown; see appendix E, table E3). What I found was a robust interactive effect among white respondents. White Democrats who viewed Obama as mixed race gave him higher thermometer ratings than white Democrats who viewed Obama as black (see figure 6.3). White Democrats who viewed Obama as black were also more likely to give Obama higher job approval ratings than white Democrats who viewed Obama as mixed race. However, there were no significant differences on the feeling thermometer or job approval measures for white Republicans or for white independents. In contrast, white Republicans who viewed Obama as black were more likely to believe Obama is Muslim than white Republicans who viewed Obama as mixed race (see figure 6.4). White Republicans who viewed Obama as black were also more likely to believe that there has been too much focus on race and gender in federal appointments than white Republicans who viewed Obama as mixed race. On these second two items, there were no significant differences for white Democrats or white independents.

These results are particularly robust because these differences are statistically significant even when controlling for age, gender, socioeconomic status, and nativity. Therefore, while perceptions of Obama's race did not

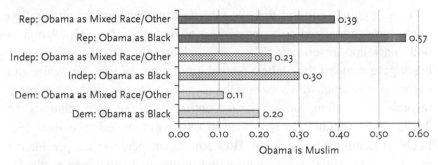

FIGURE 6.4 White Respondents' Belief That Obama Is Muslim, 2012

SOURCE: 2010–2012 Evaluations of Government and Society Study. Variable is on a 0 to 1 scale. Results are weighted to reflect the national population. Significant difference only found for white Republicans at $p < .05$.

impact white evaluations of Obama in 2009, there was a clear effect of the interaction between perceptions of Obama's race and partisanship on white evaluations of Obama in 2012. Interestingly, for white Democrats, perceiving Obama as mixed race had a deracializing effect and encouraged more positive evaluations of the president. Yet, for white Republicans, perceiving Obama as black had a racializing effect by encouraging both acceptance of erroneous rumors and the belief that Obama favored racial minorities. This comparison across time show that while it was difficult to identify any consequences to how whites perceived Obama's race when he first took office, how whites viewed Obama's race increasingly influenced their evaluations of him over time.

But while I identified these significant effects for white respondents, there were fewer consequences of the interaction between perceptions of Obama's race and partisanship on Latino evaluations of him. In 2009, I identified a deracializing effect of perceiving Obama as mixed race on Latino Democrats' and Latino independents' evaluations and a racializing effect of perceiving Obama as black among Latino Republicans. In the 2012 dataset, I found only one significant effect: for Latino Democrats, those who perceived Obama as black were more likely to believe Obama is Muslim than Latino Democrats who perceived Obama as mixed race. Therefore, there is some consistency across the two surveys for Latino Democrats, since those who perceived Obama as black were more likely to racialize him, but since there were few significant results found in 2012, this analysis shows that the interactive effect between partisanship and perceptions of Obama's race had a weakening effect on Latinos' evaluations of Obama over time.

These findings suggest that the Obama campaign and administration might have capitalized on a competitive advantage to framing Obama as both black and mixed race. Black respondents who perceived Obama as black gave some of the highest favorability ratings of him. Yet white and Latino respondents who viewed Obama as mixed race either gave more favorable evaluations or were more optimistic about race relations. In 2012, white Republicans who viewed Obama as mixed race were less likely to racialize the president. How Americans perceive the president's race is consequential, which means that frames that encourage particular racial identities can be understood as strategic messages deployed by leaders and their campaigns.

President Obama and Assignment of Racial Identity

Although President Obama was commonly described as America's first "black" president, the evidence in this chapter shows just how complex the practice of racial assignment is at the beginning of the twenty-first century. Interestingly, survey evidence shows that Americans were more than willing to apply a mixed racial identity to Obama and they continued to perceive him as mixed race throughout his first term in office. At the same time, racial background strongly mediates a respondent's perceptions of Obama's racial classification: blacks were more likely to label Obama as black, while whites and Latinos labeled Obama as mixed race.

The racial differences in how respondents racially classify Obama are indicative of how members of each racial group experience race and how they apply racial categories to others. The history of American racial classification covered in chapter 2 explains why one's own racial classification will directly inform how a person understands race and racial categories. For example, blacks have historically witnessed severe racial discrimination supported by the one-drop rule but are also inclusive in whom they classify as part of their racial group. The findings in this chapter show that blacks are the group most likely to label Obama as black. In contrast, white ethnic narratives that emphasize an ethnic identity informed by family heritage create the belief that there is a link between identity and ancestry (Waters 1990). It is understandable, then, why white respondents are more likely to see Obama as mixed race because he has parents of two different races. Interestingly, Latinos appear to be the most willing to label Obama as mixed race. For Latinos who are strongly influenced by the immigration experience, the historic norms that govern American race relations may not strongly resonate. Thus, Latino attitudes might be the least driven by tradition and American norms about race, which explains their general willingness to classify Obama as mixed race.

While individuals do view the world through their own racial lens, we also cannot discount the strategic activities deployed by the Obama campaign throughout the 2008 election, which might explain why so many Americans view Obama as mixed race. As a candidate, Obama's primary goal in 2008 was to win by courting more voters than his opponent. The evidence in this chapter confirms that emphasizing an interracial background may have offered Obama a competitive advantage, particularly among white Democrats over time. However, the fact that whites, blacks, and Latinos perceived Obama's race differently may not only be due to the ways individuals apply racial categories but also to Obama's campaign, which presented specific images to each racial group. Political scientists have long documented how candidates deploy specialized messages to targeted voting demographic groups in order to earn votes (Popkin 2012). This means that, depending on individuals' background or geographic location, they are likely subject to a distinctive and carefully cultivated message from a political candidate. Early in the presidential election cycle, the Obama campaign hired special political operatives to design strategies for groups and locales identified as key to the Obama coalition, including blacks, Latinos, battleground states, and new voters (Huffington Post 2008; Zeleny 2008). Reviewing published transcripts of Obama's speeches to African American groups like the NAACP, one sees that for black audiences Obama highlighted his African American racial identity.[15] In contrast, television advertisements targeting the general population often highlighted Obama's white mother and grandparents (Clayton 2010). These strategic aspects of the Obama campaign offer an additional explanation why black voters were more likely to racially label Obama as black than were whites and Latinos.

Yet, even after accounting for these explanations, it is striking how many Americans described Obama as mixed race even when he has both publicly and consistently asserted that he identifies as (only) African American. In many ways, there are similarities between this case with President Obama and the challenge described by the self-identified multiracial activists in chapter 3 who wanted to self-identify as multiracial even though others typically applied established monoracial categories to them. This contrast between how a person personally racially identifies and how others perceive that person's racial classification perfectly reflects the tension between racial identification and classification that exists at the beginning of the twenty-first century. A person may have a preferred identity for how she conceives herself, but this does not necessarily mean that others will apply that identity to her. Self-identification can be empowering to the individual because it offers a sense of autonomy over one's image and sense of self. However, as it has been practiced in the United States, race is persistently assigned by others. While we don't typically think about self-identification as black as a complex process, this chapter reveals that all Americans, not just self-identified multiracial individuals, experience the tension between racial identification and classification.

Conclusion | Multiracial and Beyond

RACIAL FORMATION IN THE TWENTY-FIRST CENTURY

W HILE CONDUCTING RESEARCH FOR THIS book, I came across a poster advertising a meeting for an undergraduate student group organized around the multiracial experience. The poster was lined with smiling pictures of a diverse group of students and offered the caption: "I am: ~~Black, Chinese, White, Mexican, Indian, Korean, Italian~~. I am _____ ." The poster perfectly captured a vision of identity choice: the text of a list of established racial and ethnic categories was boldly crossed out. The viewer was instead offered the opportunity to figuratively fill in the blank space. The poster did not offer a specific racial identity label for the viewer to enter but rather invoked the belief that a person could assert any racial identity label desired. It offered a clear statement that individuals should not be constrained by existing racial or ethnic categories but rather have the personal agency to assert choice in their racial identity. The viewer could wholeheartedly embrace the message presented in the poster and firmly believe that she should evoke her own preferred multiracial identity. Yet a different person could perceive the message as out of touch with reality because assignment to one of these existing racial and ethnic categories occurs regardless of one's personal preference. With a simple claim, this poster acutely portrayed the practices of both racial identification and racial classification.

Walking around a university campus populated by our country's newest generation, one would be hard pressed not to find a social embrace of personal agency and belief in the ability to define one's own identity. Assertions of multiracial identification represent a visible practice on college campuses today (Renn 2004). Outside higher education, other institutionalized practices encourage the practice of self-identification: the census has documented a growing number of Americans who are willing to self-identify as multiracial. Yet, at the same time, the country continues to face conflicts rooted in long-standing practices of racial classification. News stories cover events highlighting violence between white police officers and black residents, stark patterns of racial residential segregation, and the racial profiling of Latino immigrants as assumed "illegal" immigrants. These stories show our continued reliance on racial categorization and how consequential assignment is in the United States. In an environment that simultaneously celebrates the flexibility of racial identification along with continued reliance on the long-standing meanings attached to established (mono)racial categories, this book demonstrated how this tension between racial identification and racial classification could be found in individual political behavior and attitudes.

The evidence in this book primarily focused on individual behavior but the larger objective was to offer conceptual insight into processes of racial formation in the United States. This book embraced the view that the meanings attached to race are not simply a product of a given time, but rather are narratives in a cyclical process of reformation: the racial politics of one era is distinctly informed by those of previous periods. The key dynamic highlighted in this book is the relationship between two practices of race: assigned classification and identification. I argued that American norms about race have shifted and today are characterized by the incorporation of the view that race is a product of personal identification. As a result of this cultural shift, we find practices of what I call *identity choice*, or the practice of race as a form of personal identification, which can largely be understood as a response to historic norms that defined race as a process of assigned classification. Yet, as a lesson in racial formation, we learn that identity choice does not replace other norms but rather adds new complexity to the practice of race.

This chapter offers some reflections on the evidence presented in this book and closing insights on the trajectory of American race relations in the twenty-first century. Overall, this book demonstrates that while many Americans believe there is increased personal agency in determining how a person defines her race, the evidence shows that practices of identification continue to be constrained by other forces. This book showed that identity choices are not available to all Americans but rather some racial identities can only be asserted when there exist inviting contexts or opportunities to assert those identities. This conclusion will also argue that the identity choice approach developed in this book is not limited to studies on multiracial identities but applies to other racial identities. Indeed, those who self-identify as (only) black, or (only) Latino, or (only) Asian American are making racial identity choices. I also consider how this approach can apply to characteristics beyond race, most notably gender identities. Yet, while we can frame other race and gender identities as products of identification, as with multiracial identities, it is likely the case that the personal freedom to express a preferred identity is not unchecked but rather hindered by other processes.

Multiracial as Identity Choice

The objective of this book was to use multiracial self-identification as a way to understand changing racial norms, specifically the rise of identity choice, which I argued had occurred over the second half of the twentieth century and generally characterizes the culture at the beginning of the twenty-first century. Although all Americans can practice racial identity choice, I highlighted multiracial self-identification as a unique case that best demonstrated the growing tension between racial assignment and identification. Multiracial individuals embrace the right to conceptualize a hybrid identity along with their own monikers, such as "biracial," "swirlies," or "hapa," Yet, while some individuals assert multiracial identities, not all Americans who may want to identify as multiracial do so. In fact, most Americans continue to identify with one established racial category. This is because, in reality, multiracial identity is a direct contrast to the way racial classification has been historically practiced in the United States.

I explain the creation of the tension between the racial norms as assigned classification and as identification using a historical analysis and evidence from qualitative interviews. Chapter 2 established the original American racial tradition to conceptualize race as a process of assigned classification. Race was conceptualized as a system made up of a small set of discrete categories. As early as the drafting of the Constitution, individuals were assigned to distinctive categories of white, black, and Indian. By applying these categories to individuals, race was used to determine who was a full and equal citizen in the country and who was a partial citizen or an resident unworthy of equal membership. Furthermore, since racial categories implied certain social privileges, these categories were understood to be mutually exclusive and thus citizens could not hold overlapping racial group memberships. Because racial categorization was the justification for determining full citizenship, race represented a classification system that was imposed on individuals and has been understood to represent a biological nature. Slave was burdened with that social status *because of* their race, not because they embraced blackness and the life as a second-class citizen. The traditions of conceptualizing race as a set of discrete categories and as a system of assigned classification have generally persisted as unchallenged features of the American racial system. Even today, the idea that Americans are classified into categories such as white, black, or Asian is generally taken as a given.

But cultural changes that began to take shape during the civil rights movement of the twentieth century have encouraged individuals to challenge many of the embedded assumptions in how race is practiced in the United States. The historical events traced in chapter 2 showed how certain modern developments, at both cultural and institutional levels, helped to create a culture in which race was increasingly conceptualized as personal identity. In terms of political culture, concepts such as "diversity" and "multiculturalism" are often framed as normatively positive and desirable goals, and so individuals are encouraged to be proud of their ethnic identity. At an institutional level, certain subtle changes to how the government collects racial data also offer the opportunity of racial identity choice. In the past, the government collected data on a person's racial background by having an administrator assign and then record the race of the respondent. However, today a person's racial background is self-reported by the individual respondent. It is now common to collect racial data by asking respondents how they would describe their own race, as opposed to administrators assigning a respondent's racial classification. In 2000, the second important institutional development occurred when the US Census Bureau changed the directions on the racial identification by allowing Americans to mark one or more categories. These institutional changes may have been perceived as simple bureaucratic decisions, but they offer new cues to citizens that race is an indicator of personal identity rather than an imposed characteristic.

In addition to this historical perspective, I also incorporated qualitative data to understand how individuals have begun to describe race as a product of their personal preference and identity. Chapter 3 presented data from in-depth interviews with activists who lobbied on behalf of multiracial identities. These interviews revealed an emphasis on the importance of seeing racial identification as a product of choice. I learned that these individuals had characteristics that did not easily fit into established (mono)racial categories because they looked racially ambiguous, were children of interracial parents, or were in families with transracial adoptions. Because of this, activists reported that they were constantly assigned a racial category by others. These persistent experiences of what they felt was "forced" assignment led activists to assert their own preferred racial identity, which they believed better captured how they saw themselves. This emphasis on identity was striking given historical processes of race, which never offered individuals a chance to assert such preferences. Even more importantly, although activists firmly acknowledged the dominant process of assignment, they still believed that there were opportunities to assert their preferred identities.

The interview data in chapter 3 offered two important insights on the tension between racial identification and racial classification. First, at the activist level, multiracial identification is mobilized primarily as a *response* to the existing practices of race. Multiracial activists may express the right to have identity choice, but their demand for choice would not make sense without the existence of the established (mono)racial order. An identity highlighting racial hybridity is understood only as a contrast to existing practices of race, which are characterized by a specific set of discrete categories. Thus, like the transformation of all other racial categories, we see how the creation of "multiracial" develops as an extension from the existing racial system. Second, although I found activists who dedicated time to promoting the identity choice as multiracial, the majority of these activists insisted that established racial categories continue to define American race relations. Activists described the disadvantages of being nonwhite in the United States and believed that their organizations aligned with the politics of other civil rights organization. In this way, multiracial activists did not believe their efforts demonstrated the disappearance of race in the United States but rather were an effort to raise awareness about their preferred racial identity, which they believed should be *added* to the existing spectrum of racial categories.

After establishing the underlining cultural tension between assigned classification and identification that exists at the turn of the twenty-first century, chapters 4 and 5 highlighted multiracial identification and sought to empirically examine how individuals come to adopt their racial identities and the possible political consequences of their racial identities. Chapter 4 focused on the assertion of multiracial identities and presented an identity choice approach for interpreting empirical patterns of multiracial identification. If we accept the claim that multiracial is an adopted identity, not an automatic or inherent characteristic, then an identity choice approach would contend that we should focus on the factors and contexts that allow individuals to assert that identity. In this way, an identity choice approach pushes readers to see multiracial identities as contingent and permitting individuals to assert identity rather than adopt an assigned classification.

Chapter 4 first sought to add nuance to some of the common explanations for multiracial identification by considering to what extent multiracial identities are only proxies for being a child of interracial parents. The analyses in this chapter showed that while some children with parents of two different races see themselves as being of mixed race, there are also other children with such parents who do not see themselves as mixed race. Moreover, those who are typically classified as a monoracial minority (black or Latino) are more likely to report a perception of being mixed race, while this belief is not as common among those who are typically classified as (only) white. Therefore, chapter 4 showed that individual understandings of being mixed race are complex and are strongly informed by historic definitions of what it means to be "white" or "black." Multiracial identification cannot simply be explained by personal preference; instead, these identities are also guided by the historic racial norms that dictate assigned classification into established (mono)racial categories. Moreover, an identity choice interpretation of census data on the two-or-more-races population highlights the particular resources and contexts that offer opportunities for the assertion of multiracial identities. Those who report two or more races are more likely to be in households of higher socioeconomic status (compared to monoracial minority households) and are living in specific regions—in particular the West—that are likely to be more open to multiracial identities.

Since chapter 4 revealed that multiracial identities are asserted by those who have the opportunity to do so, chapter 5 assessed the extent to which there are possible political consequences to this identity. I evaluated if multiracial political attitudes demonstrated a similar pattern as whites, or as racial minorities, or if they revealed a unique pattern as a distinct identity group. When multiracial respondents were analyzed as one collective group, the results were mixed. Some of the findings suggested that multiracial attitudes were like those of whites, while others suggested alignment with racial minorities. However, on the whole, multiracial political attitudes still reflected identification as a nonwhite minority. In sum, the diverse results suggested that we cannot think about the multiracial population as one coherent group.

Given the findings in chapter 4, which emphasized the importance of monoracial classification, chapter 5 disaggregated multiracial respondents by racial background and found more consistent patterns. Multiracial-blacks and multiracial-Latinos demonstrated attitudes aligned with their monoracial minority counterparts. In contrast, multiracial-Asians aligned more closely with whites. Although the sample size of multiracial Asians was too small to allow firm generalizations, the evidence did demonstrate that established racial categories play an important role in multiracial political attitude formation. For those who include black or Latino as part of their racial identity, their political attitudes reflect experiences as a marginalized racial minority, while for those multiracial respondents who include Asian as part of their racial identity, an assimilation process was documented. Thus, the political consequences of a multiracial identity will depend on the racial combination of the multiracial individual.

Chapter 6 offered one case through which to understand how Americans assign race to others and examined to what extent a person's preferred racial identity corresponds with the racial assignment made by others. Chapter 6 focused on the opinions of white, black, and Latino Americans and examined how these voters perceived the race of President Barack Obama. President Obama presented a unique case of identity choice: he openly promoted being a child of an interracial couple while at the same time self-identifying as (only) African American. We can think of Obama as employing an identity choice because he could have identified instead as "multiracial." At the same time, conflicting narratives about Obama's race were promoted by his 2008 campaign and so raised an empirical question regarding how Americans chose to understand the his race. Strikingly, I found that the majority of both whites and Latinos labeled the president as mixed race rather than black and continued to see Obama as mixed race throughout the duration of his first term in office. In contrast, a larger proportion of blacks saw Obama as black rather than mixed race. Thus, Americans did not all view Obama's race in the same way, but most relied on the fact that he was a child of interracial parents rather than on his own preferred racial identity.

Chapter 6 showed that there were consequences to perceiving Obama as mixed race rather than as black. Analysis of data from 2012 showed that for white Democrats, perceiving Obama as mixed race made them more supportive of the president, while for white Republicans, those who perceived Obama as black were more likely to think Obama is Muslim and to believe that there was too much attention on race and gender in federal appointments. The analysis also suggests that perceiving Obama as mixed race had a similar deracializing effect for Latinos (particularly Latino Democrats). However, for blacks, perceptions of shared race (those who perceived Obama as black) made them more supportive of the president.

Therefore, from chapter 6 we learn that how individuals assign race to others continues to have consequences. The results in chapter 6 suggest that, over the long run, the assignment of multiracial identities could have a deracializing effect; that is, these identities discourage individuals from applying racial stereotypes to a political leader.

Racial Formation and Contemporary Identity Choice

This book emphasized identity because it became incorporated into a new narrative attached to race over the second half of the twentieth century. However, the belief that there exists greater freedom to choose one's racial identity must be distinguished from the actual practice of race in today's society. The meanings attached to the established racial categories (particularly white and black) and the consequences of those categories on individual life chances have remained largely unchanged as these new norms about race have been created. Processes and institutions that support the practice of race as assigned classification therefore continue to exist and create barriers for many Americans who might make racial identity choices. So while Americans can adopt a normative preference for identity choice, their ability to assert their preferred identities continues to be dictated by the surrounding social context, interpersonal interactions that police which identities can be evoked, and society's continued reliance on established racial categories.

One important point to be emphasized is that some Americans experience more structural constraints limiting their racial identity choices than others. Those who are able to self-identify as multiracial likely experience more flexibility in their racial classification than those who self-identify as a monoracial minority. While this book pointed to larger societal forces, such as historic norms about race, to describe how narratives of identity choice were constructed, it is also important to recognize that certain characteristics of the individual make some more likely than others to assert their own preferred racial identities. Although there may be many individual traits that could be identified, I argue that two deserve the most attention: visual appearance and socioeconomic resources. With these two characteristics in mind, it is apparent that those who self-identify as multiracial do so because they *can*, not necessarily because they are the only individuals who see race in a different way.

Since racial categorization is processed upon visual inspection of a person's phenotypic features, those whose race is visually ambiguous are not automatically classified in an existing racial category (see also Williams 1996). Studies in social psychology confirm that when respondents are presented with faces that appear racially ambiguous, respondents are less efficient in classifying those faces in categories and are less likely to remember (for example, see Pauker et al. 2009). The activists in chapter 3 often recounted that others could not easily determine their race and that, in some social activities, they could pass for a (monoracial) white person. Because those who have racially ambiguous features cannot be easily classified, they are provided more consistent opportunities to express their preferred racial identity. In particular, those who can be perceived as white experience the most opportunities to assert a preferred racial identity. In contrast, those who have prototypical features that lead others to classify that person as black, Latino, or Asian are more likely to witness social policing that enforces their assigned classification as a racial minority regardless of the individual's preferred racial identity.

Multiracial identification also shows the continued interaction between race and social class. Since the era of slavery, race has been used as a justification for an economic hierarchy in which nonwhite races were understood as fit for subordinate roles in the economy and thus subject to less than equal treatment in economic interactions. Although such practices are now outlawed, Americans experience the long-standing implications of this history and typically connect lower-class status with blacks and other nonwhite groups. Yet patterns of multiracial identification suggest that social class is connected with racial identification. Those who are counted as two or more races in the census are those who live in households with higher levels of socioeconomic status. Given the correspondence between class status and race, social class is one factor that dictates which individuals experience more flexibility in racial identification. Interestingly, research has shown that individuals use status cues to make assumptions about a person's race. For example, researchers are more likely to classify a poor person as black (Freeman et al. 2011; Saperstein and Penner 2012). Those of lower socioeconomic status could therefore be more constrained by the racial classification assigned by others and therefore not have opportunities to self-identify as multiracial.

I highlight factors such as visual appearance and resources as a way to discuss both the privileges associated with multiracial identities and the fact that for many Americans there exist real constraints on their ability to assert a preferred racial identity. One of the more deceiving assumptions that could be drawn from an identity choice approach is that personal identification overrides assignment leading to the belief that the structural features of race are disappearing. Indeed, norms that emphasize self-expression and identity embrace classic American ideologies of individual liberalism and the power of personal agency. However, all of these narratives downplay the fact that, in reality, there are not equal opportunities for individuals to exercise personal agency. Moreover, outcomes are not necessarily attributed to the strength of one's belief system or the amount of personal effort. In terms of multiracial identification, individuals who can self-identify as multiracial are not necessarily those who hold the strongest preferences or who make the most efforts to assert their preferred identities. Rather, they are individuals who are advantaged by certain factors, many of which are not under their personal control, such as visual appearance and the family resources one is born into.

While it may be argued that multiracial identities have not fundamentally changed the practice of race in the United States, this does not mean they have not resulted in new processes of racial formation. Multiracial identities do not replace existing racial categories but rather encourage us to incorporate new considerations in how we understand race. One important perspective offered by multiracial identification is that racial identities can be fluid. One of the main findings presented in this book is that those who self-identify as multiracial often do not consistently identify as such in all contexts (Doyle and Kao 2007; Harris and Sim 2002). In fact, a person who prefers to identify as multiracial may be found, in some contexts, to self-identify with an established (mono)racial category. In contrast, research shows that those who self-identify with an established racial category, such as "black" or "Asian," are more likely to consistently identify as such in all contexts (Hirschman, Farley and Alba 2000; Kiang et al. 2010; Nishina et al. 2010). This implies that for most Americans, racial categorization and racial identity go hand in hand and represent a stable characteristic that influences the life chances of the individual. In contrast, for self-identified multiracial individuals, racial categorization and racial identity do not always align, and this offers an opportunity to assert different identities in different contexts.

As a result, those who self-identify as multiracial may view racial identity as a more flexible construct and are not necessarily committed to multiracial as their only racial identity. This is not to say that multiracial individuals will always hold weak attachments to other multiracial individuals. The collective mobilization efforts of activists to change the racial identification question on the census demonstrate that collective group identities do form among multiracial individuals. However, since multiracial individuals embrace the opportunity to have fluid identities and have been found to assert different racial identities in different contexts, multiracial identities may represent a different form of racial identity than monoracial identities embraced by whites, blacks, Asian Americans, and Latinos.

Second, demands to recognize multiracial identities will add nuance to how Americans perceive and assign race to others. Rather than assume that race is an obvious, automatic, and stable trait, Americans are pushed by multiracial identities to recognize that racial classification and identification do not always align. It is no coincidence that multiracial identities have flourished during a time that Americans witnessed increased racial diversity attributed to the incorporation of a more diverse group of immigrants and legal processes that dictated increased interracial interactions. As diversity increases, Americans must adjust their assumptions to account for more varied interracial interactions. However, Americans do not necessarily know how to change their assumptions as they witness a changing demography. Demands to recognize multiracial identities offer narratives on how to understand a diversifying society and push Americans to adopt more varied approaches to how they assign race to others.

Beyond Multiracial: Application of Identity Choice to Race and Gender

Much of the book focused on the assertion of multiracial identities, which I argued was an obvious case of how identity choice is practiced. However, the cultural shift from conceiving race as primarily a product of classification to conceiving it as one of identification does not simply impact those who self-identify as multiracial, but all Americans. Moreover, I argue that we are beginning to see that cultural norms that emphasize personal agency and identity are not limited to expressions of race but also are being applied to other characteristics, such as gender. The concept of "gender identity" proposes that individuals should not be limited to the biological sex one is assigned at birth but should represent the preferred gender identity of the individual. Therefore, by examining both race and gender, we see that there is shift in how Americans perceive traits that were once thought of as inherent and immutable to the belief that these traits can be reframed and rearticulated as a sense of identity.

Latinos as Identity Choice

In the introduction of this book, I posed that race was in a process of racial formation and so the complexities of identity choices can apply to all racial groups. While this book focused on multiracial identification, I argued that it is possible to also conceptualize the assertion of being black, Latino, or Asian American as an identity choice. One way of explaining how identity choice applies to racial minorities is to point to the creation of alternative worldviews about the American racial order that rearticulate the meanings attached to racial identity (Omi and Winant 1994). For example, African Americans, particularly during the civil rights movement, have embraced counternarratives to the existing tropes of race. Instead of accepting blackness as a marker of inferiority or deviance, African Americans highlight the positive aspects of their community and demand that government treat them as equal to whites (Ture and Hamilton 1992; Young 1990). Indeed, chapter 6 presented President Barack Obama as making an identity choice in declaring his racial identity as black. In this way, by adopting more positive frames to their race, monoracial minorities are making choices to assert their racial identities.

However, the case could be made that there is variation in how minority groups experience opportunities to adopt their identity choices. I suggest that one particular racial group could be studied as a parallel to multiracial individuals because they are also given institutional opportunities to express different forms of identity: those who identify as Latino. In this book, I rely on the current American assumption that those of Latin American descent are to be classified in one collective category of "Latino" (or what is oftentimes labeled "Hispanic"). Moreover, throughout the book, the word "race" has been applied to the Latino category. Both of these decisions were deliberate on my part, given the strong imperative to offer a comparative assessment between self-identified multiracial individuals and those who self-identify as monoracial. But by making these decisions, I did not spend time in this book discussing the complex nature of what I argued are "established" racial identities. In particular, Latino identity problematizes the assumption that established racial identities are straightforward and monolithic.

The norms regarding the definition of "Latino" are not established (Hattam 2007; Rodriguez 2000). For example, the US government designates Latinos an *ethnic* group. Since 1980, the federal government has identified Latinos through a separate Hispanic ethnicity question that is commonly asked before the racial identification question (Nobles 2000). In practice, this means that Latinos are identified as a separate ethnic group but may be of any race. Using this strategy, Latinos are presented with many different identity choices: they can highlight their collective distinctiveness as a Latino ethnic group; they can emphasize their racial background as white, black, Asian, or brown, or embrace a perspective that reflects a mixture of their race and ethnicity (Rodriguez 2000, 2008). Moreover, new deliberations over how to effectively enumerate Latinos have encouraged federal officials to develop new strategies for identifying Latinos on future censuses, such as eliminating the Latino ethnicity category and instead including it as a racial category.

In everyday practice, Americans may assume that "Latino" is clearly defined and that their identity as such is straightforward and so do not problematize the existence of a Latino category. Yet the fact that even the federal government has not adopted a consistent strategy for enumerating Latinos tells us that there are institutional openings for Latinos to assert their own sense of racial and ethnic identity. In this way, Latinos are subject to many of the same complex questions that are asked about self-identified multiracial individuals.[1] The choice Latinos make to emphasize their ethnic designation or adhere to the American racial hierarchy by highlighting their racial classification has parallels to self-identified multiracial individuals who choose to emphasize their hybridity or adhere to monoracial categorization.

By making parallels between multiracial individuals and Latinos, I do not attempt to argue these two groups are subject to the same social and political circumstances. Multiracial individuals are attempting to define their own concepts of identity, while Latinos are forced to work within the confines of a category that has represented a more historic presence in the American racial spectrum (Nobles 2000; Rodriguez 2008). The challenges of identifying as multiracial are clearly different from those facing Latinos. At the same time, I would argue that Latinos represent an excellent case for a study on identity choice because, as the evidence presented in this book demonstrates, identity choice is possible when there exist both institutional and cultural openings for a group to adopt certain racial options. For self-identified multiracial individuals, the opening for identity choice is made available through institutional changes that allow Americans to select two or more racial categories for themselves. For Latinos, identity choices can be made within the unresolved tension that exists between their racial and ethnic classification.

Transgender as Identity Choice

Outside of racial categories, it may also be the case that we can apply an identity choice approach to the study of gender, particularly transgender identities. Although gender was not studied in this book, the increasing number of public demands to recognize transgender identities, I believe, also is the product of the perceived tension between assigned classification and personal identification. For example, discussions on gender identity highlight a contrast between the biological sex one is born with and the gender identity that a person believes best reflects the sense of self. The transgender movement has included individuals who have switched gender (from male to female or from female to male) and individuals who believe they identify as neither male nor female. This movement therefore privileges the power of identity and articulates a claim that a person's sense of self should trump assigned classification.

Interestingly, debates on gender identity have spurred discussions about how government and other institutions should recognize gender identity alongside assignment by biological sex. When it comes to reporting gender to institutions, there appears to be a movement, as there has been for race, to allow individuals to self-report their preferred gender identity (see also Westbrook and Saperstein 2015). Moreover, different options are given that allows for more a variety of choices in expressing one's gender identity. For example, the University of California system now offers different gender categories for new college applicants to declare: in addition to male and female, the categories of "trans male/trans man," "trans female/trans woman," "gender queer/gender non-conforming," and "different identity" are included as possible identities.

By including a discussion on gender identity in this book, I do not mean to equate race with gender because there are important differences. Race is generally recognized as a social construction in which there are societal norms that define racial categories. In contrast, the accepted biological dimension to sex encourages a stark contrast between gender and sex as two separate processes. For example, Schilt and Bratter (2015) argue that there are more institutional sanctions that constrain an individual's ability to declare a different gender identity than the sex reported on one's birth certificate. In addition they argue that scholars need to incorporate perceptions of intimidation or fear into models of explaining transgender identity. They argue that individuals are often fearful in declaring a transgender identity given the discrimination often waged against transgender people. Indeed, these authors find that individuals who have switched their gender prefer to report being male or female rather than a transgender identity even when given the opportunity to declare a transgender identity.

But by identifying correspondence between race and gender, I point out the important change in how Americans have come to understand traits that have historically believed to be inherent to the individual. Race and gender have historically both been seen as objective traits of the individual that are obvious to all and so are not subject to investigation or change. Because these traits are seen as fundamental aspects of the individual, Americans have adopted certain assumptions that can be made by observing a person's race or gender. However, today some narratives argue that when identity does not correspond with assigned classification, identity should be given greater value. Therefore, this shift away from the belief that race and gender are immutable and instead should be products of personal identification reflects a larger cultural change to how Americans understand their social and political world.

Race Still Matters

I want to close this conclusion by considering the most obvious question that could be posed by the evidence presented in this book: will race still matter? A growing self-identified multiracial population can encourage a number of grand speculations and predictions about the role of race in American life. It is common to see multiracial people used as evidence for two different but interrelated claims: that Americans today live in a color-blind society and that the American racial hierarchy that has long characterized social relations is fundamentally changing. Because race has long served as a source of social conflict in American life, it is completely understandable that many prefer to see race diminish as a fundamental categorization tool. While this is an ideal, the data presented in this book demonstrate that although multiracial individuals complicate practices of racial classification by asserting their own form of racial identity, their choices continue to be constrained by the American racial hierarchy. Rather than demonstrate that race is disappearing, this study shows that while racial identities may be in flux, key dimensions to racial classification remain firmly intact.

The first claim—that Americans will live in a color-blind society—is often made in relation to the growing number of children of interracial marriages. Proponents of this argument claim that multiracial individuals reflect evidence that American race relations are no longer characterized by conflict but rather by cooperation and intimate interactions. Accordingly, multiracial identities tend to be evoked in normative statements that Americans today are color-blind. For example, Samuel Huntington states that "if the trends toward multiracialism continue, they will at some point ... make government efforts to classify people by race 'quaintly passé.'

When it happens, the removal of race from census forms will signal a dramatic step toward the creation of a comprehensive American national identity" (2004, 309). Thus, multiracial individuals offer the opportunity for Americans to celebrate the idealized "melting pot." From this it is often concluded that because Americans are represented by a heterogeneous ethnic mixture rather than distinctive racial groups, individuals will no longer rely on race to characterize others (see also Hollinger 2005.

The second claim argues instead that race will continue to be a central feature in American life, but that the order of the American racial hierarchy is fundamentally changing. For example, Hochschild, Weaver, and Burch (2012) argue that the increasing racial heterogeneity and changing rules of racial classification will create a new racial order in which blacks will no longer be at the bottom of the racial hierarchy and will be replaced by Muslims and undocumented immigrants. A different prediction presented by Lee and Bean (2010) forecasts that rather than characterizing the American racial hierarchy along a variegated color spectrum, Americans instead will live in a bifurcated racial system of black and nonblack. Lee and Bean point to the high rates of interracial marriage and assimilation of Asian and Latino immigrants as evidence that not all nonwhite minorities face the same forms of discrimination. Rather, they argue that those classified as black continue to represent the exceptional case in American race relations (see also Bonilla Silva and Glover 2004).

Of course, only time will tell exactly what the future will bring. However, the evidence in this book suggests that a dramatic transformation may not occur as soon as many might like to hope. The most important outcome that was consistently demonstrated in all analyses conducted in this book is that even for those who self-identify as multiracial, the established racial hierarchy continues to constrain their choices and behaviors. Self-identified multiracial individuals do not entirely reject the use of established racial categories. Rather, they prefer to denote their racial identities using multiple existing racial categories, such as being both white and black or both Asian and Latino. Moreover, when I disaggregated self-identified multiracial individuals by racial background in chapter 5, I found that the racial mixture of the self-identified multiracial respondent influenced political attitude formation. In particular, there were few significant differences between monoracially identified blacks and multiracial respondents who reported being partially black.

The results also show that although self-identified multiracial individuals reflect identity choice, they do not have a range of unlimited racial options with which they may self-identify. The self-identified multiracial movement does not appear to advocate that monoracial identities be interchangeable. Most importantly, it is not seen as a flexible choice to self-identify as (only) white. Multiracial individuals advocate for a specific type of choice: the ability to assert multiple established racial categories. But beyond personal preference, the racial identity options are, in reality, limited to the selection of a nonwhite racial identity. In contrast, the white racial category remains well buffered from deliberations about racial identity. It is more likely that we find Americans considering the choice between a black versus a multiracial identity, or an Asian versus a multiracial identity, or a Latino versus a multiracial identity. It is less likely we find Americans considering between being white and being multiracial (but see Roquemore and Arend 2002). This is also distinctively clear in the analysis of how Americans view Obama's racial identity. Data collected for the American National Election Study show that Americans deliberate over Obama's racial identity as either black or biracial, but very few Americans consider Obama white. Thus, identity choice is heavily structured by the long-standing norms that preserve the white racial category, while the meanings associated with nonwhite racial categories—including multiracial—are altered to fit new and changing circumstances.

The other striking finding is that multiracial political interests generally align more closely with racial minorities than with whites. It could be perceived that by asserting an alternative racial identity, multiracial individuals intend to create social distance from monoracial minority groups. But the data presented in this book demonstrate that multiracial individuals are sympathetic to race-based policies such as affirmative action and more aware of racial discrimination than whites. Multiracial activists also foresee a growing multiracial political agenda that is in partnership with other civil rights causes. Even though multiracial individuals express their race as identity, they demonstrate a clear awareness of the disadvantages associated with a nonwhite racial status. As the interviews with activists suggested, multiracial individuals continue to be racialized and subjected to treatment like that which is given to monoracial minority groups. In fact, many of the multiracial activists I spoke with reported that their experiences with racial discrimination occurred they were assumed to be a monoracial minority.

The existence of a self-identified multiracial population therefore does not show that the American racial order is fundamentally changing but rather reflects the incorporation of new developments associated with the increased emphasis on personal identification. The established racial hierarchy continues to characterize American race relations, but now there are new complications to how Americans practice racial classification given a growing culture of identity choice.

APPENDIX A | Interview Subjects, Their Organizations, and Questions Asked

TABLE A.1 Characteristics of Interview Subjects

INTERVIEW NUMBER	AGE	GENDER	EDUCATION	RACIAL IDENTITY	PARTY ID	LOCATION OF CHILDHOOD HOME AND PRIMARY RESIDENCE
1	29	Female	Enrolled master's program	Multiracial: Jewish and Chinese	Democrat	Queens, NY
2	23	Male	Bachelor's degree	Multiracial: white and Japanese	Republican	Born in San Fernando, CA; grew up in Newton, MA
3		Female		White		Lived in Georgia and Florida
4	38	Female	Master's degree	White	Democrat	San Francisco Bay Area
5	Mid 20's	Female	enrolled PhD program	Multiracial: black and Korean		Baltimore
6	43	Female	Master's degree	White	Democrat	San Francisco Bay Area
7	27	Female	PhD program	Multiracial: Italian and Japanese	Republican	Central Massachusetts
8	43	Female	Some college	White	Republican	
9	53	Male	Some college	Multiracial: white, black, and American Indian	Independent	Virginia

(continued)

187

INTERVIEW NUMBER	AGE	GENDER	EDUCATION	RACIAL IDENTITY	PARTY ID	LOCATION OF CHILDHOOD HOME AND PRIMARY RESIDENCE
10	53	Female	Master's degree	White		New Jersey
11	26	Female	Bachelor's degree	Multiracial: white and Japanese	Democrat	San Francisco Bay Area
12	39	Male	PhD	Multiracial: Japanese and Mexican	Democrat	Hawaii
13		Male		Multiracial: Japanese and German		Sacramento, CA
14	56	Female	Some graduate courses	Multiracial: black and white	Independent	
15		Male	PhD	Multiracial: black, white, and Native American	Democrat	Illinois
16		Female	Bachelor's degree	Multiracial: white and Native American	Democrat	San Francisco
17	28	Male	Master's degree	Multiracial: Belgian and Japanese		Washington, DC
18	29	Male	Bachelor's degree	Multiracial: Latino and white	Democrat	Seattle
19	55	Male	Master's degree	White	Democrat	Long Island, NY
20	54	Female	Master's degree	White	Independent	New Jersey
21	25	Female	Bachelor's degree	Multiracial: white and Japanese	No party	Oakland, CA
22	37	Female	Master's degree	Black	Democrat	Washington. DC
23	26	Male	Some college	Multiracial: white and Native American	Libertarian	Central Illinois
24	47	Female	Some college	Puerto Rican	Democrat	Chicago
25	25	Female	Bachelor's degree	Multiracial: white and Japanese	Independent	Eugene, OR
26	50+	Female	Bachelor's degree	White		
27	33	Female	Bachelor's degree	White and Japanese	Democrat	Seattle
28	52	Female	Master's degree	Multiracial and black	Independent	In the South

List of Multiracial Organizations

ORGANIZATION	LOCATION
A Place for Us Arkansas	Little Rock, AR
Association of Multiethnic Americans	Los Angeles, CA
Biracial Family Network	Chicago, IL
Getting Interracial Families Together	Montclair, NJ
Honor Our New Ethnic Youth	Eugene, OR
Interracial Family Circle	Washington, DC
Interracial Intercultural Pride (IPride)	Berkeley, CA
Interracial Voice	College Point, NY
LovingDay	New York, NY
MAVIN Foundation	Seattle, WA
Multiethnics of Southern Arizona in Celebration	Tempe, AZ
Multiracial Americans of Southern California	Los Angeles, CA
Oregon Council on Multiracial Affairs	Portland, OR
Project RACE	Los Banos, CA
Swirl, Boston	Boston, MA
Swirl, New York	New York, NY
Swirl, San Francisco	San Francisco, CA
The Multiracial Activist	Alexandria, VA

List of Interview Questions

The list of questions below represents the general topics and related questions asked of interview subjects. In each interview, I employed a semistructured technique, which means that questions were not necessarily asked in the exact order presented in this list. Respondents were encouraged to expand on their answers and were allowed to deviate from the questions asked in order to allow their personal narratives to be communicated rather than impose answers by the researcher. However, every attempt was made to ensure that interviews covered all seven areas listed here.

1 Individual Involvement
   a Please describe your position and role in [organization]
   b When did you join [organization]?
   c How did you come to join [organization]?
   d Why do you feel it is important that there be an organization such as this one?
   e Why did you feel it was important to be personally involved in this organization?
   f Are you personally involved with other political organizations?
      (1) If yes, are you involved with organizations focusing on the policy needs of blacks, Latinos, or Asian Americans?
      (2) What is your involvement with these organizations?

2 For Founders Only: Organization Founding
  a What experiences led you to establish this organization?
  b Why did you feel a "new" organization was needed (as opposed to joining an established organization)?
  c What were your initial goals?
   (1) Why these goals?
   (2) Do you feel the goals have changed since the organization's formation?
    (i) How?
    (ii) Why?
  d What were the initial activities of the group?
  e Did these activities change over time?
  f Are/were you personally involved with other political organizations?
   (1) If yes, are you involved with organizations focusing on the policy needs of blacks, Latinos, or Asian Americans?
   (2) What is your involvement with these organizations?
3 Organizational Activities, and Goals
  a What are the primary goals of your organization?
  b What are the main activities/projects sponsored by your organization?
  c How do these activities help to accomplish your primary goals?
  d Would you consider any of these activities to be directed at politics?
  e Is there an example of which you encountered opposition to accomplishing one of your primary goals?
  f Do you regularly inform your members about these activities/projects? If so, how do you communicate these projects to your members
  g Do you regularly inform non-members or the general public about these activities? If so, how do you communicate these projects to the general public?
  h What benefits do your members expect from membership in your organization?
  i Over the next ten years, what do you hope your organization will accomplish?
4 Politicized Identities
  a What do you feel are major problems facing multiracial peoples today?
  b What do you feel needs to be done to correct these problems?
   (1) Do you feel that your organization plays a role in correcting these problems? If so, how?
   (2) Do you feel the government should play a role in solving these problems? How?
  c Currently, do you feel multiracial identities are properly represented in politics?
   (1) If so, how do you feel they are represented?
   (2) Why do you think political representation of multiracial identities is important?
  d Does your organization sponsor activities that encourage greater public recognition of multiracial peoples? If so, what are they?
  e Do you encourage your members to become involved in politics?
   (1) Why do you feel that it is important for your members to become involved in politics?

5 Social Context
   a Your organization is located in [city]. Why do you think this location is ideal for a multiracial organization?
   b Is your organization active in other parts of the country? Which areas?
      (1) Why the focus on these areas?
   c Have you found that multiracial identities are generally recognized by your surrounding community?
      (1) Have you found your surrounding community to be accepting of your organization's purpose? Why do you think that is the case?
   d How would you describe the racial makeup of your surrounding community?
      (1) To your knowledge, are there other active minority organizations in your surrounding community?
      (2) To your knowledge, are there other active multiracial organizations in your surrounding community?
6 Coalition Building
   a What other organization(s) do you work with?
      (1) Why did the partnership form? [ask for each organization]
      (2) What are the shared goals?
   b Generally speaking, have you found that multiracial organizations share common problems/issues with black political organizations such as the NAACP, Urban League, etc.?
      (1) On what problems or issues?
      (2) Have you found black organizations to be open to building partnerships with your organization? If so, can you provide an example of a shared project?
      (3) Have you found black organizations to be resistant to building partnerships with your organization?
   c Generally speaking, have you found that multiracial organizations share common problems/issues with Latino political organizations such as MALDEF, LULAC, etc.?
      (1) On what problems or issues?
      (2) Have you found Latino organizations to be open to building partnerships with your organization? If so, can you provide an example of a shared project?
      (3) Have you found Latino organizations to be resistant to building partnerships with your organization? Why?
   d Generally speaking, have you found that multiracial organizations share common problems/issues with Asian American organizations such as the JACL, NAPALA etc.?
      (1) On what problems or issues?
      (2) Have you found Asian American organizations to be open to building partnerships with your organization?
         (i) If so, can you provide an example of a shared project?
      (3) Have you found Asian American organizations to be resistant to building partnerships with your organization? Why?
7 Respondent Socio-demographics
   a How old are you?
   b Gender [record from interview]

c   What was the last grade you completed in school?

d   What was your total household income last year?

e   How do you choose to identify yourself racially?

f   Under what circumstances do you emphasize your [answer from #6d] racial identification?

g   How does your mother identify racially/ethnically?

h   How does your father identify racially/ethnically?

i   On official forms that do not provide a "multiracial/check all that apply" option on the racial identification question, what racial category do you normally select?

j   Where did you grow up?

k   Growing up, what was the racial makeup of your neighborhood?

   (1)   What about your neighborhood today?

l   Have you ever experienced racial discrimination?

   (1)   Do you believe it was because you are multiracial/mixed race?

m   What was your occupation before joining organization?

n   Are you registered to vote?

o   Did you vote in the last election?

p   What is your political partisanship?

| Washington Post / Kaiser Family
Foundation / Harvard University, *Race
and Ethnicity in 2001: Attitudes,
Perceptions, and Experiences* (WKH 2001)

Survey Question Wording

Q#7: Now please tell me how much discrimination there is against each of these groups in our society today. How about (insert racial group)? Would you say there is a lot of discrimination, some, only a little, or none at all?

[Racial groups were randomly ordered]
a) African Americans
b) Hispanic Americans
c) Asian Americans
d) White Americans

Q#12. Do you believe it is the responsibility or isn't the responsibility of the federal government to make sure minorities have equality with whites in each of the following areas, even if it means you will have to pay more in taxes? Making sure minorities have:

[Items were randomly ordered]
a) Jobs equal in quality to whites
b) Schools equal in quality to whites
c) Health care services equal to whites
d) Treatment by the courts and police equal to whites

Q#26: How much discrimination do you think there is against multi-racial Americans in our society today? Would you say there is a lot of discrimination, some, only a little, or none at all?

Q#28: Do you think multiracial children face more problems or fewer problems growing up than children of a single race do, or isn't there much difference?
1) A lot more
2) Somewhat more
3) Somewhat fewer

4) A lot fewer
5) Not much difference

Q#29: Is your mother White, Black, Hispanic, Asian, or of some other race?

Q#32: Is your father White, Black, Hispanic, Asian, or of some other race?

Q#35: Some people say they're of more than one race even if their parents are of the same race. Do you consider yourself to be of mixed race, that is, belonging to more than one racial group, or not?

Q#36: Please name the groups you consider yourself to be part of. (answer was recorded)

Q#51: Do you favor or oppose employers and colleges making an extra effort to find and recruit qualified minorities?

Q#57. Do you live in a racially integrated neighborhood, or are almost all of the families in your neighborhood of the same race?

Q#59. In your day-to-day life, how often do any of the following things happen to you because of your racial or ethnic background? [Read items a-d]. Would you say very often, fairly often, once in a while, or never?
a) You are treated with less respect than other people
b) You receive poorer service than other people at restaurants or stores
c) People act as if they are afraid of you
d) You are called names or insulted

Q#60. How important is religion in your everyday life:
1) The most important thing in your life
2) Very important but not the most important thing
3) Somewhat important
4) Not too important
5) Don't know
6) Refused

Q#61. For each of the following, please tell me whether or not it is something you and your family have had to deal with recently:
a) You have problems paying rent or mortgage for yourself or your family
b) You have delayed or had trouble getting medical care for yourself and your family
c) You have been unable to save money for future needs

D01: In politics today, do you consider yourself a Republican, a Democrat, an Independent or something else?

D01a: [If Independent] Do you consider yourself closer to the Republican Part or Democratic Party?

D02. Would you say your views in most political matters are liberal, moderate, conservative, something else or haven't you given this much thought?

D13a. I have one final question, this one is about me. What race or ethnicity do you think I am?

TABLE B.1 Sample Demographics

	WHITE	BLACK	ASIAN	LATINO
N	779	323	254	315
Age				
18–29	14%	30%	30%	36%
30–44	32%	36%	44%	39%
45–59	29%	19%	19%	17%
60+	24%	15%	4%	8%
Refused	1.4%	0.6%	2.4%	0.6%
% Female	54%	57%	48%	52%
Education				
Less than HS degree	7%	11%	9%	27%
HS degree	26%	35%	9%	23%
Some college	27%	30%	20%	24%
Bachelor's or more	39%	24%	61%	25%
Refused	0.3%	0.0%	0.8%	0.3%
Household income				
less than 15K	8%	15%	7%	12%
15K–30K	14%	27%	14%	27%
30K50K	22%	27%	23%	25%
50K–75K	19%	15%	13%	14%
75K–100K	11%	5%	13%	6%
100K+	14%	5%	20%	7%
Refused	13%	7%	10%	10%
Region				
Northeast	20%	15%	27%	17%
Midwest	27%	16%	9%	7%
South	33%	59%	15%	41%
West	21%	10%	49%	36%
Language of interview				
% taken in non-English	0.1%	0.3%	11.4%	18.7%
Party affiliation				
Republican	37%	6%	18%	21%
Democrat	29%	65%	41%	41%

TABLE B.2 Responses to Follow-Up Question to Mixed-Race
Background Question

	NUMBER OF RESPONDENTS	%
Asian	15	5%
Asian-Latino	9	3%
Asian-white	14	4%
Black	5	2%
Black-Latino	9	3%
Black-Latino-white	10	3%
Black–Native Am.	26	8%
Black–Native Am.–white	21	7%
Black-white	20	6%
Latino	13	4%
Latino–Native Am.	7	2%
Latino-white	54	17%
Native Am.	18	6%
Native Am.–white	31	10%
White	18	6%
Other	35	11%
Don't know / refused	12	4%
Total	**317**	**100%**

NOTE: The survey question is "[If self-identify as multiracial] Please name the groups you consider yourself to be part of." SOURCE: WKH 2001.

TABLE B.3 Cross Tabulation of Parental Ancestry Questions by Parents' Race

		RACE OF FATHER					
		WHITE	BLACK	LATINO	ASIAN	OTHER	TOTAL
Race of mother	White	795	7	32	5	9	*848*
	Black	1	283	5	0	10	*299*
	Latino	29	7	205	2	2	*245*
	Asian	10	1	3	229	1	*244*
	Other	21	19	5	0	12	*57*
	Total	*856*	*317*	*250*	*236*	*34*	*1,693*

NOTE: Numbers in cells represent the raw number of respondents in the survey that fit into the designated category. SOURCE: WKH 2001.

APPENDIX C | American National Election Study 2008 Time Series Study (ANES)

Survey Question Wording

v083097: Generally speaking, do you usually think of yourself as a Democrat, a Republican, an Independent or what? [order of parties is randomly assigned]

v083098a: [If R a Democrat or Republican] Would you call yourself a strong [Democrat/Republican] or a not very strong [Democrat/Republican]

v083098b: [If Independent, no preference or other party] Do you think of yourself as closer to the Republican party or to the Democratic party?

v085079: Some people feel that if black people are not getting fair treatment in jobs, the government in Washington ought to see to it that they do. Others feel that this is not the federal government's business. Have you had enough interest in this question to favor one side over the other?

v085079a: [In has interest in issue of fair treatment] How do you feel? Should the government in Washington see to it that black people get fair treatment in jobs or is this not the federal government's business?

v085082: Do you think the number of immigrants from foreign countries who are permitted to come to the United States to live should be increased a lot, increased a little, left the same as it is now, decreased a little or decreased a lot?

v085143: "Irish, Italians, Jewish and many other minorities overcame prejudice and worked their way up. Blacks should do the same without any special favors." Do you agree strongly, agree somewhat, neither agree nor disagree, disagree somewhat or disagree strongly with this statement?

v085144: "Generations of slavery and discrimination have created conditions that make it difficult for blacks to work their way out of the lower class." Do you agree strongly, agree somewhat, neither agree nor disagree, disagree somewhat or disagree strongly with this statement?

v085145: "Over the past few years, blacks have gotten less than they deserve" Do you agree strongly, agree somewhat, neither agree nor disagree, disagree somewhat or disagree strongly with this statement?

v085146: "It's really a matter of some people not trying hard enough; if blacks would only try harder they could be just as well off as whites." Do you agree strongly, agree somewhat, neither agree nor disagree, disagree somewhat or disagree strongly with this statement?

v085157: What about your opinion: are you for or against preferential hiring and promotion of blacks?

v085157a: [If support preferential hiring] Do you favor preference in hiring and promotion strongly or not strongly?

v085157b: [If oppose preferential hiring] Do you oppose preference in hiring and promotion strongly or not strongly?

TABLE C.1 Sample Demographics

	WHITE	BLACK	LATINO	MULTIRACIAL
N	1177	558	427	48
Age				
18–29	15%	18%	25%	23%
30–44	24%	28%	34%	33%
45–59	30%	31%	21%	38%
60+	29%	22%	19%	6%
Refused	2.3%	1.3%	1.2%	0%
% Female	56%	60%	59%	44%
Education				
Less than HS degree	8%	20%	27%	19%
HS degree	32%	38%	32%	29%
Some college	32%	30%	28%	35%
Bachelor's or more	28%	12%	13%	15%
Refused	0.2%	0.2%	0.5%	2%
Household income				
Less than 15K	27%	40%	40%	31%
15K–30K	21%	26%	21%	25%
30K–50K	21%	18%	20%	25%
50K–75K	13%	5%	7%	8%
75K–100K	5%	3%	2%	2%
100K+	7%	1%	3%	6%
Refused	6%	7%	7%	2%
Region				
Northeast	12%	10%	7%	8%
Midwest	21%	22%	2%	21%
South	41%	60%	56%	29%
West	27%	9%	35%	42%
Foreign born (Latinos only)				
% foreign born	n/a	n/a	28.3%	n/a
Party affiliation				
Republican	30%	2%	11%	15%
Democrat	27%	71%	49%	33%

APPENDIX D | *Racial Attitudes in America II*, Pew Research Center for the People and the Press

Survey Question Wording

Q5. Now I'd like your views on some people. As I read some names, please tell me if you have a favorable or unfavorable opinion of each person. First, Barack Obama, would you say your overall opinion of Barack Obama is

Very favorable
Mostly favorable
Mostly unfavorable
Very unfavorable

Q7. Do you think Barack Obama is paying too much attention, not enough attention, or about the right amount of attention to the concerns of blacks?

Q10. Which of these two statements comes closer to your own views—even if neither is exactly right:

1) Our country has made the changes needed to give blacks equal rights with whites [OR]
2) Our country needs to continue making changes to give blacks equal rights with whites

Q37: Please tell me how much discrimination there is against each of these groups in our society today. How about [Insert group]? Would you say there is a lot of discrimination, some, only a little, or none at all?
[Groups randomly ordered]
a) African Americans
b) Hispanic Americans
c) Asian Americans
d) White Americans

Q52: Thinking about the neighborhood where you live, are all, most, some or only a few people [respondent's race]?

Q59: Has Barack Obama's election as president led to better race relations in the United States, worse race relations or hasn't it made a difference?
1) Better
2) Worse
3) Not made a difference

Q63: Do you mostly think of Obama as:
1) A black person [Or mostly as]
2) A person of mixed race

Q64: Thinking about opposition to Barack Obama's policies, do you think that his race is a major reason, a minor reason or not a reason people oppose Barack Obama's policies?
1) Major reason
2) Minor reason
3) Not a reason

Q68: And thinking about the news. . .do you regularly [insert media] or not?
a) Read a daily newspaper
b) Watch the local television news about your area
c) Watch the national news on major network or cable news

Q71: Please tell me which of the following, if any, apply to you. Do you:
a) Consider yourself to be of mixed race
b) Have a child of mixed race

REGIST: These days, many people are so busy they can't time find to register to vote, or move around so often they don't get a change to re-register. Are you NOW registered to vote in your precinct or election district or haven't you been able to register so far?
1) Yes, registered
2) No, not registered

PARTY: In politics today, do you consider yourself a Republican, Democrat or Independent?
1) Republican
2) Democrat
3) Independent

PARTYSTR: [If Republican/Democrat] Do you consider yourself a STRONG [Republican/Democrat] or NOT strong [Republican/Democrat]
1) Strong
2) Not strong

PARTYLN: [If Independent or no party] As of today do you lean more to the Republican Party or to the Democratic Party?
1) Republican
2) Democrat

TABLE D.1 Sample Demographics

	WHITE	BLACK	LATINO	MULTIRACIAL
N	1444	807	363	58
18–29	12%	19%	30%	24%
30–44	19%	20%	30%	36%
45–59	30%	31%	23%	24%
60+	37%	27%	13%	16%
Refused	1.8%	2.4%	4.1%	0%
% Female	54%	57%	56%	62%
Education				
Less than HS degree	4%	14%	26%	2%
HS degree	23%	30%	30%	21%
Some college	29%	31%	22%	26%
Bachelor's or more	43%	24%	19%	52%
Refused	0.6%	0.5%	3.0%	0%
Household Income				
Less than 20K	10%	23%	28%	12%
20K–40K	16%	26%	25%	17%
40K–75K	22%	21%	12%	28%
75K–100K	14%	9%	6%	21%
100K+	21%	9%	10%	14%
Refused	17%	13%	20%	9%
Region				
Northeast	20%	15%	16%	10%
Midwest	28%	21%	4%	19%
South	33%	57%	26%	41%
West	19%	7%	53%	29%
Foreign born				
% foreign born	5.2%	5.3%	59.2%	10%
Party affiliation				
Republican	32%	4%	12%	16%
Democrat	27%	75%	35%	50%

TABLE D.2 Factors Predicting Perceptions of Obama's Race, 2009 Pew

| | RACE OF RESPONDENT | | | | | |
| | WHITE | | BLACK | | LATINO | |
	PR (OBAMA AS BLACK) VS. PR (OBAMA AS MR)	PR (NO POSITION) VS. PR(OBAMA AS MR)	PR (OBAMA AS BLACK) VS. PR (OBAMA AS MR)	PR (NO POSITION) VS. PR(OBAMA AS MR)	PR (OBAMA AS BLACK) VS. PR (OBAMA AS MR)	PR (NO POSITION) VS. PR(OBAMA AS MR)
Demographics						
Age	-.01 (.01)	.02 (.01)*	.003 (.01)	.07 (.01)**	.003 (.02)	.03 (.02)*
Education	.19 (.10)*	-.05 (.11)	.19 (.12)	.06 (.21)	-.09 (.29)	-.27 (.20)
Income	.07 (.05)	.01 (.05)	-.04 (.06)	-.18 (.15)	.14 (.12)	.12 (.15)
Female	-.13 (.20)	-.002 (.23)	-.08 (.24)	-.08 (.43)	-.83 (.47)	.34 (.56)
Foreign born	.47 (.50)	.62 (.52)	-.41 (.61)	.69 (.73)	-.07 (.42)	-.72 (.70)
Politics						
Republican	.32 (.26)	-.11 (.31)	-.28 (.55)	-.52 (.70)	.55 (.70)	1.04 (1.17)
Independent	-.28 (.26)	-.22 (.30)	-.54 (.31)	.10 (.75)	.42 (.52)	1.05 (.85)
Decline to state partisanship	1.38 (.56)*	1.13 (.57)*	-.36 (.65)	-1.43 (.89)	.69 (.91)	2.33 (1.12)*
Registered to vote	.29 (.30)	-.16 (.32)	-.24 (.34)	.04 (.59)	.98 (.44)*	1.12 (.87)

(continued)

TABLE D.2 (Cont.)

	RACE OF RESPONDENT					
	WHITE		BLACK		LATINO	
	PR (OBAMA AS BLACK) VS. PR (OBAMA AS MR)	PR (NO POSITION) VS. PR(OBAMA AS MR)	PR (OBAMA AS BLACK) VS. PR (OBAMA AS MR)	PR (NO POSITION) VS. PR(OBAMA AS MR)	PR (OBAMA AS BLACK) VS. PR (OBAMA AS MR)	PR (NO POSITION) VS. PR(OBAMA AS MR)
Media effects						
High news consumption[a]	-.01 (.10)	.09 (.12)	.07 (.12)	-.19 (.22)	-.25 (.24)	.71 (.38)
Racial attitudes						
Discrimination[b]	.16 (.22)	-.19 (.22)	.43 (.19)*	.80 (.34)*	-.35 (.38)	-.14 (.59)
Racial optimism[c]	.02 (.22)	-.26 (.25)	-.31 (.33)	.19 (.60)	-.91 (.47)	-1.26 (.68)
Contextual effects						
Have a MR child	.09 (.37)	.80 (.42)	-.94 (.35)**	1.39 (.50)**	-.05 (.52)	.07 (.56)
Neighborhood context[d]	-.05 (.13)	-.10 (.16)	-.09 (.12)	-.06 (.19)	-.24 (.22)	-.19 (.27)
Region: West[e]	.02 (.25)	-.48 (.32)	.73 (.50)	.67 (.66)	.24 (.22)	-.04 (.69)
Constant	-1.83 (.68)**	-1.02 (.81)	-.28 (.73)	-5.95 (1.41)	.12 (1.30)	-4.17 (1.61)*
N	1015		602		243	
Log likelihood	-17073.718		-2552.36		-2523.18	

NOTE: Results derived from multinomial logit with those who perceive "Obama as Mixed Race" as the comparison group. Standard errors in parentheses. Results are weighted. Partisanship was measured as dichotomous variables, each representing one of three partisan identifications of Democrat, independent, and Republican. Since there were respondents who declined to state one of these identities, a variable representing those who did not answer the partisanship question was also included in the model. In the models, Democrat is the excluded category. SOURCE: Pew Research Center 2009.

[a] The High news consumption variable was constructed as an index variable that added together the respondent's reporting that she or he regularly (1) read a daily newspaper; (2) watched the local television news about your area; and (3) watched the national news on major network or cable channels. The highest value on this variable reflected regular consumption of all three forms of media. The Cronbach's alpha for the variables in this index is .49.

[b] The Discrimination variable was constructed as an index variable that added together responses to three separate questions about the degree to which there was discrimination against (1) blacks; (2) Latinos and (3) Asian Americans. The highest value on this variable reflected perceptions of "a lot" of discrimination against all three minority groups. The Cronbach's alpha for the variables in this index is .69.

[c] The Racial Optimism variable is represented by the question: "Which of these two statements comes closer to your own views—even if neither is exactly right: (1) Our country has made the changes needed to give blacks equal rights with whites OR (2) Our country needs to continue making changes to give blacks equal rights with whites." The Racial Optimism variable is a dichotomous variable with respondents who believe the country as made the changes needed are given a value of 1.

[d] The Neighborhood context variable represents the self-reported diversity of the respondent's neighborhood. The highest value on this variable is given to those respondents who report that "all" of the respondent's neighborhood is of the same race as the respondent.

[e] Region is a dichotomous variable that compares respondents living in the West and respondents living in all other regions of the United States.

*p < .05 **p < .01

TABLE D.3 Evaluation of President by Perceptions of Obama's Race and Partisanship, White and Latino Respondents Only, 2009

	MEAN FAVORABILITY	TOO MUCH ATTENTION TO BLACKS	BETTER RACE RELATIONS	PEOPLE OPPOSE POLICIES BECAUSE OF OBAMA'S RACE
White respondents				
Dem: Obama as black	.77 (.04)	.49 (.03)	.77 (.04)	.55 (.04)
Dem: Obama as mixed race	.79 (.02)	.48 (.02)	.75 (.03)	.45 (.04)
Indep: Obama as black	.53 (.04)	.48 (.05)	.58 (.05)	.37 (.05)
Indep: Obama as mixed race	.53 (.03)	.53 (.02)	.60 (.03)	.37 (.03)
Rep: Obama as black	.34 (.04)	.61 (.03)	.45 (.04)	.30 (.04)
Rep: Obama as mixed race	.32 (.03)	.57 (.03)	.43 (.03)	.28 (.03)
Latino respondents				
Dem: Obama as black	.90 (.04)	.47 (.04)	.86 (.05)	.55 (.11)
Dem: Obama as mixed race	.81 (.04)	.45 (.05)	.70 (.04)	.54 (.06)
Indep: Obama as black	.84 (.05)	.61 (.09)	.77 (.07)	.59 (.09)
Indep: Obama as mixed race	.79 (.03)	.49 (.03)	.72 (.07)	.55 (.06)
Rep: Obama as black	.45 (.17)	.73 (.09)	.44 (.13)	.51 (.05)

NOTE: All variables on a 0 to 1 scale. Standard errors in parentheses.

APPENDIX E | 2010–2012 Evaluations of Government and Society Survey, Wave 4

Question Wording

A1. Some people seem to follow what's going on in government and public affairs most of the time, whether there's an election going on or not. Others aren't that interested. Would you say you follow what's going on in government and public affairs most of the time, some of the time, only now and then or hardly at all?

C2. Please look at the graphic below. We'd like to get your feelings toward some of our political leaders and other people who are in the news these days. We'll show the name of a person and we'd like you to rate that person using something we call the feeling thermometer. Ratings between 50 and 100 degrees mean you feel favorable and warm toward the person. Ratings between 0 and 50 degrees mean that you don't feel favorable toward the person and that you don't care too much for that person. You would rate the person at the 50 degree mark if you don't feel particularly warm or cold toward the person.

How would you rate Barack Obama?

D1. Are you registered to vote or not?

G1. Do you approve, disapprove or neither approve nor disapprove of the way Barack Obama is handling his job as president?

Do you [approve/disapprove] Extremely strongly, Moderately strongly or Slightly strongly

N1–N6. Generally speaking, do you consider yourself a Republican, Democrat or Independent?

[If Republican/Democrat] Do you consider yourself a STRONG [Republican/Democrat] or NOT strong [Republican/Democrat]

[If Independent or no party] Do you think of yourself closer to the Republican Party or to the Democratic Party?

Republican

Democrat

Neither

S1–S8. How much discrimination is there in the United States today against each of the following groups? A great deal, A lot, A moderate amount, A little, or None at all

- Blacks
- Latinos
- Whites
- Gays and Lesbians
- Women
- Men
- Christians
- Muslims

Z3–Z8. Do you think what happens generally to [black/Hispanic/white] people in this country will have something to do with what happens in your life?
Yes
No

Will it affect you a lot, some or not very much?

ZA.1–ZA.4. Do you agree strongly, agree somewhat, neither agree nor disagree, disagree somewhat or disagree strongly with each of the following statements?

- Irish, Italians, Jewish and many other minorities overcame prejudice and worked their way up. Blacks should do the same without any special favors.
- Generations of slavery and discrimination have created conditions that make it difficult for blacks to work their way out of the lower class.
- Over the past few years, blacks have gotten less than they deserve
- It's really a matter of some people not trying hard enough; if blacks would only try harder they could be just as well off as whites.

ZM16. What is Barack Obama's religion?
Protestant
Catholic
Jewish
Muslim
Mormon
Something else
Not religious

ZP0. How would you describe Barack Obama's race? Mark all that apply [Racial categories randomized]
White
Black
Hispanic
Mixed race
Asian
Other race

ZP7. In appointing people to his administration, do you think Barack Obama as paid too much attention to selecting people on the basis of race and gender, has paid too little attention or has paid just the right amount of attention?

TABLE E.1 Sample Demographics

	WHITE	BLACK	LATINO
N	1,038	94	114
Age			
18–29	14%	18%	22%
30–44	19%	23%	34%
45–59	31%	26%	24%
60+	36%	33%	20%
% Female	**53%**	**53%**	**48%**
Education			
Less than HS degree	6%	10%	18%
HS degree	27%	30%	31%
Some college	29%	39%	29%
Bachelor's or more	37%	21%	23%
Household income			
Less than 20K	9%	15%	14%
20K–40K	17%	26%	25%
40K–75K	29%	29%	24%
75K–100K	15%	18%	14%
100K+	30%	13%	24%
Region			
Northeast	20%	14%	20%
Midwest	28%	18%	9%
South	32%	57%	33%
West	20%	11%	38%
Foreign born			
% foreign born	1.9%	8.5%	14.0%
Party affiliation			
Republican	34%	1%	19%
Democrat	28%	76%	45%

TABLE E.2 Factors Predicting Perceptions of Obama's Race as Black, EGSS 2012

	RACE OF RESPONDENT		
	WHITE	BLACK	LATINO
Sociodemographic			
Age	−.00 (.01)	−.03 (.06)	.12 (.07)
Education	.16 (.17)	−.03 (.60)	−.15 (.52)
Income	−.06 (.04)	−.69 (.28)	−.06 (.10)
Female	−.29 (.26)	.24 (.1.06)	−.54 (.89)
Foreign born		−3.96 (2.10)	1.95 (1.57)
Politics			
Republican	−.22 (1.13)		2.41 (4.51)
Independent	−.39 (.61)	−4.41 (2.63)	−.59 (3.13)
Other pol. party	−.03 (.22)	.01 (.90)	−.22 (1.08)
Media effects			
Follow politics	−.05 (.15)	1.08 (.96)	−1.19 (.78)
Racial attitudes			
Discrimination[a]	−.01 (.08)	.15 (.23)	−.07 (.32)
Racial resentment[b]	.08 (.05)	−.27 (.51)	.07 (.19)
Racial linked fate	−.09 (.12)	−.56 (.37)	−1.32 (.61)*
Contextual effects			
Live in West[c]	.26 (.33)	−.41 (1.91)	1.02 (1.02)
Constant	−1.12 (1.02)	11.08 (7.97)	−.42 (4.01)
N	479	43	56
Log likelihood	−232.46	−17.98	−30.99

NOTE: Results derived from logistic regression, Results compare perceptions of Obama as "black" compared to perceptions of Obama as "mixed race" or two or more races. Excludes respondents who did not respond to the question or who reported Obama as "white." Standard errors in parentheses. Results are weighted. Partisanship was measured as dichotomous variables, each representing one of three partisan identifications of Democrat, independent, and Republican. Since there were respondents who chose not to state one of these three partisan identities, a variable representing those who did not answer the partisanship question was also included in the model. In the models, Democrat is the excluded category. SOURCE: EGSS 2012.
[a] The Discrimination variable was constructed as an index variable that added together responses to three separate questions about the degree to which there was discrimination against (1) blacks and (2) Latinos. The highest value on this variable reflected perceptions of "a lot" of discrimination against both groups. The Cronbach's alpha for the variables in this index is .81.
[b] Racial resentment was constructed as an index variable that combined responses to four questions typically used in the racial resentment index (see Kinder and Sanders 1990). The Cronbach's alpha for the index is .82.
[c] Region is a dichotomous variable that compares respondents living in the West and respondents living in all other regions of the United States.
$*p < .05$ $**p < .01$

TABLE E.3 Evaluation of President by Perceptions of Obama's Race and Partisanship, White and Latino Respondents Only, 2012

	FEELING THERM.	JOB APPROVAL	OBAMA IS MUSLIM	TOO MUCH FOCUS ON RACE & GENDER
White respondents				
Dem: Obama as black	.64 (.04)	.59 (.04)	.20 (.06)	.52 (.02)
Dem: Obama as mixed race / other	.75 (.02)	.69 (.03)	.11 (.03)	.49 (.02)
Indep: Obama as black	.44 (.04)	.33 (.04)	.30 (.06)	.55 (.03)
Indep: Obama as mixed race / other	.43 (.02)	.35 (.02)	.23 (.03)	.57 (.02)
Rep: Obama as black	.15 (.03)	.11 (.02)	.57 (.06)	.72 (.03)
Rep: Obama as mixed race / other	.19 (.02)	.14 (.02)	.39 (.04)	.64 (.02)
Latino respondents				
Dem: Obama as black	.69 (.12)	.70 (.08)	.59 (.14)	.47 (.03)
Dem: Obama as mixed race / other	.69 (.07)	.63 (.08)	.27 (.11)	.45 (.05)
Indep: Obama as black	.54 (.12)	.56 (.04)	[a]	.56 (.10)
Indep: Obama as mixed race / other	.50 (.10)	.48 (.11)	[a]	.44 (.05)
Rep: Obama as black	.47 (.15)	.33 (.11)	.41 (.19)	.54 (.07)
Rep: Obama as mixed race / other	.26 (.08)	.25 (.11)	.18 (.13)	.68 (.10)

NOTE: All variables on a 0 to 1 scale. Standard errors in parentheses
[a] Results omitted due to nonresponse to the question.

NOTES

Chapter 1

1. Emphasis in original.

2. Haya El Nasser, "Multiracial No Longer Boxed in by the Census," *USA Today*, March 15, 2010, online edition, http://www.usatoday.com/news/nation/census/2010-03-02-census-multi-race_N.htm.

3. Todd Lewan, "Attitudes toward Multiracial Americans Evolving," *USA Today*, June 15, 2008, online edition, http://www.usatoday.com/news/nation/2008-06-15-race_N.htm.

4. Since the Supreme Court decision in the *Loving v. Virginia* case in 1967, which ruled antimiscegenation laws unconstitutional, the number of reported interracial marriages has grown from 150,000 in 1960 to 5 million in 2000 (Lee and Edmonston 2005). A Pew study estimates that approximately 8.4% of all marriages in the United States are interracial and 15.1% of new marriages in 2010 were interracial (Wang 2012).

5. I recognize that the focus on only four groups—whites, blacks, Asian Americans, and Latinos—does not reflect an exhaustive set of the racial categories used in the United States. The federal government recognizes indigenous groups such as American Indian, Alaskan Native, Native Hawaiians, and Pacific Islanders as distinctive racial groups. Because of data limitations and because these indigenous groups hold a unique legal status in the United States that is different from that held by whites, blacks, Asian Americans, and Latinos, these indigenous groups will be excluded from most analyses in this book. I hope that future research will incorporate the experiences of these indigenous groups.

6. At its most extreme, a growing contingent of Americans believe that race is now irrelevant to American life and so the country can now engage in decisions that are "color-blind." These frames fortify American liberalism and a public belief that individual merit is the primary factor in personal success. At the same time, scholars have been critical of the color-blind perspective; see Bonilla-Silva 2003.

7. For more information, see the "Federal Guidance on Maintaining, Collecting and Reporting Racial and Ethnic Data to the U.S. Department of Education," *Federal Register* 72(202): 59266–59279. See also http://nces.ed.gov/ipeds/reic/resource.asp.

8. US Congress, House, Subcommittee on Census, Statistics and Postal Personnel, Committee on Post Office and Civil Service, *Hearings on the Review of Federal Measurement of Race and Ethnicity*, testimony by Carlos Fernandez, June 30, 1993, 127. Downloaded from http://amea.site/classification/tstmny93.asp

9. For the transcript see http://www.cnn.com/2007/POLITICS/07/23/debate.transcript/.

10. Of course, identification with a racial category represents one of many dimensions reflecting how an individual understands race. Other scholarship has developed different measures to document how an individual processes race, such as level of racial prejudice or resentment, implicit racial attitudes, and personality scales such as ethnocentrism (Dovidio, Kawakami, and Gaertner 2002; Kinder and Kam 2009; Kinder and Sanders 1996; Sears et al. 1997). However, many of these scales involve assessment of out-groups and perceptions of racial conflict. In contrast, racial identification is an indicator of how the individual understands her own orientation in the context of the American racial hierarchy (Masuoka and Junn 2013). Moreover, Americans practice racial identification often in their everyday life. A person is more often asked to describe her racial identity than, for example, asked to deliberate the implications of institutionalized racism.

11. We know that racial identity is associated with other many important factors, such as self-esteem and belonging to groups (Goodstein and Ponterotto 1997; Phinney and Chavira 1992; Rumbaut 1994; Steele 2010). Although studies on early childhood and adolescent development show that early in life, racial identities are flexible and subject to surrounding social contexts (Phinney 1990; Quintana 2007), it is typically the case that the majority of even young adults report the same racial identity across contexts and that their attachment to their ethnic identities increases with age (Harris and Sim 2002; Kiang et al. 2010; Nishina et al. 2010). So while not all possible social identities a person could use to characterize her sense of self reflect purposeful and meaningful descriptions, how a person describes her race is generally recognized by Americans to have social or political consequence.

12. In this book, "Latinos" will be designated as one group and in most discussions will be labeled as a racial group, or "monoracial." However, those who claim to be Latino but also assert a multiracial identity will be included in the self-identified multiracial population. I acknowledge that describing Latinos as one racial group is not consistent with Latinos' official federal classification as an "ethnic" group. Today, the federal government defines Latinos as an ethnicity, which means one can be Latino and one of the six racial categories of white, black, Asian, American Indian / Alaska Native or Pacific Islander / Native Hawaiian, or "some other race." Because the objective of this book is to understand and explain multiracial identification, I choose not to focus on the problematized classification of Latinos as an "ethnic" group and rather treat Latinos as a group to be contrasted with the three other major racial groups: whites, blacks, and Asian Americans. Because I believe that a discussion about race in the United States should include a discussion that incorporates Latinos, I made the decision toinclude rather than to exclude Latinos. For a more extensive discussion of Latinos as an "ethnic" or "racial" group, see Rodriguez 2000.

13. This is the term Tiger Woods infamously used in a1997 interview on the Oprah Winfrey show. Some hypothesize that this interview helped garner greater public recognition that there are multiracial identities (Cole and Andrews 2011; Ibrahim 2009).

14. There is indeed a growing literature that explores these topics. See Hochschild, Weaver, and Burch 2011; Pauker et al. 2009; Rockquemore and Brunsma 2007.

Chapter 2

1. Labor practices were generally governed by English law—drawn from the Elizabethan Statute of Artificers. These laws protected white servants, for example, by limiting the total number of hours worked per day. These laws were not extended to black slaves, but since there was minimal distinction between black slaves and white servants in practice, laws that protected servants tended to protect slaves (Berlin 2000).

2. These early images brought over by explorers were promoted in brochures and other documentation about the indigenous people in the New World and played a role in creating popular racialized stereotypes of Native Americans among Europeans (Berkhofer 1979; Powell 2005; Smedley and Smedley 2012; Smits 1987). Because of this, settlers often had specific expectations of Native Americans before they reached North America. Early anthropological studies also characterized Native Americans as a distinctive race. Linnaeus's influential *Systema naturae* in 1735 described four races of humans, with Native Americans representing one of the four and characterized them as "reddish, single-minded and guided by tradition" (cited in Powell 2005, 30). Native Americans were conceived as a race inferior to European whites and, though they recognized distinct tribes, Europeans often referred to Native Americans as one homogenized category of "Indian" (Berkhofer 1979; Wilkins and Lomawaima 2001).

3. Acceptance of intermarriages between whites and Native Americans varied by European group. The French and Spanish often viewed intermarriage as a pragmatic practice in the New World. In contrast, the English were generally averse to white–Native American marriages (Smits 1987). In 1691, English settlers in Virginia passed a law prohibiting Anglo–Native American marriages (Smits 1987). In contrast, early Spanish policy encouraged Spanish–Native American mixing, as it was perceived to spread Spanish identity in the New World population (Martinez 2008).

4. American leaders witnessed how these tribes entered agreements with other European nations and organized alliances with the British during the Revolutionary War. As a result, the new American government established relationships with tribes through (international) treaties. The federal government also recognized the national autonomy of the tribes by enumerating Native Americans as "Indians not taxed" in the census (see also Smith 1999). Although these practices could have implied that Native Americans were seen as equal to whites, the fact that treaties were often signed under trickery, ignored, or broken when convenient does suggest that, in practice, whites did not view Native Americans as equals.

5. The Dawes Allotment Act of 1887 sought to divide Native American reservation land, which was originally held by tribal governments, into smaller parcels that would be owned by individuals. In order to determine which individuals would be eligible for land grants under the act, the Dawes Commission established a rule of blood quantum to define a Native American person (Gross 2008).

6. Woods (2003) traces documents recorded by the Cherokee Nation—the first tribe to formally record tribal rules regarding marriage—and finds that over time, the tribe's attitudes toward blacks increasingly align with those of whites. In 1819, the Cherokee tribe regulated rights awarded to white-Cherokee marriages and then declared a ban on black-Cherokee marriages in 1924. In 1827, the New Echota Constitution eliminates tribal citizenship rights for those of partial black descent. Other tribes besides the Cherokee held blacks as slaves (McCloughlin 1974). However, it may not be the case that

all tribes sought to discriminate against blacks. For example, some historians argue that black members of the Seminole Nation in Florida were integrated as equals into the tribe (Gross 2008).

7. The history of indigenous peoples in the United States is extremely rich. While the topic is worthy of attention, it is too complex to document distinctive tribal relationships in this chapter. The federal government—as described in the policies under the Department of the Interior—officially recognizes 561 distinctive tribes, all of which hold sovereign powers as a distinct nation (Wilkins 2002). However, because most indigenous people are subject to a similar relationship with the federal government, I discuss them as one group in the remainder of this book. My decision to exclude a comparison between multiracial individuals and Native Americans is rooted in the fact that Native Americans do not have the same relationship with the federal government as do American racial groups (see Deloria and Wilkins 2000; Wilkins 2002). Indigenous tribes are simultaneously sovereign nations and wards of the state, but one set of laws governs relationships between indigenous tribes and the US government (Wilkins and Lomawaima 2001; see also Smith 1999). It should also be noted that Native Hawaiians are subject to a different set of rules and are not a recognized tribe by the Department of the Interior (Wilkins 2002).

8. In addition, early European perspectives often justified the status of African slaves on religious grounds. Africans were thought of as barbaric peoples who practiced heathen rituals. Their lack of a civilized culture and Christian religion was perceived to be punished by God. Europeans characterized Africans as descendants of Noah's son, Ham; their black skin was a visible curse made by God. Africans were thus fated to live as slaves because of their ancient sins (Fredickson 2003; Myrdal 1944).

9. It was the invention of the cotton gin in 1793 that dramatically changed the economy in the South. Global demand for cotton created a new economic sector and need for slave labor (Foner 1983).

10. By counting blacks as three-fifths of a person in the census enumeration, the Framers also ensured greater political power to southern states, allowing southern representatives to protect their interests in future legislatures. Foner (1999) notes that between 1788 and 1848, all but four presidents were southern slave-owners. These decisions helped to protect the practice from political interference, which ultimately helped to institutionalize slavery in the American political culture.

11. Ideals of liberty and equality were understood as political rights and could only be awarded to those individuals who were able to take part in governance. A democratic government requires that citizens deliberate and make appropriate decisions regarding what is best for the political community. Early liberal thinkers, such as Locke, argued that those incapable of governance, such as children, should be placed under the guardianship of capable minds (their parents) until they were capable to taking part in the political community (Schuck and Smith 1985). Black slaves were assumed to be intellectually unable to contribute to governance.

12. Nativists targeted this law as too generous given the relatively short period of residency of two years. This law was very quickly changed by extending this residency period in 1795. Further restrictions were made through the Alien and Sedition Acts of 1798, which extended the residency requirement to fourteen years (Tichenor 2002).

13. This argument was later echoed in other state court cases deciding black citizenship rights in the southern states (Foner 2014). Throughout the antebellum period, those

who challenged the assumptions of the racial order were increasingly threatened and targeted. Free blacks began losing many liberties originally provided to them. In fact, the harshest laws against free blacks were passed in the years immediately preceding the Civil War.

14. Original federal policy toward tribal lands recognized tribes as sovereign nations but then shifted to a policy framing Indians as dependents (Wilkins 2002). The 1787 Northwest Ordinance and the 1790 Trade and Intercourse Act established that land transfers were to be made through international treaty. But with the 1823 ruling *Johnson v. McIntosh* the Supreme Court upheld a doctrine of discovery that upheld the European right to land and diminished the power of Indian land rights. During the first half of the nineteenth century under a policy of removal, Indians were removed to reservations and placed under administrative oversight by the Bureau of Indian Affairs within the Department of the Interior.

15. The first case to reach the Supreme Court in 1922 was *Ozawa v. United States*, in which the plaintiff claimed whiteness on the basis of his skin color. Ozawa, a Japanese immigrant, claimed to be white since his skin was the same visible color as others who were classified as white. The Supreme Court ruled that race was not determined solely by skin color. In the second case to reach the Supreme Court, *Thind v. United States* (1923), the plaintiff, who was born in India, claimed to be of the Caucasian race based on anthropological studies that declared India to be a part of the Caucasus region. The Supreme Court ruled that the definition of white must meet the "understanding of the common man" and a common man would not say Indians are white. See Haney-Lopez 2006.

16. Interestingly, while nonwhite classification appeared to be clear for immigrants arriving from East and Southeast Asia, the federal courts could not decide the "whiteness" of Syrians, Armenians, Arabs, and Mexicans. Court decisions on the racial classification of these groups contradicted one another. See Haney Lopez 2006.

17. However, Snipp (2003) argues that classification for Native Americans has increasingly followed the rule of hyperdescent, which meant that individuals who deemed to have an insufficient amount of Native American ancestry are excluded from classification as Native American.

18. For extensive histories on these three major policies see Davidson and Grofman 1994; Grofman 2000; Tichenor 2002. On explaining the rise of the modern civil rights movement, see McAdam 1999.

19. A more detailed examination on the patterns of interracial marriage still reveals significant racial and gendered biases. When comparing groups, there is a lower rate of interracial marriages among blacks than among Latinos and Asians. Most interracial marriages involve one white partner. In terms of gender, Asian women are more likely to be in an interracial marriage than Asian men, while black men are more likely to be in an interracial marriage than black women. See Lee and Edmonston 2005 and Wang 2012.

20. It is an incorrect assumption that the current US population is now more diverse than historical populations (Higham 2002). Immigration statistics, for example, show that the level of immigration today is no higher than at the turn of the twentieth century. Jill Lepore (2003) estimates that the percentage of nonnative English speakers in the United States was greater in 1790 than in 1990 (see also Schuck 2003).

21. In contrast to the growing anti-immigrant sentiment at the time, Kallen argued that cultural diversity was essential to American intellectual and economic growth since

cultural retention allowed people to embrace their individuality. He directly opposed theories of assimilation that advocated cultural homogeneity. At the same time, Kallen emphasized a collective sense of national unity and offered the insight that solidarity could be rooted in shared democratic ideals rather than a shared Anglo-Protestant culture (see also Gerstle 2001). While some might see scholars such as Kallen as ahead of their time, others would argue that scholars who privileged national unity largely ignored institutionalized practices that formally excluded certain segments of the population, such as women, immigrants, and racial minorities (Rathner 1984). Iris Marion Young (1990) insists that establishment of one dominant meaning, such as those attached to national identity, assumes that all individuals share the same experiences. Young argues that dominant meanings reflect the worldviews of the dominant group, which, in turn, render excluded groups as irrelevant. Modern scholars who defend diversity thus do not necessarily advocate for one shared identity or set of values but rather that the governing system allow unique policies for different groups (see also Carens 2000; Kymlicka 1996; Taylor 1994).

22. I note that American opinion does not always correspond with actual behavior. Wang et al.'s (2008) study, which reported American preference for living in diverse environments also showed that in reality, most Americans live in largely homogenous environments. However, positive orientation to diversity and multiculturalism is important for multiracial identification because it creates a cultural environment in which the public is accepting of these identities.

23. Opponents proclaimed that a multicultural curriculum promoted ethnic balkanization and potentially erroneous facts about American history (Schlesinger 1998; Thernstrom and Thernstrom 1997). Yet in 1997, vocal critic of the multicultural perspective Nathan Glazer (1998) proclaimed in the title of his book that "we are all multiculturalists now." While Glazer did not necessarily change his views, he found that the multicultural ideal had become fully integrated into the American education system.

24. The embrace of equality and diversity as public goods can be seen as a cultural change that occurred primarily among white Americans. The civil rights movement indeed influenced all Americans, but attitude changes found among racial minority groups are substantively different from those among white Americans. As the victims of racial discrimination, racial minorities have historically rejected racist ideologies employed to justify the racial order. For example, public opinion analyses by Schuman et al. (1997) show that blacks have long rejected old-fashioned racist ideas and have long desired diversity and inclusion. In general, black values of equality and incorporation have remained consistent since the 1960s civil rights changes. Furthermore, legal challenges against racial segregation and exclusion waged by Asian and Latino groups suggest that these groups also rejected white supremacist ideals (Acuna 2010; Hing 1994; Takaki 1998).

25. The assimilationist ideal has been revised and rearticulated over the course of the twentieth century but in general embraces the preference that all Americans share an Anglo-Protestant culture. See, for example, Huntington 2004.

26. The first scholarly association for ethnic studies, the National Association of Interdisciplinary Studies for Native American, Black, Chicano, Puerto Rican and Asian Americans was formed in 1972. Today the association is entitled the National Association

of Ethnic Studies. Documentation of this association's history is found at http://ethnic-studies.org/about/naes-history.

27. The Census Bureau website has published most of the directions distributed to the enumerators. The directions for 1940 can be found at https://www.census.gov/history/www/through_the_decades/census_instructions/1940_instructions.html.

28. Special footnotes were provided on how to deal with unique populations such as the Melungeon population, a mixed-race population that resulted from the interaction between runaway slaves, Native Americans, and isolated whites who lived in the Appalachian Mountains (see also Gross 2008).

29. I emphasize the importance of self-report, but not every single American gets to self-report his or her own race. The census is a household survey in which one person completes the survey for all members of the household. Therefore, while enumerators do not impose race, it is possible that the head of the household could assign a race to a member of the household that does not match that person's self-identification.

30. See also arguments on the rise of self-identification on the census by Dacosta 2007; Rodriguez 2000; Yanow 2003

31. Although Williams (2006) documents the lobbying efforts by a specific group of activists, Wallman, Evinger, and Schechter (2000) also show that a sizable number of Americans wrote in some form of multiracial identity in their responses to the race question on the 1990 census. Thus, there was also evidence from census data to support the claims made by multiracial activists.

32. Scholars identify both positive and negative consequences to the "mark one or more" option. On the one hand, it may encourage multiracial identification, but, on the other hand, it makes monitoring racial discrimination more difficult. For example, can an individual who identifies as both white and black file a legal case citing racial discrimination as a black person? Since 2000, the federal government has included in the black population individuals who mark multiple races so long as black is one of them. See discussions by Goldstein and Morning 2002; Harrison 2002; Persily 2002; Williams 2006.

33. For identified concerns and criticisms of the continued practice of collecting racial data, see Hirschman, Alba, and Farley 2000; Prewitt 2013; Skerry 2000. For an argument why data on racial categories need to be collected by the census, see Goldstein and Morning 2002.

34. See an interesting work by social psychologist, Marilynn Brewer (1991,) who argues that individuals strive to attain what she calls "optimal distinctiveness." Brewer argues that humans have a dual need to both feel included in a group and be identified as uniquely distinctive. These two desires largely explain group identity formation.

35. As Roediger (2006) highlights, early European immigrants could not freely celebrate their ethnic identities during the period that their white racial status was being questioned.

36. Latinos were not always classified as an ethnic group. In 1930, "Mexican" appeared on the census as a racial category, in an attempt to trace the influx of Mexican migrants into the United States. Concerned that the federal government would use that racial data to impose discriminatory measures, Mexican American civic groups and the Mexican government lobbied to remove Mexican from the list of racial categories (Hattam 2007; Nobles 2000). It was omitted from the 1940 and later censuses.

Chapter 3

1. Early theories of social group identity revealed how quickly and easily individuals became attached to a group identity. Experiments showed that people could develop strong identities from inconsequential characteristics such as the same eye color (Tajfel and Turner 1979; Tajfel 1981). Brewer (1991) showed that they key factors that determined the strength of social group identification were a desire for social belonging and the ability to maintain some individuality.

2. The federal government uses what is called a maximum allocation formula. For example, the black population comprises both those who select "black" as their racial category and those who select two or more races with "black" as one of them.

3. One of the groups was located in Canada and so was excluded from the sample of organizations.

4. At the time these interviews were conducted in 2006, only certain federal entities, for example, the Census Bureau, had implemented the Office of Management and Budget's guidelines for the mark-one-or-more option. However, other federal agencies and state and local agencies later adopted the option so their data would be consistent with census data. For example, the Department of Education published new guidelines in 2007 that included the option, and public schools were required to follow the guidelines. When state and local government entities use federal funds to provide services, their data collection practices must correspond with federal guidelines.

5. I spoke with one respondent who was involved in the lobbying efforts to pass SB 1615 in California that was not a member of a multiracial organization but rather a local chapter of the Japanese American Citizens League (JACL). This self-identified multiracial respondent had been organizing activities involving multiracial issues within his JACL chapter and had collaborated with other multiracial organizations to mobilize support for SB 1615.

6. This was a viewpoint expressed by Republican leaders during committee hearings to change the 2000 census race question (Williams 2006). This viewpoint also was publicly prominent when Ward Connerly, a conservative activist, sought to pass a voter initiative in California, Proposition 54, entitled the Racial Privacy Initiative, that aimed to eliminate the race question from official forms (Hosang 2010). Connerly argued that if racial categories were eliminated, citizens would be less likely to emphasize racial boundaries, which in turn would reduce problems associated with race. This proposition was placed on the ballot in 2003, three years prior to the time I conducted these interviews.

Chapter 4

1. Some analyses presented in this chapter have been published in an article in *American Politics Research* (see Masuoka 2011).

2. This is a Hawaiian term, originally *hapa haole*, which means "half foreigner" or, in practice, "half white." Recently, the term *hapa* has been embraced by some Asian Americans to refer to the Asian multiracial population more broadly (Takaki 1998). The rise of self-identified hapas has been documented in texts on Asian American history and society (see, for example, Kibria 2002; Okihiro 2004; Takaki 1998). However, others are more critical of the term. Chang (2014) argues that the more inclusive meaning of the term lumps together Asian Americans and Native Hawaiians, as if there were minimal

differences among them. Moreover, she argues that the colonial history that led to the mixing of Native Hawaiians with other racial groups has different political meaning than does the process of interracial marriage experienced by Asian Americans.

3. In general, there are relatively fewer academic studies on Latinos and multiracial identities. However, Jimenez's (2010) study on multiethnic Mexican Americans in California suggests that Latino children of interracial marriages face experiences similar to those that have been found for black and Asian American children of interracial marriages.

4. It should be noted, however, that while racial self-identification is increasingly the norm for public opinion surveys, some major surveys continued to use interviewer-assigned race in their data collection procedures after the census changed its procedures. For example, the General Social Survey, which has collected data on American social life since 1952, used interviewer assigned race as a measure until 2000. Research by Smith (2001) and Saperstein (2006) shows that racial demographics of a survey population differ when researchers use a self-identification measure than when interviewers assign race.

5. Hirschman, Alba, and Farley (2000) conducted a study for the Census Bureau to test the willingness of individuals to use the multiple-races option as compared to a multiracial category (as activists lobbied for). They found that that the multiracial population was actually larger using the mark-one-or-more option. Their study thus suggested that Americans were less willing to designate themselves as multiracial when forced to only select one racial category. Therefore, enumerators were more likely to identify a larger multiracial population when respondents were given the option to declare multiple races. This study demonstrates the importance of measurement when accounting for race.

6. This telephone survey, conducted between March 8 and April 22, 2001, provides a nationally representative sample of 1,790 adults, with oversamples of African American, Latino, and Asian American respondents. Respondents were given the option to be interviewed in English, Spanish, Korean, Mandarin, Cantonese, Vietnamese, or Japanese. The interviews were conducted by ICR/International Communications Research using the Computer Assisted Telephone Interviewing (CATI) system. The minority oversample was obtained through a stratified sample determined by the Optimal Sample Allocation sampling technique. Utilizing the American Association for Public Opinion Research (AAPOR) Response Rate 4, the overall response rate for this survey was 40%. The margin of sampling error for the entire sample is +/− 3. The margin of error for blacks is +/− 6, for Latinos +/− 7, and for Asians +/− 9. Table B2 in the appendix presents summary statistics of the sample.

7. For full question wording on all the measures used for the WKH 2001 analysis, see appendix B.

8. Table B3 in the Appendix reports how respondents answered this question.

9. In the WKH 2001 survey, respondents were offered the opportunity to declare themselves to be of mixed race after answering questions regarding their parents' racial backgrounds. See appendix B, table B2 for a summary of how respondents answered this survey item

10. The WKH survey fortunately offered multiple measures to identify the respondent's financial hardship beyond income. Income is the most common measure of a respondent's financial resources, but is not the most valid measure. Respondents often choose not to answer the income question. More importantly, research has shown that

annual household income is not the same as family wealth (Oliver and Shapiro 2006). Since there were multiple available measures on this survey, I included an additional variable accounting for financial hardship in this model. This variable is an index variable that adds together the experience of three forms of financial hardship: difficulty paying rent, difficulty paying for healthcare, and difficulty saving money for future needs. The Cronbach's alpha for this index is .60. There is a moderate correlation between income and financial hardship of .31.

11. Urban residence is a variable created by WKH researchers using census data and definitions. It is operationalized as a nominal variable with three categories of urban, suburban, and rural. In my specified models, urban is the excluded category.

12. In the WKH 2001 dataset, the correlation between living in a racially integrated neighborhood and living in an urban area is only .14. Thus, I am able to include both variables in the analysis.

13. For Perceived discrimination, I created an index variable adding together the respondent's perceived level of racial discrimination against each of the major three minority groups: blacks, Latinos, and Asian Americans. The Cronbach's alpha for this index is .77. For the Experience discrimination measure, the WKH 2001 included questions that offered different everyday circumstances in which an individual may experience racial discrimination, such as poor treatment in restaurants or being called names. I used an index variable that added together the total number of experiences witnessed by the respondent. This offered a more nuanced measure of discrimination than the commonly employed dichotomous measure, which bluntly asks the respondent whether or not he or she has experienced racial discrimination. The Cronbach's alpha for this Experience discrimination index is .72.

14. The WKH 2001 survey unfortunately did not include a question about immigrant status, I considered including a proxy for immigration: if the survey was conducted in a non-English language. However, given the small number of respondents who conducted the survey in a non-English language and lack of variation across the dependent variable, this proxy was dropped from the analysis by STATA. Given these problems, I did not include the variable in the final multivariate model presented in table 4.2.

15. In this model, I operationalized political ideology as a nominal variable with four categories: liberal, moderate, conservative, and nonideological. The WKH 2001 offered respondents the opportunity to state that they did not have a clear political ideology; 31% of the respondents reported being nonideological, likely because of the large oversamples of Asian American and Latino respondents (see Hajnal and Lee 2011 for an explanation of Asian and Latino nonpartisanship). Therefore, by operationalizing ideology as a nominal variable I could ensure that all respondents were included in the analysis. In my specified model, liberal is the excluded category.

16. This is an appropriate sequence that eliminates any question order effects that might occur through nonrandomization of questions. Nearly all demographic and major political attitude surveys today ask about racial background using the "established method." Thus, respondents should not be surprised or primed differently than they would in any other survey by being asked the Hispanic and racial identification questions first. Consistent with federal practice, the WKH 2001 asked first a Hispanic ethnicity question, then a racial classification question. To calculate the frequencies for the *Established method*, I combined responses to the Hispanic ethnicity question and racial

identification question to identify non-Latino whites, non-Latino blacks, non-Latino Asians, and Latinos.

17. It is difficult to say how the rule of hypodescent applies to Mexicans. Originally Mexicans were classified as white by virtue of their citizenship status after the Mexican-American War (Haney Lopez 2006). Although in practice Mexicans were not treated as equal to whites, social norms that incorporated rules of blood quantum to exclude Mexicans from the white racial category did not apply given Mexican's white racial classification (Hollinger 2005).

18. The total sample sizes presented in table 4.3 do not directly correspond with the sample sizes reported in table 4.1. Respondents were dropped from the analysis for table 4.3 if they failed to answer either the parental ancestry or the self-as-mixed-race questions. As already noted, some respondents reported having parents of the same race but reported a race for themselves that is different from the parents; race. These respondents were also dropped from the analysis in this table.

19. This is consistent with other findings. Herman (2004) examined how children with parents of two different races racially identify in instances when they are allowed to choose only one racial category. These children were more likely to say they were a racial minority. However, the racial mixture of the child did influence the results: those with a black parent were more likely to identify as a racial minority than those with an Asian or Latino parent.

20. I define identity consistency as responses to survey items that might not expectedly match; however, scholars measure identity inconsistency using other strategies. For example, Doyle and Kao's (2007) longitudinal study of adolescents found that a good share of self-identified multiracials change their preferred racial identities over time, while those who identify with monoracial identities—white, black, and Asian—hold consistent identities over time.

21. These findings do contradict the conclusions by Lee and Bean (2006), who argue that those of Asian American or Latino descent have more flexible options for self-identifying as multiracial than those of black descent. These authors argue that because Asian Americans and Latinos conceive their racial/ethnic identities to be defined by narrow and exclusive group boundaries, those who believe they are of mixed racial descent are encouraged to identify as multiracial rather than as monoracial. In contrast, since the black category has been defined as a broad and inclusive category in which a person of any level of black ancestry is considered "black," Lee and Bean argue that those of mixed black ancestry are encouraged to self-identify as (monoracial) black.

22. *Racial Attitudes in America II* is a telephone survey of 2,884 adults. The interviews were completed between October 28 and November 30, 2009, and were conducted in both English and Spanish. Both black and Latino respondents were targeted for oversampling. The study also targeted both cell phone and landlines to improve the quality of the data. The AAPOR Response Rate 3 for the entire sample is approximately 22.9%. Please see table D1 in the appendix for summary statistics of the sample.

23. See appendix D for full question wording of the survey measures used in the 2009 Pew analysis.

24. For this measure, I used a variable operationalized by Pew researchers. This variable integrated population data from the 2000 census and ranked the respondent's county

on the degree of population density. The variable is operationalized as an ordinal variable on a range of 1 indicating low density to 5 indicating high density.

25. For Perceived discrimination, I created an index variable adding together the respondent's perceived level of racial discrimination against each of the major three minority groups: blacks, Latinos, and Asian Americans. The Cronbach's alpha for this index is .69. Given the significant results for the experience of discrimination in the WKH 2001 analysis, it would be ideal to examine the effects of experiences of discrimination. Unfortunately, the 2009 Pew survey did not include an item to identify if a respondent had personally experienced discrimination. Future studies will need to test for the effect of experiencing discrimination on multiracial identity choice.

26. In the Pew survey, respondents were asked if their political views were liberal, moderate, or conservative. Unlike the respondents in the WKH 2001, the overwhelming majority in the Pew survey identified with a political ideology. Only 6% of respondents responded "don't know" or refused to answer. Given this, I operationalized ideology as an ordinal variable with the highest value attached to those who identify as "very liberal."

27. All detailed data from the 2010 census had not yet been publicly released at the time this analysis was conducted. However, every attempt was made to compare 2000 and 2010 figures on as many demographic features as possible. Data analysis that has been conducted so far reveals that the two-or-more-races population has grown, but this growth has not dramatically changed the patterns originally identified in the 2000 data.

28. The PUMS dataset is a stratified sample of 15.8 million Americans who answered the census long form in 2000. The first stratum of respondents reported in the PUMS dataset was derived from a sample of households, and a second stratum was derived from a sample of people in institutions or other group quarters. The 1% PUMS that I analyze here uses the first stratum of respondents and has a total sample size of 2.8 million people.

29. According to the census, Latinos can be of any race. Commonly, the federal government clarifies this by listing racial groups as "non-Hispanic white" or "non-Hispanic black." However, I do not use such designations in this chapter. Unless specifically noted, all references to "whites," "blacks," "Asian Americans," and "Native Americans" exclude those who also identify as Latino.

30. Pilot tests conducted on the census questionnaire found that Latinos are more likely to leave the racial identification question blank than other racial groups (Hirschman, Alba, and Farley 2000). Thus, the racial characteristics of the Latino population in the census are more likely to rely on imputed data than data for other groups.

31. In her analysis of Latinos in California, Tafoya (2003) finds that the foreign born are much more likely to denote their children as "some other race," while the native born are more likely to designate their children "white." Thus, racial identification among Latinos may reflect a different pattern as the current Latino population moves into the second and third generations.

32. The exponential growth of American Indian identification since 1960 is well documented by demographers, who argue that this growth cannot be attributed purely to birth rates (Passel 1997; Thornton 1997). Nagel (1995) argues that there has been a cultural resurgence in Americans willingness to self-identify as Native American. Individuals who previously did not identify as Native American became increasingly willing to identify as such in the second half of the twentieth century. While Nagel's argument is that an increased sense of ethnic consciousness largely explains this population

increase, others argue that this identity has become more culturally popular among white Americans (Hollinger 2005; Strum 2010). Proponents of this argument claim that white Americans' desire for ethnic attachments and symbolic identity leads more to denote a Native American, often Cherokee, identity. As with American Indians, declaring two or more races among Hawaiians and other Pacific Islanders is also common. For example, see Kana'iaupuni and Liebler 2005.

33. This is the median age for all Americans who reported themselves to be of Latino descent. If one disaggregates Latinos by race, the median age for white Latinos is 28.9, for black Latinos 24, and for Some Other Race Latinos 26.5.

34. In terms of educational attainment, 19.9% of two-or-more-races adults obtained a college degree or higher. In contrast, among Asian Americans, the group with the highest average educational attainment, 44.4% had at least a college degree. Latinos represented the group with the overall lowest levels of higher education: 10.5% held a college degree. The median family income for the two-or-more-races population was approximately $42,000. Asian Americans reported the highest median family income of $58,580, while blacks reported the lowest median family income of $33,600.

35. This geographic pattern characterizing the two-or-more-races population in 2000 is also consistent with the pattern of interracial marriage in 2000. Lee and Edmonston (2005) found that while interracial couples make up only 5.4% of all married couples, they make up 9.8% of married couples in the West.

36. The two-or-more-races population is the largest in New York and Los Angeles, which, of course, are the two largest cities in the United States. When we examine cities with the highest percentage of the two-or-more-races population, less obvious places top the list but are still larger, more urban metropolitan areas. The two-or-more-races population makes up 16.3% of the Honolulu census area. Cities that have a two-or-more-races population that is 8% or larger include Fairfield, CA, Anchorage, AK, and Tacoma, WA. These results show that cities with a large percentage of the two-or-more-races population have large indigenous populations.

Chapter 5

1. A version of this chapter was published in an article in *Political Research Quarterly* (see Masuoka 2008).

2. Although research suggests that other nonethnic characteristics, such as socioeconomic status, most strongly inform political attitude formation among whites, other research has shown that white ethnic identities continue to inform group based preferences for some whites in particular regions. For example, Gimpel and Cho (2004) find that white ethnic identities continue to influence partisan preferences among whites in New England. However, this finding was contingent on the existence of a strong concentration of white ethnics. Therefore, consistent with Waters's (1990) conclusions, whites will rely on ethnic identities when there are incentives or contexts for doing so.

3. Today, most self-identified multiracials today report being two races, with "white" as one of their racial backgrounds. If, in the future, a multiracial identity is characterized by a diverse number of racial combinations, then we will not be able to determine which racial identity trumps the others. However, for the time being, scholars can examine to what extent a minority racial category informs political attitude formation.

4. The racial resentment index is made up of responses to the following statements: (1) "Irish, Italians, Jewish and many other minorities overcame prejudice and worked their way up. Blacks should do the same without any special favors"; (2) "Generations of slavery and discrimination have created conditions that make it difficult for blacks to work their way out of the lower class"; (3) "Over the past few years, blacks have gotten less than they deserve"; and (4) "It's really a matter of some people not trying hard enough; if blacks would only try harder they could be just as well off as whites." The Cronbach's alpha for this scale in the ANES is .70. See Kinder and Sanders (1996) for a detailed explanation of the racial resentment index.

5. Exact question wording on all of these dependent variable measures is provided in appendices C and D.

6. The American National Election Study 2008 Time Series Study is a two-wave panel survey in which respondents were surveyed both before and after the 2008 election. For the pre-election study, 2,470 citizen adult respondents were contacted as well as oversamples of black and Latino respondents. In total, 2,323 respondents completed the pre-election survey and 2,102 respondents completed the second postelection survey. Respondents were interviewed face to face in either English or Spanish, but some questions were asked by Audio Computer-Assisted Self-Interviewing (ACASI). The pre-election study was conducted between September 2 and November 3, 2008. The post-election study was conducted between November 5 and December 20, 2008. For the pre-election study, the AAPOR Response Rate 3 is 63.7%; it is 57.7% for the postelection study. The dependent variables used in this study were asked in the postelection study. See table C1 for summary statistics about this sample.

7. There are other surveys that could have been used in this analysis. For example, after 2000, the General Social Survey (GSS) employed a mark-one-or-more format on its racial identification question. However, the GSS is a survey dedicated to understanding American social life more broadly and so has a limited number of political and racial attitude measures. Because most of the relevant measures available in the GSS are similar to those found in the ANES, I chose to not to use GSS data in this analysis.

8. The two studies used slightly different wording for the racial identification question. The ANES question was, "What racial or ethnic group or groups best describes you?" The Pew question was, "Which of the following describes your race? You can select as many as apply." For both surveys, respondents were allowed to list as many racial groups as they preferred. In both surveys 2% of the sample identified with two or more races. See appendices C and D for details on sample demographics.

9. All differences across means are significant at $p < .01$.

10. All differences of means across monoracial groups are significant at $p < .01$.

11. Differences across means for monoracial groups are all statistically significant at $p < .01$.

12. Differences across means for monoracial groups on support for government intervention and affirmative action are all significant at $p < .01$.

13. Difference between Latinos and whites and between Latinos and blacks is significant at $p < .01$. There is no significant difference between white and black attitudes on immigration policy measure.

14. In the WKH 2001, "Latino" is offered as a distinctive racial identity, alongside with white, black, Asian, and "Some other race." Thus, we cannot break down the Latino

respondents by race for this analysis. Although the survey codes Latinos as a distinctive racial group, I acknowledge that defining Latinos is not consistent with the method outlined by the federal government.

15. Sample sizes for each multiracial category are 168, 91, 102, and 38 respectively. For a complete breakdown on the racial background of the self-identified multiracial respondents in this sample, see appendix B.

16. Respondents who acknowledged being mixed race but only reported one racial group in the follow-up question were coded as multiracial. Since these respondents only identified with one racial group, they are the only cases which do not overlap in the coded multiracial categories in this analysis.

17. I acknowledge that the most ideal comparison would be to disaggregate by specific racial combination. The WKH 2001 does allow me to identify specific multiracial combinations (for example, distinguish white-blacks from black-Asians). However, the sample size of multiracial respondents is not large enough to allow tests of statistical significance, since disaggregating multiracial groups by each possible combination of multiracial identities would result in sample populations of less than 10. The only limitation of my chosen strategy is that I cannot compare across multiracial groupings. In reality, my strategy is no different from other comparative designs that compare across social groupings. Take, for example, a study that groups respondents by shared party identification. It is the case that respondents can be disaggregated by party identification but will overlap in terms of gender (Republican women and Democratic women share the same gender). Comparative design requires scholars to privilege one trait over others. My operationalization strategy simply groups together multiracial respondents who share one common monoracial identity. The findings offered in this section using my chosen strategy offer as much substantive value as other social comparisons made in other social science studies.

18. However, question wording on these questions in the WKH 2001 does vary with those measures in the ANES and Pew. See appendices for exact question wording.

19. This evidence is consistent with scholars' general expectation that Asian American and Latino attitudes are subject to contextual effects of the survey and sampling design (see Barreto et al. 2006; Wong et al. 2011). We should thus not be concerned that the inconsistent findings are unique to the surveys analyzed here but demonstrate the general challenge to studying Latino and Asian American public opinion. There exists such a diversity in both the Latino and Asian American populations that we should expect differences due to sampling procedures.

20. Any differences in mean scores across monoracial groups shown in table 5.4 on the party identification variable are significant at $p < .01$.

21. On support for government intervention, the WKH 2001 asked respondents to consider support for government intervention to ensure equality in four different areas of social and political life: jobs, schools, healthcare services, and treatment by the courts and police. Given that there were a total of four questions, the government intervention variable analyzed here is an index variable that adds together responses to all four questions (Cronbach's alpha for this scale is .79). For full question wording, see appendix B.

22. High standard errors may not truly depict diverse attitudes within multiracial groupings but rather may be due to the fact that the multiracial groupings are relatively

small in sample size—for example there are only 38 total multiracial-Asian respondents in this sample. Alternatively, high standard errors could be due to the fact that the variable is coded as a dichotomous variable. However, the standard errors on the other survey measures are relatively lower than those found on the affirmative action question. So relative to the other survey items analyzed here, there does appear to be greater diversity in opinion on the affirmative action measure than the other measures.

23. While this book was being written, Pew Research Center released findings on a public opinion survey that targeted multiracial Americans (Pew Research Center 2015). The researchers of this report defined multiracial respondents as those who either self-identified as multiracial or who reported having parents of two different races. However, even though researchers used a broad definition of multiracial, many of their findings correspond with the patterns presented in this chapter. For example, a comparison between monoracial and multiracial black respondents found that the two groups shared similar political attitudes, while a comparison between monoracial and multiracial Asian respondents found differences in political attitudes. In the 2015 Pew study, multiracial Asian respondents were found to be more politically liberal and more supportive of government intervention than the data presented in this chapter. However, monoracial Asian respondents in the 2015 Pew study were also found to be more politically liberal than they are according to the data presented in this chapter.

Chapter 6

1. "Candidate Obama's Sense of Urgency," *60 Minutes*, CBS News, February 9, 2007, http://www.cbsnews.com/stories/2007/02/09/60minutes/main2456335.shtml.

2. Obama, of course, is not the only case in which a person classified as nonwhite was seen as a viable candidate for president. For example, Jesse Jackson campaigned to be the Democratic nominee in 1984 and 1988. But unlike Obama, Jackson did not complicate his racial background and solidly promoted his status as a black American (see Tate 1994). This comparison between Jackson and Obama is a good case to see how candidates can use personal narratives to complicate race and racial background.

3. Abigail Thernstrom, "Obama's Census Identity," *Wall Street Journal*, 15, April 10, 2010, http://online.wsj.com/article/SB10001424052702303720604575169783.

4. http://articles.nydailynews.com/2006-11-02/news/18339455_1_black-world-alan-keyes-people-of-african-descent, November 2, 2006.

5. *Meet the Press* interview with Tom Brokaw, October 19, 2008, http://www.clipsandcomment.com/2008/10/19/transcript-colin-powell-on-meet-the-press-endorses-barack-obama-october-19/.

6. Leslie Fulbright, "Obama's Candidacy Sparks Debates on Race," *SF Gate*, February 19, 2007,. http://www.sfgate.com/politics/article/Obama-s-candidacy-sparks-debates-on-race-Is-he-2616419.php

7. Transcript of John McCain's concession speech, *New York Times*, http://www.nytimes.com/2008/11/04/us/politics/04text-mccain.html.

8. Between 2010 and 2012, the American National Election Study implemented the Evaluations of Government and Society Study (EGSS), which included a series of four nationally representative surveys on adult citizens. These surveys were conducted in English and over the Internet. The survey was implemented by Knowledge Networks, Inc. The data I use in this chapter come from the fourth wave of EGSS, which was

collected from February 18 through February 23, 2012. The sample size of this survey was $n = 1,253$ and included 1,038 whites, 94 blacks, and 114 Latinos. The AAPOR Response Rate 3 is 2.5%. For survey question wording, see appendix E. Summary statistics of the sample is provided in table E1.

9. Also see Wilson and Hunt 2014, who offer their own analysis of the Pew survey.

10. The Asian American Election Eve study was a telephone survey implemented by Latino Decisions / Asian American Decisions. This survey was a nationally representative sample of Asian American respondents and was conducted in English, Mandarin, Korean, and Vietnamese. The survey was implemented between November 1 and November 5, 2012. The purpose of the study was to evaluate Asian American preferences during the 2012 election, so only registered voters were included in the study. The total sample size for the study was $n = 804$.

11. Since there were so many respondents who took no clear position on Obama's racial identity, I wanted to include them in the analysis. Since this resulted in three unordered options of Obama's racial identity (black person, mixed-race person, no clear position), I employed multinomial logit and used perceptions of Obama as mixed race as the comparison group in this analysis.

12. I also found that among white respondents, those who declined to state their political affiliation were more likely to perceive Obama as black than were Democrats. However, these results are difficult to interpret since they are the respondents who chose not to designate a party identification.

13. Deracialized campaigns could also be seen as a generational change in black leadership rather than a particular strategy used selectively by certain candidates. Gillespie (2010) argues that today's black candidates represent a third generation of black leadership. These "new" black candidates were born after the civil rights movement and have been found to use campaign strategies distinctly different from earlier generations of black candidates. Today's third generation of black leaders employs more universal claims that appeal to a general audience rather than primarily black audiences. They also highlight more conservative policy agendas that focus on middle-class concerns such as economic development. These strategies force new discussions regarding the definition of a "deracialized" campaign, as some would argue that campaign strategies targeting a general audience are more in tune with today's political context.

14. In addition to the public deliberation over Obama's race, there were other proposed claims that Obama was not straightforward about his true religion or nationality. In terms of religion, some Americans deliberated over whether Obama was Christian or Muslim. In terms of nationality, what was labeled the "birther movement" sought to disseminate the claim that Obama was not a natural born citizen of the United States and so was ineligible for the presidency. While all three of these topics could be considered similar in nature because they represented public deliberations over Obama's identity, the public debate over race is substantively different from claims about Obama's religion or nationality. Claims challenging Obama's religion or nationality represented erroneous statements used to prime voter anxiety. Thus, a study examining voter beliefs about Obama's religion or nationality is more applicable for understanding the role of political knowledge, racism, or use of conspiracy theories, rather than revealing the effects of legitimate public debate on voter attitudes (see also Hollander 2010; Marable 2009; Parker and Barreto 2013; Tesler and Sears 2010).

15. Obama's speeches to black audiences offered specific comments tailored to their shared black experience that often sparked controversy in the media. Obama's speech to the NAACP on July 14, 2008, in Cincinnati, Ohio garnered public attention when he spoke to the largely black audience about black family values. For a transcript see http://www.presidentialrhetoric.com/campaign2008/obama/07.14.08.html. His speech to the NAACP Centennial Convention on July 17, 2009, included comments about traveling to Africa and learning about his African heritage and the shared black experience of discrimination. For a transcript, see http://www.whitehouse.gov/the-press-office/remarks-president-naacp-centennial-convention-07162009.

Conclusion

1. Cristina Beltran posits that Latinos are not homogenous, nor do they necessarily share the same political goals. Thus, she argues that "Latino" is a created political category rather than a descriptive one. She claims that by "approaching *Latinidad* as action—as something we *do* rather than something we *are*—this definition sees Latino politics as inherently coalitional" (2010, 19; see also Oboler 1995).

REFERENCES

Acuna, Rodolfo. 2010. *Occupied America: A History of Chicanos*. New York: Prentice Hall.

Alba, Richard, and Victor Nee. 2005. *Remaking the American Mainstream: Assimilation and Contemporary Immigration*. Cambridge, MA: Harvard University Press.

Allport, Gordon. 1954. *The Nature of Prejudice*. Cambridge, MA: Addison-Wesley.

Anderson, Margo. 1988. *The American Census: A Social History*. New Haven: Yale University Press.

Anderson, Terry. 2004. *The Pursuit of Fairness: A History of Affirmative Action*. New York: Oxford University Press.

Aptheker, Herbert. 1939. "Maroons within the Present Limits of the United States." *Journal of Negro History* 24(2): 167–184.

Bailey, Stanley R. 2008. "Unmixing for Race Making in Brazil." *American Journal of Sociology* 114(3): 577–614.

Ball, Portia, and Gordon Cantor. 1974. "White Boys' Ratings of Pictures of Whites and Blacks Are Related to Amount of Familiarization." *Perceptual and Motor Skills* 39(2): 883–890.

Banks, James. 1993. "Multicultural Education: Historical Development, Dimensions and Practice." *Review of Research in Education* 19: 3–49.

Barreto, Matt. 2010. *Ethnic Cues: The Role of Shared Ethnicity in Latino Political Participation*. Ann Arbor: University of Michigan Press.

Barreto, Matt, Fernando Guerra, Mara Marks Stephen Nuno, and Nathan Woods. 2006. "Controversies in Exit Polling: Implementing a Racially Stratified Homogenous Precinct Approach." *PS: Political Science and Politics* 39(3): 477–483.

Beltran, Cristina. 2010. *The Trouble with Unity: Latino Politics and the Creation of Identity*. New York: Oxford University Press.

Berkhofer, Robert, Jr. 1979. *The White Man's Indian: Images of the American Indian from Columbus to the Present*. New York: Random House.

Berkinsky, Adam. 1999. "The Two Faces of Public Opinion." *Journal of Politics* 43(4): 1209–1230.

Berlin, Ira. 2000. *Many Thousands Gone: The First Two Centuries of Slavery in North America*. Cambridge, MA: Belknap Press of Harvard University Press.

Bernstein, Mary, and Marcie de la Cruz. 2009. "'What Are You?' Explaining Identity as a Goal of the Multiracial Hapa Movement." *Social Problems* 56(4): 722–745.

Blassingame, John. 1979. *The Slave Community: Plantation Life in the Antebellum South*. Rev. ed. New York: Oxford University Press.

Blee, Kathleen 2002. *Inside Organized Racism: Women in the Hate Movement*. Berkeley: University of California Press.

Bobo, Lawrence. 2000. "Race and Beliefs about Affirmative Action: Assessing the Effects of Interests, Group Threat, Ideology and Racism." In *Racialized Politics: The Debate about Racism in the America*, ed. David Sears, Jim Sidanius, and Lawrence Bobo. Chicago: University of Chicago Press. Pp 137–164.

Bobo, Lawrence, James Kluegel, and Ryan Smith. 1997. "Laissez Faire Racism: The Crystallization of a 'Kinder, Gentler' Anti-black Ideology." In *Racial Attitudes in the 1990's: Continuity and Change*, ed. Steven Tuch and Jack Martin. Westport, CT: Praeger. Pp 15–44.

Bonilla-Silva, Eduardo. 2003. *Racism without Racists: Color-Blind Racism and the Persistence of Racial Inequality in the United States*. Lanham, MD: Rowman and Littlefield.

Bonilla-Silva, Eduardo. 2004. "From Bi-racial to Tri-racial: Towards a New System of Racial Stratification in the USA." *Ethnic and Racial Studies* 27(6): 931–950.

Bonilla-Silva, Eduardo, and Karen Glover. 2004. "'We Are All Americans': The Latin Americanization of Race Relations in the U.S." In *The Changing Terrain of Race and Ethnicity*, ed. Maria Krysan and Amanda Lewis. New York: Russell Sage Foundation. Pp 149–186.

Bowler, Shaun, and Gary M. Segura. 2012. *The Future Is Ours: Minority Politics, Political Behavior, and the Multiracial Era of American Politics*. Washington, DC: Congressional Quarterly Press.

Brace, Paul, and Barbara Hinckley. 1991. "The Structure of Presidential Approval: Constraints within and across Presidencies." *Journal of Politics* 53(4): 993–1017.

Bratter, Jenifer. 2007. "Will 'Multiracial' Survive to the Next Generation? The Racial Classification of Children of Multiracial Parents." *Social Forces* 86(2): 821–849.

Brewer, Marilynn. 1988. "A Dual Process Model of Impression Formation." In *A Dual-Process Model of Impression Formation: Advances in Social Cognition*, vol. 1, ed. Thomas Srull and Robert Wyer. Hillsdale, NJ: Erlbaum. 1–36.

Brewer, Marilynn. 1991. "The Social Self: On Being the Same and Different at the Same Time." *Personality and Social Psychology Bulletin* 17: 475–482.

Brown, Nancy, and Ramona Douglas. 2003. "Evolution of Multiracial Organizations: Where We Have Been and Where We are Going." In *New Faces in a Changing America: Multiracial Identity in the 21st Century*, ed. Loretta Winters and Herman DeBose. Thousand Oaks, CA: Sage. 111–124.

Brown, Ursula. 2001. *The Interracial Experience: Growing Up Black/White Racially Mixed in the United States*. Westport, CT: Praeger.

Brubaker, Rogers. 1992. *Citizenship and Nationhood in France and Germany*. Cambridge, MA: Harvard University Press.

Brunsma, David. 2006. "Public Categories, Private Identities: Exploring Regional Differences in the Biracial Experience." *Social Science Research* 35: 555–576.

Brunsma, David. 2005. "Interracial Families and the Racial Identification of Mixed-Race Children: Evidence from the Early Childhood Longitudinal Survey." *Social Forces* 84(2): 1131–1157.

Camarillo, Albert. 1984. *Chicanos in California: A History of Mexican Americans.* Sparks, NV: Materials for Today's Learning.

Campbell, Angus, Philip Converse, Warren Miller, and Donald Stokes. 1960. *The American Voter.* Chicago: University of Chicago Press.

Campbell, Mary E., and Lisa Troyer. 2007. "The Implications of Racial Misclassification by Observers." *American Sociological Review* 72(5): 750–65.

Campbell, Mary E., Jenifer Bratter, and Wendy Roth. 2016. "Measuring the Diverging Components of Race: An Introduction." *American Behavioral Scientist* 60(4): 381–389.

Carens, Joseph. 2000. *Culture, Citizenship and Community: A Contextual Exploration of Justice as Evenhandedness.* New York: Oxford University Press.

Carmines, Edward, and James Stimson. 1981. "Issue Evolution, Population Replacement and Normal Partisan Change." *American Political Science Review* 75(1): 107–118.

Chan, Sucheng. 1991. *Asian Americans: An Interpretive History.* New York: Twayne.

Chang, Sharon. 2014. "Say Hapa, with Care." *AAPI Voices.* June 18. Online at: http://multiasianfamilies.blogspot.com/2016/10/say-hapa-with-care.html.

Chavez, Leo. 2008. *The Latino Threat: Constructing Immigrants, Citizens and the Nation.* Palo Alto, CA: Stanford University Press.

Cheng, Simon, and Brian Powell. 2007. "Allocation to Young Children from Biracial Families." *American Journal of Sociology* 112(4): 1044–1094.

Cho, Wendy Tam. 1999. "Naturalization, Socialization, Participation: Immigrants and (Non-)Voting." *Journal of Politics* 61(4): 1140–1155.

Chong, Dennis, and Dukhong Kim. 2006. "The Experiences and Effects of Economic Status among Racial and Ethnic Minorities." *American Political Science Review* 100(3): 335–351.

Chong, Dennis, and Reuel Rogers. 2005. "Racial Solidarity and Political Participation." *Political Behavior* 27(4): 327–372.

Clayton, Dewey. 2010. *The Presidential Campaign of Barack Obama: A Critical Analysis of a Racially Transcendent Strategy.* New York: Routledge.

Cole, C. L., and David L. Andrews. 2011. "America's New Son: Tiger Woods and America's Multiculturalism." In *Commodified and Criminalized: New Racism and African Americans in Contemporary Sports*, ed. David Leonard and C. Richard King. New York: Rowman and Littlefield. 23–40.

Conover, Pamela J. 1984. "The Influence of Group Identification on Political Perception and Evaluation." *Journal of Politics* 46: 760–785.

Conover, Pamela J. 1988. "The Role of Social Groups in Political Thinking." *British Journal of Political Science* 18(1): 51–76.

Cornell, Stephen, and Douglas Harmann. 2007. *Ethnicity and Race: Making Identities in a Changing World.* Thousand Oaks, CA: Pine Forge Press.

Dacosta, Kimberly McClain. 2007. *Making Multiracial Individuals: State, Family and Market in the Redrawing of the Color Line.* Palo Alto, CA: Stanford University Press.

Dahl, Robert. 1961. *Who Governs? Democracy and Power in an American City.* New Haven: Yale University Press.

Dalmage, Heather. 2000. *Tripping on the Color Line: Black-White Multiracial Families in a Racially Divided World*. New Brunswick, NJ: Rutgers University Press.

Dalmage, Heather. 2004. "Protecting Racial Comfort, Protecting White Privilege." In *The Politics of Multiracialism: Challenging Racial Thinking*, ed. Heather Dalmage. Albany: State University of New York Press. 203–218.

Daniel, Reginald. 2002. *More Than Black? Multiracial Identity and the New Racial Order*. Philadelphia: Temple University Press.

Davidson, Chandler, and Bernard Grofman, eds. 1994. *Quiet Revolution in the South: The Impact of the Voting Rights Act, 1965–1990*. Princeton, NJ: Princeton University Press.

Davis, F. James. 1991. *Who Is Black? One Nation's Definition?* University Park: Pennsylvania State University Press.

Dawson, Michael. 1994. *Behind the Mule: Race and Class in African American Politics*. Princeton, NJ: Princeton University Press.

Dawson, Michael. 2001. *Black Visions: The Roots of Contemporary African-American Political Ideologies*. Chicago: University of Chicago Press.

de la Garza, Rodolfo, and Louis DeSipio. 1997. "Save the Baby, Change the Bathwater, Scrub the Tub: Latino Electoral Participation after Twenty Years of Voting Rights Coverage." In *Pursuing Power: Latinos and the Political System*, ed. F. Chris Garcia. South Bend, IN: University of Notre Dame Press. 72–126.

de la Garza, Rodolfo, Louis DeSipio, F. Chris Garcia, and Angelo Falcon. 1992. *Latino Voices: Mexican, Puerto Rican and Cuban Perspectives on American Politics*. Boulder, CO: Westview Press.

Deloria, Vine, and David Wilkins. 2000. *Tribes, Treaties and Constitutional Tribulations*. Austin: University of Texas Press.

DeSipio, Louis. 1996. *Counting on the Latino Vote: Latinos as the New Electorate*. Charlottesville: University Press of Virginia.

Dovi, Suzanne. 2002. "Preferable Descriptive Representation: Will Just Any Woman, Black or Latino Do?" *American Journal of Political Science* 96(4): 729–743.

Dovidio, John, Kerry Kawakami, and Samuel Gaertner. 2002. "Implicit and Explicit Prejudice and Interracial Interaction." *Journal of Personality and Social Psychology* 82(1): 62–68.

Dowling, Julie A. 2014. *Mexican Americans and the Question of Race*. Austin: University of Texas Press.

Doyle, Jamie, and Grace Kao. 2007. "Are Racial Identities of Multiracial Individuals Stable? Changing Self-Identification among Single and Multiple Race Individuals." *Social Psychology Quarterly* 70(4): 405–423.

Escott, Paul. 1979. *Slavery Remembered: A Record of Twentieth Century Slave Narratives*. Chapel Hill: University of North Carolina Press.

Espiritu, Yen Le. 1993. *Asian American Panethnicity: Bridging Institutions and Identities*. Philadelphia: Temple University Press.

Farley, Reynolds. 2002. "Racial Identities in 2000: The Response to the Multiple-Race Response Option." In *The New Race Question: How the Census Counts Multiracial Individuals*, ed. Joel Perlmann and Mary Waters. New York: Russell Sage Foundation. 33–61.

Feldman, Stanley, and Leonie Huddy. 2005. "Racial Resentment and White Opposition to Race-Conscious Programs: Principles or Prejudice?" *American Journal of Political Science* 49(1): 168–183.

Fhagen-Smith, Peony. 2010. "Social Class, Racial/Ethnic Identity and the Psychology of 'Choice.'" In *Multiracial Americans and Social Class: The Influence of Social Class on Racial Identity*, ed. Kathleen Odell Korgen. New York: Routledge. Pp 30–38.

Foner, Eric. 1999. *The Story of American Freedom*. New York: Norton.

Foner, Eric, 2014. *Reconstruction: America's Unfinished Revolution, 1863–1877.* Updated ed. New York: Harper Perennial Modern Classics.

Foner, Philip. 1983. *History of Black Americans: From the Emergence of the Cotton Kingdom to the Eve of the Compromise of 1850*. Westport, CT: Greenwood Press.

Fraga, Luis, John Garcia, Gary Segura, Michael Jones-Correa, Rodney Hero, and Valerie Martinez-Ebers. 2010. *Latino Lives in America: Making It Home*. Philadelphia: Temple University Press.

Fraga, Luis, John Garcia, Gary Segura, Michael Jones-Correa, Rodney Hero, and Valerie Martinez-Ebers. 2011. *Latinos in the New Millennium: An Almanac of Opinion, Behavior, and Policy Preferences*. New York: Cambridge University Press.

Frasure, Lorrie. 2010. "The Burden of Jekyll and Hyde: Barack Obama, Racial Identity, and Black Political Behavior." In *Whose Black Politics? Cases in Post-racial Black Leadership*, ed. Andra Gillespie. New York: Routledge. 133–154.

Fredrickson, George. 2003. *Racism: A Short History*. Princeton, NJ: Princeton University Press.

Freeman, Jonathan B., Andrew M. Penner, Aliya Saperstein, Matthias Scheutz, and Nalini Ambady. 2011. "Looking the Part: Social Status Cues Shape Race Perception." PLoS ONE 6(9):e25107.

Frymer, Paul. 1999. *Uneasy Alliances: Race and Party Competition in America*. Princeton, NJ: Princeton University Press.

Funderburg, Lise. 1994. *Black, White, Other: Biracial Americans Talk about Race and Identity*. New York: William Morrow.

Gallagher, Charles. 2015. "Colour-Blind Egalitarianism as the New Racial Norm." In *Theories of Race and Ethnicity: Contemporary Debates and Perspectives*, ed. Karim Murji and John Solomos. Cambridge: Cambridge University Press. Pp 40–56.

Gallup Poll News Service. 2013. "Gallup Poll: Social Series: Minority Rights and Relations." Gallup Brain. http://institution.gallup.com.ezproxy.library.tufts.edu/documents/questionnaire.aspx?STUDY=P1306008&p=5.

Gans, Herbert. 1979. "Symbolic Ethnicity: The Future of Ethnic Groups and Cultures in America." *Ethnic and Racial Studies* 2(1): 1–20.

Gans, Herbert. 1999. "The Possibility of a New Racial Hierarchy in the Twenty-First Century United States." In *The Cultural Territories of Race: Black and White Boundaries*, ed. Michele Lamont. New York: Russell Sage. Pp 371–390.

Garcia, F. Chris. 1994a. "Latinos and the Affirmative Action Debate: Wedge or Coalition Issue?" In *Pursuing Power: Latinos and the Political System*, ed. F. Chris Garcia. South Bend, IN: University of Notre Dame Press. 368–400.

Garcia, F. Chris, ed. 1994b. *Pursuing Power: Latinos and the Political System*. South Bend, IN: University of Notre Dame Press.

Garcia Bedolla, Lisa. 2005. *Fluid Borders: Latino Power, Identity and Politics in Los Angeles*. Berkeley, CA: University of California Press.

Gerstle, Gary. 2001. *American Crucible: Race and Nation in the Twentieth Century*. Princeton, NJ: Princeton University Press.

Gillespie, Andra. 2010. "Meet the New Class: Theorizing Young Black Leadership in a 'Postracial' Era." In *Whose Black Politics? Cases in Post-racial Black Leadership*, ed. Andra Gillespie. New York: Routledge. 9–42.

Gimpel, James, and Wendy Tam Cho. 2004. "The Persistence of White Ethnicity in New England Politics." *Political Geography* 23(8): 987–1008.

Gitlin, Todd. 1995. *The Twilight of Common Dreams: Why America Is Wracked by Culture Wars*. New York: Metropolitan Books.

Glaszer, Nathan. 1998. *We Are All Multiculturalists Now*. Cambridge, MA: Harvard University Press.

Goff, Phillip, Claude Steele, and Paul Davies. 2008. "The Space between Us: Stereotype Threat and Distance in Interracial Contexts." *Journal of Personality and Social Psychology* 94(1): 91–107.

Goldstein, Joshua, and Ann Morning. 2002. "Back in the Box: The Dilemma of Using Multiple-Race Data for Single-Race Laws." In *The New Race Question: How the Census Counts Multiracial Individuals*, ed. Joel Perlmann and Mary Waters. New York: Russell Sage Foundation. 119–136.

Gomez, Laura. 2008. *Manifest Destinies: The Making of the Mexican American Race*. New York: New York University Press.

Goodstein, Renee, and Joseph Ponterotto. 1997. "Racial and Ethnic Identity: Their Relationship and Their Contribution to Self-Esteem." *Journal of Black Psychology* 23(3): 275–292.

Gordon, Milton. 1964. *Assimilation in American Life: The Role of Race, Religion and National Origins*. New York: Oxford University Press.

Graham, Hugh Davis. 2000. "The Civil Rights Act and the American Regulatory State." In *Legacies of the 1964 Civil Rights Act*, ed. Bernard Grofman. Charlottesville: University of Virginia Press. 9–32.

Grofman, Bernard, ed. 2000. *Legacies of the 1964 Civil Rights Act*. Charlottesville: University of Virginia Press.

Gross, Ariela. 2008. *What Blood Won't Tell: A History of Race on Trial in America*. Cambridge, MA: Harvard University Press.

Gutmann, Amy. 2003. *Identity and Democracy*. Princeton, NJ: Princeton University Press.

Hajnal, Zoltan. 2001. "White Residents, Black Incumbents and a Declining Racial Divide." *American Political Science Review* 95(3): 603–617.

Hajnal, Zoltan, and Takeu Lee. 2011. *Why Americans Don't Join the Party: Race, Immigration and the Failure of Political Parties to Engage the Electorate*. Princeton, NJ: Princeton University Press.

Halberstadt, Jamin, Steven J. Sherman, and Jeffrey W. Sherman. 2011. "Why Barack Obama Is Black: A Cognitive Account of Hypodescent." *Psychological Science* 22(1): 29–33.

Hamm, Norman, Michael Baum, and Kenneth Nikels. 1975. "Effects of Race and Exposure on Judgments of Interpersonal Favorability." *Journal of Experimental Social Psychology* 11(1): 14–24.

Haney-Lopez, Ian. 1999. "The Social Construction of Race: Some Observations on Illusion, Fabrication, and Choice." *Harvard Civil Rights and Civil Liberties Law Review* 29: 1–62.

Haney Lopez, Ian. 2006. *White by Law: The Legal Construction of Race*. 10th anniversary ed. New York: New York University Press.

Hansen, Marcus Lee. 1928. "The Problem of the Third Generation Immigrant." Augustana College Library Occasional Papers Number 16. Rock Island, IL: Augustana Historical Society Publications.

Harris, David, and Jeremiah Joseph Sim. 2002. "Who Is Multiracial? Assessing the Complexity of Lived Race." *American Sociological Review* 67(4): 614–627.

Harrison, Roderick. 2002. "Inadequacies of Multiple-Response Race Data in the Federal Statistical System." In *The New Race Question: How the Census Counts Multiracial Individuals*, ed. Joel Perlmann and Mary Waters. New York: Russell Sage Foundation. 137–160.

Hattam, Victoria. 2007. *In the Shadow of Race: Jews, Latinos and Immigrant Politics in the United States*. Chicago: University of Chicago Press.

Herman, Melissa. 2004. "Forced to Choose: Some Determinants of Racial Identification in Multiracial Adolescents." *Child Development* 75(3): 730–748.

Hero, Rodney. 1992. *Latinos and the U.S. Political System: Two-Tiered Pluralism*. Philadelphia: Temple University Press.

Hero, Rodney, and Robert Preuhs. 2013. *Black-Latino Relations in U.S. National Politics*. New York: Cambridge University Press.

Hickman, Christine. 1996. "The Devil and the One Drop Rule: Racial Categories, African Americans and the U.S. Census." *Michigan Law Review* 95: 1161–1265.

Higham, John. 2002. *Strangers in the Land: Patterns of American Nativism, 1860–1925*. New Brunswick, NJ: Rutgers University Press.

Highton, Benjamin. 2004. "White Voters and African American Candidates in Congress." *Political Behavior* 26(1): 1–25.

Hing, Bill Ong. 1994. *Making and Remaking Asian America through Immigration Policy 1850–1990*. Palo Alto, CA: Stanford University Press.

Hing, Bill Ong. 2003. *Defining America through Immigration Policy*. Philadelphia: Temple University Press.

Hirschman, Charles, Richard Alba, and Reynolds Farley. 2000. "The Meaning and Measurement of Race in the U.S. Census: Glimpses into the Future." *Demography* 37(3): 381–393.

Hitlin, Steven, J. Scott Brown, and Glen Elder Jr. 2006. "Racial Self-Categorization in Adolescence: Multiracial Development and Social Pathways." *Child Development* 77(5): 1298–1308.

Hochschild, Jennifer, Vesla Weaver, and Traci Burch. 2012. *Creating a New Racial Order: How Immigration, Multiracialism, Genomics and the Young Can Remake Race in America*. Princeton, NJ: Princeton University Press.

Hodes, Martha. 1997. *White Women, Black Men: Illicit Sex in the 19th Century South*. New Haven: Yale University Press.

Hollander, Barry. 2010. "Persistence in the Perception of Barack Obama as a Muslim in the 2008 Presidential Campaign." *Journal of Media and Religion* 9: 55–66.

Hollinger, David. 2003. "Amalgamation and Hypodescent: The Question of Ethnoracial Mixture in the History of the United States." *American Historical Review* 108(5): 1363–1390.

Hollinger, David. 2005. *Postethnic America: Beyond Multiculturalism*. New York: Basic Books.

Hosang, Daniel. 2010. *Racial Propositions: Ballot Initiatives and the Making of Postwar California*. Berkeley: University of California Press.

Huber, Gregory, and John Lapinski. 2006. "The 'Race Card' Revisited: Assessing Racial Priming in Policy Contests." *American Journal of Political Science* 50(2): 421–440.

Huddy, Leonie, and Nayda Terkildsen. 1993. "The Consequences of Gender Stereotypes for Women Candidates at Different Levels and Types of Office." *Political Research Quarterly* 46(3): 503–525.

Huffington Post. 2008. "Patty Solis Doyle, Former Clinton Campaign Manager, Hired by Obama Camp." June 24. http://www.huffingtonpost.com/2008/06/16/obama-hires-new-campaign_n_107361.html.

Huntington, Samuel. 2004. *Who Are We? America's National Identity and the Challenges It Faces*. New York: Simon & Schuster.

Ibrahim, Habiba. 2009. "Toward Black and Multiracial 'Kinship' after 1997, or How a Race Man Became Cablinasian." *Black Scholar* 39(3–4): 23–31.

Ignatiev, Noel. 2009. *How the Irish Became White*. New York: Routledge.

Iijima Hall, Christine, and Trude Cooke Turner. 2001. "The Diversity of Biracial Individuals: Asian-White and Asian-Minority Biracial Identity." In *The Sum of Our Parts: Mixed Heritage Asian Americans*, ed. Teresa Williams-Leon and Cynthia Nakashima. Philadelphia: Temple University Press. 81–92.

Jacobson, Matthew Frye. 1998. *Whiteness of a Different Color: European Immigrants and the Alchemy of Race*. Cambridge, MA: Harvard University Press.

Jimenez, Tomas. 2010. *Replenished Ethnicity: Mexican Americans, Immigration and Identity*. Berkeley: University of California Press.

Johnson, Kimberly. 2008. "Jim Crow Reform and the Democratization of the South." In *Race and American Political Development*, ed. Joseph Lowndes, Julie Novkov, and Dorian Warren. New York: Routledge. Pp 155–179.

Johnson, Troy. 2008. *The American Indian Occupation of Alcatraz Island: Red Power and Self-Determination*. Lincoln: University of Nebraska Press.

Jolivette, Andrew, ed. 2012. *Obama and the Biracial Factor: The Battle for the New American Majority*. Chicago: Policy Press.

Junn, Jane, and Natalie Masuoka. 2008. "Asian American Identity: Shared Racial Status and Political Context." *Perspectives on Politics* 6(4): 729–740.

Kallen, Horace. 1970. *Culture and Democracy in the United States*. New York: Arno Press.

Kana'iaupuni, Shawn, and Carolyn Liebler. 2005. "Pondering Poi Dog: Place and Racial Identification of Multiracial Native Hawaiians." *Ethnic and Racial Studies* 28(4): 687–721.

Karenga, Maulana. 2010. *Introduction to Black Studies*. 4th ed. Los Angeles: Sankore Press.

Karis, Terri. 2004. "'I Prefer to Speak of Culture': White Mothers of Multiracial Children." In *The Politics of Multiracialism: Challenging Racial Thinking*, ed. Heather Dalmage. Albany: State University of New York Press. 161–174.

Kertzer, David, and Dominique Arel. 2002. "Censuses, Identity Formation and the Struggle for Political Power." In *Census and Identity: The Politics of Race, Ethnicity and Language in National Censuses*, ed. David Kertzer and Dominque Arel. New York: Cambridge University Press. Pp 1–42.

Ketcham, Ralph Lewis. 2003. *The Political Thought of Benjamin Franklin*. Indianapolis: Hackett.

Key, V. O. 1977. *Southern Politics in State and Nation*. Knoxville: University of Tennessee Press.

Khanna, Nikki. 2001. "The Role of Reflected Appraisals in Racial Identity: The Case of Multiracial Asians." *Social Psychology Quarterly* 67(2): 115–131.

Kiang, Lisa, Melissa Witkow, Oscar Baldelomar, and Andrew Fuligni. 2010. "Change in Ethnic Identity across the High School Years among Adolescents with Latin American, Asian and European Backgrounds." *Journal of Youth and Adolescence* 39(6): 683–693.

Kibria, Nazli. 2002. *Becoming Asian American: Second-Generation Chinese and Korean American Identities*. Baltimore: Johns Hopkins University Press.

Kim, Claire Jean. 1999. "The Racial Triangulation of Asian Americans." *Politics and Society* 27(1): 105–138.

Kim, Claire Jean. 2000. *Bitter Fruit: The Politics of Black-Korean Conflict in New York*. New Haven, CT: Yale University Press.

Kinder, Donald, and Cindy Kam. 2009. *Us against Them: Ethnocentric Foundations of American Opinion*. Chicago: University of Chicago Press.

Kinder, Donald, and Lynn Sanders. 1996. *Divided by Color: Racial Politics and Democratic Ideals*. Chicago: University of Chicago Press.

King-O'Riain, and Rebecca Chiyoko. 2006. *Pure Beauty: Judging Race in Japanese American Beauty Pageants*. Minneapolis: University of Minnesota Press.

Korgen, Kathleen Odell. 1998. *From Black to Biracial: Transforming Racial Identity among Americans*. Westport, CT: Praeger.

Kymlicka, Will. 1996. *Multicultural Citizenship: A Liberal Theory of Minority Rights*. New York: Oxford University Press.

Lee, Jennifer, and Frank Bean. 2010. *The Diversity Paradox: Immigration and the Color Line in Twenty-First Century America*. New York: Russell Sage Foundation.

Lee, Sharon, and Barry Edmonston. 2005. "New Marriages, New Families: U.S. Racial and Hispanic Intermarriage." *Population Bulletin* 60(2). Washington, DC: Population Reference Bureau.

Lee, Taeku. 2008. "Race, Immigration and the Identity-to-Politics Link." *Annual Review of Political Science* 11: 457–478.

Lerman, Amy and Meredith Sadin. 2016. "Stereotyping or Projection?: How White and Black Voters Estimate Black Candidates' Ideology." *Political Psychology*. 37(2): 147-163.

Lien, Pei-te. 2001. *The Making of Asian America through Political Participation*. Philadelphia: Temple University Press.

Lien, Pei-te, M. Margaret Conway, and Janelle Wong. 2004. *The Politics of Asian Americans: Diversity and Community*. New York: Routledge.

Loewen, James. 1971. *The Mississippi Chinese: Between Black and White*. 2nd ed. Cambridge, MA: Harvard University Press.

Lofquist, Daphne, Terry, Lugaila, Martin O'Connell, and Sarah Feliz. 2012. "Households and Families: 2010." 2010 Census Briefs #C2010BR-14. April. Washington, DC: US Department of Commerce.

Long, J. Scott, and Jeremy Freese. 2006. *Regression Models for Categorical Dependent Variables Using Stata*. 2nd ed. College Station, TX: Stata Press.

MacLin, Otto H., and Roy S. Malpass. 2001. "Racial Categorization of Faces: The Ambiguous Race Face Effect." *Psychology, Public Policy, and Law* 7(1): 98–118.

Macrae, C. Neil, and Gail Bodenhausen. 2000. "Social Cognition: Thinking Categorically about Others." *Annual Review of Psychology* 51: 93–120.

Mansbridge, Jane. 1999. "Should Blacks Represent Blacks and Women Represent Women? A Contingent 'Yes.'" *Journal of Politics* 61(3): 628–657.

Marable, Manning. 2009. "Racializing Obama: The Enigma of Post-black Politics and Leadership." *Souls* 11(1): 1–15.

Martinez, Maria Elena. 2008. *Genealogical Fictions: Limpieza de Sangre, Religion and Gender in Colonial Mexico*. Palo Alto, CA: Stanford University Press.

Marx, Anthony. 1998. *Making Race and Nation: A Comparison of South Africa, the United States and Brazil*. New York: Cambridge University Press.

Massey, Douglas. 2007. *Categorically Unequal: The American Stratification System*. New York: Russell Sage Foundation.

Masuoka, Natalie. 2008. "Political Attitudes and Ideologies of Multiracial Americans: The Implications of Mixed Race in the U.S." *Political Research Quarterly* 61(2): 253–267.

Masuoka, Natalie. 2011. "The 'Multiracial' Option: Social Group Identity and Changing Patterns of Racial Categorization." *American Politics Research* 39(1): 176–204.

Masuoka, Natalie, and Jane Junn. 2013. *The Politics of Belonging: Race, Public Opinion and Immigration*. Chicago: University of Chicago Press.

McAdam, Doug. 1999. *Political Process and the Development of Black Insurgency, 1930–1970*. Chicago: University of Chicago Press.

McCormick, Joseph, and Charles E. Jones. 1993. "The Conceptualization of Deracialization." In *Dilemmas of Black Politics*, ed. Georgia Persons. New York: HarperCollins College Publishers. 66–84.

McGraw, Kathleen. 2003. "Political Impressions: Formation and Management." In *Oxford Handbook of Political Psychology*, ed. David Sears, Leonie Huddy, and Robert Jervins. New York: Oxford University Press. Pp 394–432.

McLoughlin, William. 1974. "Red Indians, Black Slavery and White Racism: America's Slaveholding Indians." *American Quarterly* 26(4): 367–385.

Menchaca, Martha. 2002. *Recovering History, Constructing Race: The Indian, Black and White Roots of Mexican Americans*. Austin: University of Texas Press.

Mendelberg, Tali. 2001. *The Race Card: Campaign Strategy, Implicit Messages and the Norm of Equality*. Princeton, NJ: Princeton University Press.

Miller, Arthur H., Patricia Gurin, Gerald Gurin, and Oksana Malanchuk. 1981. "Group Consciousness and Political Participation." *American Journal of Political Science* 25(3) 494–511.

Miyawaki, Michael Hajime. 2015. "Part-Latinos and Racial Reporting in the Census: An Issue of Question Format?" *Sociology of Race and Ethnicity*. 2(3): 289–306.

Moran, Rachel. 2003. *Interracial Intimacy: The Regulation of Race and Romance*. Chicago: University of Chicago Press.

Morgan, Edmund. 1975. *American Slavery, American Freedom*. New York: Norton.

Morgan, Philip. 1999. "Interracial Sex in the Chesapeake and the British Atlantic World, c. 1700–1820." In *Sally Hemings and Thomas Jefferson: History, Memory and Civic Culture*, ed. Jan Ellen Lewis and Peter Onuf. Charlottesville: University of Virginia Press. Pp 52–86.

Morris, Aldon. 1986. *The Origins of the Civil Rights Movement: Black Communities Organizing for Change*. New York: Free Press.

Myrdal, Gunnar. 1944. *An American Dilemma: The Negro Problem and American Democracy*. New York: Harper and Row.

Nagel, Joane. 1995. "American Indian Ethnic Renewal: Politics and the Resurgence of Identity." *American Sociological Review* 60(6): 947–965.

Nagel, Joane. 2003. *Race, Ethnicity and Sexuality: Intimate Intersections, Forbidden Frontiers*. New York: Oxford University Press.

Newport, Frank. 2013. "In U.S., 87% Approve of Black-White Marriage, vs 4% in 1958." http://www.gallup.com/poll/163697/approve-marriage-blacks-whites.aspx.

Ngai, Mae. 2005. *Impossible Subjects: Illegal Aliens and the Making of Modern America*. Princeton, NJ: Princeton University Press.

Nishime, Leilani. 2014. *Undercover Asian: Multiracial Asian Americans in Visual Culture*. Urbana: University of Illinois Press.

Nishina, Adrienne, Amy Bellmore, Melissa Witkow, and Karen Nylund-Gibson. 2010. "Longitudinal Consistency of Adolescent Ethnic Identification across Varying School Ethnic Contexts." *Developmental Psychology* 46(6): 1389–1401.

Nobles, Melissa. 2000. *Shades of Citizenship: Race and the Census in Modern Politics*. Stanford, CA: Stanford University Press.

Norton, Michael, Samuel Sommers, Evan Apfelbaum, Natassia Pura, and Dan Ariely. 2006. "Color Blindness and Interracial Interaction: Playing the Political Correctness Game." *Psychological Science* 17(11): 949–953.

Obama, Barack. 2004. *Dreams from My Father: A Story of Race and Inheritance*. New York: Crown.

Obama, Barack. 2008. "Keynote Address at the 2004 Democratic National Convention." http://www.barackobama.com/2004/07/27/keynote_address_at_the_2004_de.php.

Oboler, Suzanne. 1995. *Ethnic Labels, Latino Lives Identity and the Politics of (Re) Presentation in the United States*. Minneapolis: University of Minnesota Press.

Okihiro, Gary. 2004. *The Columbia Guide to Asian American History*. New York: Columbia University Press.

Oliver, Melvin, and Thomas Shapiro. 2006. *Black Wealth / White Wealth: A New Perspective on Racial Inequality*. New York: Taylor Francis.

Omi, Michael, and Howard Winant. 1994. *Racial Formation in the United States: From the 1960s to the 1990s*. 2nd ed. New York: Routledge.

Parenti, Michael. 1967. "Ethnic Politics and the Persistence of Ethnic Identification." *American Political Science Review* 61(4): 717–726.

Park, Robert. 1928. "Human Migration and the Marginal Man." *American Journal of Sociology* 33: 881–893.

Parker, Christopher, and Matt Barreto. 2013. *Change They Can't Believe In: The Tea Party and Reactionary Politics in America*. Princeton, NJ: Princeton University Press.

Passel, Jeffrey. 1997. "The Growing American Indian Population, 1960–1990: Beyond Demography." *Population Research and Policy Review* 16: 11–31.

Pauker, Kristin, Max Weisbuch, Nalini Ambady, Samuel Sommers, Reginald Adams Jr., and Zorana Ivcevic. 2009. "Not So Black and White: Memory for Ambiguous Group Members." *Journal of Personality and Social Psychology* 96(4): 759–810.

Peery, Destiny, and Galen Bodenhausen. 2008. "Black + White = Black: Hypodescent in Reflexive Categorization of Racially Ambiguous Faces." *Psychological Science* 19(10): 973–977.

Pellegrini, Gino Michael. 2013. "Creating Multiracial Identities in the Work of Rebecca Walker and Kip Fulbeck: A Collective Critique of American Liberal Multiculturalism." *MELUS: Multi-Ethnic Literature of the U.S.* 38(4): 171–190.

Perez, Efren. 2010. "Explicit Evidence on the Import of Implicit Attitudes: The IAT and Immigration Policy Judgments." *Political Behavior* 32(4): 517–545.

Perez, Efren. 2012. "Self-Fulfilled Prophecy: Xenophobic Rhetoric and Its Political Effects on Latinos." Paper presented at the Annual Meeting of the Midwest Political Science Association, Chicago, April.

Perry, Huey. 1991. "Deracialization as an Analytical Construct in American Urban Politics." *Urban Affairs Review* 27: 181–191.

Persily, Nathaniel. 2002. "The Legal Implications of a Multiracial Census." In *The New Race Question: How the Census Counts Multiracial Individuals*, ed. Joel Perlmann and Mary Waters. New York: Russell Sage Foundation. 161–188.

Peters, B. Guy. 1999. *Institutional Theory in Political Science: The "New" Institutionalism.* New York: Continuum.

Pettigew, Thomas. 1998. "Intergroup Contact Theory." *Annual Review of Psychology* 49: 65–85.

Pew Research Center for the People and the Press. 2009, December. *Racial Attitudes in America II.*

Pew Research Center for the People and the Press. 2015. "Multiracial in America: Proud, Diverse and Growing in Numbers." June 11. Washington, DC.

Phillips, Anne. 1995. *The Politics of Presence.* New York: Oxford University Press.

Phinney, Jean. 1990. "Ethnic Identity in Adolescents and Adults: Review of Research." *Psychological Bulletin* 108(5): 499–514.

Phinney, Jean, and Victor Chavira. 1992. "Ethnic Identity and Self-Esteem: An Exploratory Longitudinal Study." *Journal of Adolescence* 15(3): 271–281.

Pichardo, Nelson. 1997. "New Social Movements: A Critical Review." *Annual Review of Sociology* 23: 411–430.

Plant, E. Ashby and Patricia Devine. 2003. "The Antecedents and Implications of Interracial Anxiety." *Personality and Social Psychology Bulletin.* 29(6): 790-801.

Popkin, Samuel. 2012. *The Candidate: What it Takes to Win—and Hold—the White House.* New York: Oxford University Press.

Powell, Joseph. 2005. *The First Americans: Race, Evolution and the Origin of Native Americans.* New York: Cambridge University Press.

Prewitt, Kenneth. 2013. *What Is Your Race? The Census and Our Flawed Efforts to Classify Americans.* Princeton, NJ: Princeton University Press.

Qian, Zhenchao. 2004. "Options: Racial/Ethnic Identification of Children of Intermarried Couples." *Social Sciences Quarterly* 85(3): 746–766.

Quintana, Stephen. 2007. "Racial and Ethnic Identity: Developmental Perspectives and Research." *Journal of Counseling Psychology* 54(3): 259–270.

Ramakrishnan, S. Karthick. 2005. *Democracy in Immigrant America: Changing Demographics and Political Participation.* Stanford, CA: Stanford University Press.

Rathner, Sidney. 1984. "Horace M. Kallen and Cultural Pluralism." *Modern Judaism* 4(2): 185–200.

Reeves, Keith. 1997. *Voting Hopes or Fears? White Voters, Black Candidates and Racial Policies in American Politics.* New York: Oxford University Press.

Renn, Kristen. 2004. *Mixed Race Students in College: The Ecology of Race, Identity and Community on Campus*. Albany: State University of New York Press.

Reuter, Edward Byron. 1918. *The Mulatto in the United States*. Boston: Richard G. Badger.

Rhode, Douglas, Steve Olson, and Joseph Chang. 2004. "Modeling the Recent Common Ancestor of All Living Humans." *Nature* 431(7008): 562–566.

Rice, James. 2012. *Tales from a Revolution: Bacon's Rebellion and the Transformation of Early America*. New York: Oxford University Press.

Roberts, Sam, and Peter Baker. 2010. "Asked to Declare His Race, Obama Checks 'Black.'" *New York Times*, April 2, A9. http://www.nytimes.com/2010/04/03/us/politics/03census.html.

Rockquemore, Kerry Ann, and Patricia Arend. 2002. "Opting for White: Choice, Fluidity and Racial Identity Construction in Post Civil-Rights America." *Race and Society* 5: 49–64.

Rockquemore, Kerry Ann, and David Brunsma. 2007. *Beyond Black: Biracial Identity in America*. New York: Rowman and Littlefield.

Rockquemore, Kerry Ann, David Brunsma, and Daniel Delgado. 2009. "Racing to Theory or Retheorizing Race? Understanding the Struggle to Build a Multiracial Identity Theory." *Journal of Social Issues* 65(1): 13–34.

Rockquemore, Kerry Ann, and Tracey Laszloffy. 2005. *Raising Biracial Children*. Lanham, MD: AltaMira Press.

Rodriguez, Clara. 2000. *Changing Race: Latinos, the Census, and the History of Ethnicity in the United States*. New York: New York University Press.

Rodriguez, Gregory. 2008. *Mongrels, Bastards, Orphans and Vagabonds: Mexican Immigration and the Future of Race in America*. New York: Vintage.

Roediger, David. 1991. *Wages of Whiteness: Race and the Making of the American Working Class*. New York: Verso.

Roediger, David. 2005. *Working toward Whiteness: How America's Immigrants Became White. The Strange Journey from Ellis Island to the Suburbs*. New York: Basic Books.

Rogers, Reuel. 2006. *Afro-Caribbean Immigrants and the Politics of Incorporation: Ethnicity, Exception or Exit*. New York: Cambridge University Press.

Root, Maria, ed. 1992. *Racially Mixed People in America*. Thousand Oaks, CA: Sage.

Root, Maria. 1996a. "A Bill of Rights for Racially Mixed People." In *The Multiracial Experience: Racial Borders as the New Frontier*, ed. Maria Root. Thousand Oaks, CA: Sage. 3–14.

Root, Maria, ed. 1996b. *The Multiracial Experience: Racial Borders as the New Frontier*. Thousand Oaks, CA: Sage.

Root, Maria. 2001. "Factors Influencing the Variation in Racial and Ethnic Identity of Mixed-Heritage Persons of Asian Ancestry." In *The Sum of Our Parts: Mixed Heritage Asian Americans*, ed. Teresa Williams-Leon and Cynthia Nakashima. Philadelphia: Temple University Press. 61–70.

Rosales, F. Arturo, and Francisco Rosales. 1997. *Chicano! The History of the Mexican American Civil Rights Movement*. Houston, TX: Arte Publico Press.

Roth, Wendy D. 2012. *Race Migrations: Latinos and the Cultural Transformation of Race*. Stanford, CA: Stanford University Press.

Roth, Wendy D. 2005. "The End of the One-Drop Rule? Labeling of Multiracial Children in Black Intermarriages." *Sociological Forum* 20(1): 35–66.

Rothman, Joshua. 2003. *Notorious in the Neighborhood: Sex and Families across the Color Line in Virginia, 1787–1861.* Chapel Hill: University of North Carolina Press.

Rumbaut, Ruben. 1994. "The Crucible Within: Ethnic Identity, Self-Esteem and Segmented Assimilation among Children of Immigrants." *International Migration Review* 28(4): 748–794.

Sanchez, Gabriel. 2006. "The Role of Group Consciousness in Latino Public Opinion." *Political Research Quarterly* 59: 435–446.

Saperstein, Aliya. 2006. "Double-Checking the Race Box: Examining Inconsistency between Survey Measures of Observed and Self-Reported Race." *Social Forces* 85(1): 57–74.

Saperstein, Aliya, and Andrew M. Penner. 2012. "Racial Fluidity and Inequality in the United States." *American Journal of Sociology* 118(3): 676–727.

Schildkraut, Deborah. 2011. *Americanism in the Twenty-First Century: Public Opinion in the Age of Immigration.* New York: Cambridge University Press.

Schilt, Kristen, and Jenifer Bratter. 2015. "From Multiracial to Transgender? Assessing Attitudes toward Expanding Gender Options on the US Census." *Transgender Studies Quarterly* 2(1): 77–100.

Schlesinger, Arthur. 1998. *The Disuniting of America: Reflections of a Multicultural Society.* New York: Norton.

Schneider, Monica, and Angela Bos. 2011. "An Exploration of the Content of Stereotypes of Black Politicians." *Political Psychology* 32(2): 205–233.

Schuck, Peter. 2003. *Diversity in America: Keeping Government at a Safe Distance.* Cambridge, MA: Harvard University Press.

Schuck, Peter, and Rogers Smith. 1985. *Citizenship without Consent: Illegal Aliens in the American Polity.* New Haven: Yale University Press.

Schuman, Howard, Charlotte Steeh, Lawrence Bobo, and Maria Krysan. 1997. *Racial Attitudes in America: Trends and Interpretation.* Cambridge, MA: Harvard University Press.

Schwede, Laurie, Theresa F. Leslie, and Deborah H. Griffin. 2002. "Interviewers' Reported Behaviors in Collecting Race and Hispanic Origin Data." Working Paper. Washington D.C.: Statistical Research Division, U.S. Census Bureau. Online at: http://www.census.gov/library/working-papers/2002/acs/2002_Schwede_01.html.

Sears, David, Collete Van Laar, Mary Carrillo, and Rick Kosterman. 1997. "Is it Really Racism? The Origins of White Americans' Opposition to Race-Targeted Policies." *Public Opinion Quarterly* 61(1): 16–53.

Sidanius, Jim, and Felicia Pratto. 1999. *Social Dominance: An Intergroup Theory of Social Hierarchy and Oppression.* New York: Cambridge University Press.

Sidanius, Jim, Pam Singh, John Hetts, and Chris Federico. 2000. "It's Not Affirmative Action, It's the Blacks: The Continuing Relevance of Race in American Politics." In *Racialized Politics: The Debate about Racism in the America*, ed. David Sears, Jim Sidanius, and Lawrence Bobo. Chicago: University of Chicago Press. Pp 191–235.

Shingles, Richard. 1981. "Black Consciousness and Political Participation: The Missing Link." *American Political Science Review* 75(1): 76–91.

Skerry, Peter. 2000. *Counting on the Census? Race, Group Identity, and the Evasion of Politics.* Washington, DC: Brookings Institution.

Skrentny, John. 2002. *The Minority Rights Revolution*. Cambridge, MA: Belknap Press of Harvard University Press.

Smedley, Audrey, and Brian Smedley. 2012. *Race in North America: Origin and Evolution of a Worldview*. 4th ed. Boulder, CO: Westview Press.

Smith, Rogers. 1999. *Civic Ideals: Conflicting Visions of Citizenship in U.S. History*. New Haven: Yale University Press.

Smith, Rogers, 2003. *Stories of Peoplehood: The Politics and Morals of Political Membership*. New York: Cambridge University Press.

Smith, Tom. 2001. "Aspects of Measuring Race: Race by Observation vs. Self-Reporting and Multiple Mentions of Race and Ethnicity." GSS Methodological Report 93. Chicago: National Opinion Research Center.

Smits, David. 1987. "'Abominable Mixture': Toward the Repudiation of Anglo-Indian Intermarriage in Seventeenth-Century Virginia." *Virginia Magazine of History and Biography* 95(2): 157–192.

Sniderman, Paul, and Thomas Piazza. 1993. *The Scar of Race*. Cambridge, MA: Belknap Press of Harvard University Press.

Snipp, C. Matthew. 2003. "Racial Measurement in the American Census: Past Practices and Implications for the Future." *Annual Review of Sociology* 29(1): 563–588.

Spencer, Rainier. 2010. *Reproducing Race: The Paradox of Generation Mix*. Boulder, CO: Lynne Rienner.

Spickard, Paul. 1986. "Injustice Compounded: Amerasians and Non-Japanese Americans in World War II Concentration Camps." *Journal of American Ethnic History* 5(2): 5–22.

Spickard, Paul. 1991. *Mixed Blood: Intermarriage and Ethnic Identity in Twentieth Century America*. Madison: University of Wisconsin Press.

Spickard, Paul. 2003. "Does Multiraciality Lighten? Me-Too Ethnicity and the Whiteness Trap." In *New Faces in a Changing America: Multiracial Identity in the 21st Century*, ed. Loretta Winters and Herman DeBose. Thousand Oaks, CA: Sage. 89–300.

Spruhan, Paul. 2006. "A Legal History of Blood Quantum in Federal Indian Law to 1935." *South Dakota Law Review* 51(1): 1–50.

Steele, Claude. 2010. *Whistling Vivaldi: And Other Clues to How Stereotypes Affect Us*. New York: Norton.

Stimson, James. 2004. *Tides of Consent: How Public Opinion Shapes American Politics*. New York: Cambridge University Press.

Stonequist, Everett. 1937. *The Marginal Man: A Study in Personality and Culture Conflict*. New York: Russell & Russell.

Stout, Christopher. 2010. "Black Empowerment in the Age of Obama." PhD dissertation, University of California, Irvine.

Strum, Circe. 2010. *Becoming Indian: The Struggle over Cherokee Identity in the Twenty-First Century*. Santa Fe, NM: School for Advanced Research Press.

Symcox, Linda. 2002. *Whose History? The Struggle for National Standards in American Classrooms*. New York: Teachers College Press.

Tafoya, Sonia. 2003. "Latinos and Racial Identification in California." *California Counts: Population Trends and Profiles*. Vol 4, no. 4. San Francisco: Public Policy Institute of California.

Tajfel, Henry. 1981. *Human Groups and Social Categories*. Cambridge: Cambridge University Press.

Tajfel, Henry, and John Turner. 1979. "The Social Identity Theory of Intergroup Behavior." In *Psychology of Intergroup Relations*, ed. Stephen Worchel and William Austin. Chicago: Nelson-Hall. Pp 7–24.

Takaki, Ronald. 1998. *Strangers from a Different Shore: A History of Asian Americans*. Rev.ed. New York: Little, Brown.

Tam Cho, Wendy. 1999. "Naturalization, Socialization, Participation: Immigrants and (Non-)Voting." *Journal of Politics* 61(4): 1140–1155.

Tate, Katherine. 1994. *From Protest to Politics: The New Black Voters in American Elections*. New York: Russell Sage Foundation.

Tate, Katherine. 2010. *What's Going On? Political Incorporation and the Transformation of Black Public Opinion*. Washington, DC: Georgetown University Press.

Taylor, Charles. 1994. "The Politics of Recognition." In *Multiculturalism: Examining the Politics of Recognition*, ed. Amy Gutmann. Princeton, NJ: Princeton University Press. 25–74.

Teixeira, Ruy, John Halpin, Matt Barreto, and Adrian Pantoja. 2013. "Building an All-In Nation: A View from the American Public." October 22. Washington, DC: Center for American Progress. http://www.americanprogress.org/issues/race/report/2013/10/22/77665/building-an-all-in-nation/.

Telles, Edward, Mark Sawyer, and Gaspar Rivera-Salgado, eds. 2011. *Just Neighbors? Research on African American and Latino Relations in the United States*. New York: Russell Sage Foundation.

Terkildsen, Nayda. 1993. "When White Voters Evaluate Black Candidates: The Processing Implications of Candidate Skin Color, Prejudice and Self-Monitoring." *American Journal of Political Science* 37(4): 1032–1053.

Tesler, Michael. 2012. "The Spillover of Racialization into Health Care: How President Obama Polarized Public Opinion by Racial Attitudes and Race." *American Journal of Political Science* 56(3): 690–704.

Tesler, Michael, and David Sears. 2010. *Obama's Race: The 2008 Election and the Dream of a Post-racial America*. Chicago: University of Chicago Press.

Thernstrom, Stephan, and Abigail Thernstrom. 1997. *America in Black and White: One Nation, Indivisible*. New York: Simon & Schuster.

Thornton, Russell. 1997. "Tribal Membership Requirements and the Demography of 'Old' and 'New' Native Americans." *Population Research and Policy Review* 16: 33–42.

Tichenor, Daniel. 2002. *Dividing Lines: The Politics of Immigration Control in America*. Princeton, NJ: Princeton University Press.

Torres, Andres. 1998. *The Puerto Rican Movement: Voices from the Diaspora*. Philadelphia: Temple University Press.

Tuan, Mia. 1998. *Forever Foreigners or Honorary Whites? The Asian Ethnic Experience Today*. New Brusnwick, NJ: Rutgers University Press.

Ture, Kwame, and Charles Hamilton. 1992. *Black Power: The Politics of Liberation*. New York: Vintage Books.

Verba, Sidney, Kay Schlozman, and Henry Brady. 1995. *Voice and Equality: Civic Volunteerism in American Politics*. Cambridge, MA: Harvard University Press.

Wallman, Katherine K., Suzann Evinger, and Susan Schechter. 2000. "Measuring Our Nation's Diversity: Developing a Common Language for Data on Race/Ethnicity." *American Journal of Public Health* 90: 1704–1708.

Wang, Wendy. 2012. *The Rise of Intermarriage: Rates, Characteristics Vary by Race and Gender*. February 16. Washington, DC: Pew Social and Demographic Trends. http://www.pewsocialtrends.org/2012/02/16/the-rise-of-intermarriage/?src=prc-hcadline.

Wang, Wendy, Richard Fry, D'Vera Cohen, and Daniel Dockterman. 2008. "Americans Say They Like Diverse Communities; Election, Census Trends Suggest Otherwise." Pew Social and Demographic Trends. http://www.pewsocialtrends.org/2008/12/02/americans-say-they-like-diverse-communities-election-census-trends-suggest-otherwise/.

Washington Post, Kaiser Family Foundation, and Harvard University (WKH). 2001. *Race and Ethnicity in 2001: Attitudes, Perceptions, and Experiences*.

Waters, Mary. 1990. *Ethnic Options: Choosing Identities in America*. Berkeley: University of California Press.

Weaver, Vesla. 2012. "The Electoral Consequences of Skin Color: The 'Hidden' Side of Race in Politics." *Political Behavior* 34(1): 159–192.

Westbrook, Laurel, and Aliya Saperstein. 2015. "New Categories Are Not Enough: Rethinking the Measurement of Sex and Gender in Social Surveys." *Gender and Society* 29(4): 534–560.

White, Deborah Gray. 1999. *Ar'n't I a Woman? Female Slaves in the Plantation South*. New York: Norton.

White, Ismail. 2007. "When Race Matters and When It Doesn't: Racial Group Differences in Response to Racial Cues." *American Political Science Review* 101(2): 339–354.

Wilkins, David. 2002. *American Indian Politics and the American Political System*. Lanham, MD: Rowman and Littlefield.

Wilkins, David, and K. Tsianina Lomawaima. 2001. *Uneven Ground: American Indian Sovereignty and Federal Law*. Norman: University of Oklahoma Press.

Williams, Kim. 2006. *Mark One or More: Civil Rights in Multiracial America*. Ann Arbor: University of Michigan Press.

Williams, Teresa. 1996. "Race as Process: Reassessing the 'What Are You?' Encounters of Biracial Individuals." In *The Multiracial Experience: Racial Borders as the New Frontier*, ed. Maria Root. Thousand Oaks, CA: Sage. 191–210.

Williams-Leon, Teresa, and Cynthia Nakashima, eds. 2001. *The Sum of Our Parts: Mixed Heritage Asian Americans*. Philadelphia: Temple University Press.

Wilson, David, and Matthew Hunt. 2014. "The First Black President? Cross Racial Perceptions of Barack Obama's Race." In *American Identity in the Age of Obama*, ed. Amilcar Barreto and Richard O'Bryant. New York: Routledge. 222–244.

Wolfinger, Raymond. 1965. "The Development and Persistence of Ethnic Voting." *American Political Science Review* 59(4): 896–908.

Wong, Janelle. 2006. *Democracy's Promise: Immigrants and American Civic Institutions*. Ann Arbor: University of Michigan Press.

Wong, Janelle, S. Karthick Ramakrishnan, Taeku Lee, and Jane Junn. 2011. *Asian American Political Participation: Emerging Constituents and Their Political Identities*. New York: Russell Sage.

Woods, Karen. 2003. "A 'Wicked and Mischievous Connection': The Origins of Indian-White Miscegenation Law." *Legal Studies Forum* 23: 37–70.

Xie, Yu, and Kimberly Goyette. 1997. "The Racial Identification of Biracial Children with One Asian Parent: Evidence from the 1990 Census." *Social Forces* 76(2): 547–570.

Yang, Philip. 2000. *Ethnic Studies: Issues and Approaches*. Albany: State University of New York.

Yanow, Dvora. 2003. *Constructing Race and Ethnicity in America: Category-Making in Public Policy and Administration*. Armonk, NY: M. E. Sharpe.

Young, Iris Marion. 1990. *Justice and the Politics of Difference*. Princeton, NJ: Princeton University Press.

Zack, Naomi. 1993. *Race and Mixed Race*. Philadelphia: Temple University Press.

Zebrowitz, Leslie, P. Matthew Bronstad, and Hoon Koo Lee. 2007. "The Contribution of Face Familiarity to Ingroup Favoritism and Stereotyping." *Social Cognition* 25(2): 306–338.

Zeleny, Jeff. 2008. "Saying Race Is No Barrier, Obama Still Courts Blacks." *New York Times*, January 2. http://www.nytimes.com/2008/01/02/us/politics/02race.html?pagewanted=all.

Zimmerman, Jonathan. 2004. "*Brown*-ing the American Textbook: History, Psychology and the Origins of Modern Multiculturalism." *History of Education Quarterly* 44(1): 46–69.

INDEX

Page references followed by a "*t*" indicate table; "*f*" indicate figure.

civil rights. *see also* laws
  Civil Rights Act (1964), 37, 40
  Crandall v. State of Connecticut and, 29
  US Census and, 68–69
Civil Rights Act (1964), 37, 40
civil rights movement
  for diversity, 39–41, 172, 218n24
  history of, 37–43
  for identity politics, 41–43
  for institutional opportunities, 37–38
  for political attitudes, 7
  racial classification and, 50
class
  activism and, 58
  for children, 81
  in identification, 106–8, 107*f*–108*f*
  in multiracial identity, 106–8,
    107*f*–108*f*
  in organizations, 191–92
  race compared to, 25, 49
  in social hierarchy, 25
  in WKH 2001 survey, 221n10
classification. *See* assigned classification;
    social assignment
conventional biracial groups. *See*
    multiracial identity
Crandall v. State of Connecticut, 29
Crouch, Stanley, 147
culture. *See also* multiculturalism
  genetics in, 61
  historic norms in, 50, 111, 173
  hypodescent rule in, 25, 73–74, 85–87,
    88–89*t*, 90
  identity choice in, 169–70
  monoracial identity in, 65,
    150–52, 151*t*
  multiracial identity in, 14, 43,
    50–51, 60
  racial categorization in, 35, 36, 69
  racial identification and, 5, 8, 16
  racial norms in, 179, 229n13
  stereotypes in, 63

data. *See* empirical data
Dawes Allotment Act, 215n5
deracialization hypothesis

Americans and, 19
  for race, 158–59, 162–63
descent. *See* ancestry
discrimination, 222n13, 224n25. *See also*
    Jim Crow; segregation
  against children, 138–39, 139*f*
  religion and, 162–65, 165*f*, 175, 184,
    208, 229n14
  self-identification and, 69–70,
    178–79, 184–85
  in surveys, 193–94, 200–201
  in United States, 67–68
  in WKH 2001 survey, 136–40, 138*f*–139*f*
diversity
  Americans and, 3
  civil rights movement for, 39–41,
    172, 218n24
  Ku Klux Klan against, 7
  public opinion polls on, 39
  public policy for, 40, 42–43
  in United States, 1–2, 39, 217n20
  for voters, 42–43
DuBois, W. E. B., 42

education
  activism in, 43, 60
  identity choice in, 59–60
  in interviews, 187*t*–188*t*
  for multiculturalism, 40, 218n23
  in multiracial activism, 58
  multiracial identity in, 54, 225n34
  in US Census, 106–7, 107*f*
EGSS. *See Evaluations of Government
    and Society Study*
empirical data. *See also* WKH
    2001 survey
  for Americans, 4, 109–11
  for identity choice, 4–5, 13, 173–74
  from individuals, 78–79
  from multiracial activism, 56–57
  Pew for, 154–55
  for political attitudes, 14, 113–14,
    121, 159–66, 160*t*, 162*t*–163*t*,
    164*f*–165*f*
  race in, 76, 172–73
  for racial attitudes, 121

multiracial populations (*Cont.*)
    political attitudes for, 130–31
    public policy for, 133–34, 133*t*
    race for, 134–36, 135*t*
    racial constraints for, 131–33, 131*t*
    in US Census, 1
    WKH 2001 survey for, 129–34, 131*t*,
        133*t*, 227n17
Muslims. *See* religion

National Association for the Advancement
    of Colored People (NAACP), 55
nationalism, 42, 58–59
National Opinion Research Council
    (NORC), 37
Native Americans, 216n7, 224n32
    ancestry for, 24–25
    in interracial relationships, 24
    laws and, 27, 215nn4–5, 217n14
    stereotypes for, 215n2
Negroes. *See* blacks
NORC. *See* National Opinion Research
    Council

Obama, Barack
    for Americans, 143–45, 148–53, 150*f*,
        151*t*, 152*f*, 175, 185
    ancestry for, 15, 146–47
    assigned classification for, 166–68
    for individuals, 153–55
    leadership for, 159–66, 160*t*, 162*t*–
        163*t*, 164*f*–165*f*, 200–201, 207–8
    for monoracial identity, 19
    racial categories for, 12
    racial classification of, 145–48,
        202*t*–206*t*, 229n11
    racial identification for, 9–11
    self-identification for, 146, 167–68, 180
    stereotypes and, 148–49
    for voters, 18–19, 63, 156–59, 228n2
online communities, 59
optimal distinctiveness, 219n34
organizations
    for activism, 55, 68–69, 73
    class in, 191–92
    individuals in, 189

interviews and, 187*t*–188*t*, 189–92
leadership in, 59, 190
Mavin Foundation, 56
    for multiracial activism, 56–60, 120
    multiracial populations for, 190–91
    Swirl, 56
Ozawa v. United States, 217n15

parental ancestry. *See* ancestry
pedigree. *See* genetics
Perez, Anthony, 2
personal identification. *See also*
    identity choice
    for Americans, 17
    in identity choice, 11–14
    race and, 9, 11–14, 46, 49–50
    racial identification in, 11–14
Pew Research Center for the People and
    the Press (Pew)
    for empirical data, 154–55
    for racial attitudes, 123–29, 124*f*, 125*t*,
        126*f*, 127*t*–128*t*
    for surveys, 18, 96, 98, 102
Plessy v. Ferguson, 35
political attitudes, 224n26, 225n2. *See*
    also voters
    ANES for, 123–29, 124*f*, 125*t*, 126*f*,
        127*t*–128*t*
    for Asians, 115–16
    assimilation theory and, 140–42
    for blacks, 115
    civil rights movement for, 7
    empirical data for, 14, 113–14,
        121, 159–66, 160*t*, 162*t*–163*t*,
        164*f*–165*f*
    identity choice and, 19
    in interviews, 66–70
    for Latinos, 115–16
    in monoracial identity, 112–13, 115,
        120–29, 122*f*, 124*f*, 125*t*, 126*f*,
        127*t*–128*t*
    in multiracial identity, 118–29,
        122*f*, 124*f*, 125*t*, 126*f*,
        127*t*–128*t*, 143
    for multiracial populations, 130–31
    race and, 5–6, 16, 134–36, 135*t*, 184